MORE THAN A LABOUR OF LOVE

THIS IS THE SECOND VOLUME IN THE WOMEN'S PRESS
DOMESTIC LABOUR SERIES. ALSO INCLUDED IS:

Fox, Bonnie (ed.): *Hidden In The Household.*
Toronto: Women's Press, 1980.

MORE THAN A
LABOUR OF LOVE

Three Generations Of
Women's Work In The Home

Meg Luxton

The Women's Press

For
Fenella Earwicker Macdiarmid
Heather Roberts
Lynn Brown
Ardy Braughten
Angie Simpson
Jean Cameron Macdiarmid

Canadian Cataloguing in Publication Data

Luxton, Meg.
    More than a labour of love

Bibliography: p.
ISBN 0-88961-062-2 pa.

1. Housewives. 2. Housewives - Manitoba - Flin Flon -
Case studies. 3. Flin Flon, Man. I. Title.

HD6055.L89   305.4'3   C80-094670-7

Lithographed by union labour at Alger Press Limited
Oshawa, Ontario, Canada

Printed and bound in Canada
Published by the Women's Educational Press
Toronto, Ontario, Canada

CONTENTS

ACKNOWLEDGMENTS

Thanks are due to many people. The period I spent in Flin Flon was one of the most significant and important times of my life. If it were not for the women I met there, this book would not exist. To all those women in Flin Flon, my appreciation and thanks.

I have been motivated throughout the study by the women's liberation movement. As I researched, wrote and revised the book, I was assimilating the ideas of the thousands of women involved in the movement. Without them, this book would not have been possible. I received direct support from the Women's Studies Programme of the University of Toronto, especially from Kathryn Petersen; from the Campus Community Co-operative Day Care Centre and Jesse Ketchum Day Care Centre; from the Marxist Institute; and from The Women's Press, particularly from Bonnie Fox and Jane Springer.

I would like to thank all those who have generously encouraged, helped and supported me in one way or another: Neal Barras, Ardy Braughten, Lynn Brown, Sue Colley, Theresa Doga, Laszlo Gyongyossy, Joanne Kates, Ester Reiter Koulack, Heather Jon Maroney, Alexa Petersen, Jim Petersen, Adrie Pringle, Brenda Pringle, Jim Pringle, Julie Pringle, Chris Roberts, Heather Roberts, John Ruttner, Angie Simpson, and Helena Wehrstein.

Some of my teachers have been particularly instrumental in helping me. Jill Conway and Kathleen Gough not only educated me but provided vitally important role models, which showed that women can be scholars and scientists. My thesis committee gave me lots of guidance and encouragement. Thanks to Stuart Philpott (supervisor), Peter Carstens, Richard Lee, Rayna Rapp Reiter and Janet Salaff.

Some specific people have been especially important. Paul Campbell has been involved in the project from the start. His fine sense of Canadian social history, his ability to move from abstract theory to concrete fact and back again and his painstaking editorial skills have informed my research and writing all along. Maureen FitzGerald and Harriet Rosenberg taught me to write, edit and work collectively. For two years we met weekly and they taught me to question all my assumptions and to concretize my flights of theoretical abstraction. Their love and sisterly support transformed both the book and me. Wally Seccombe, a friend and comrade, read everything and provided enthusiasm, criticism and support.

The Canada Council and the Ontario Arts Council provided the financial support that made this study possible. Thanks to Brenda Roman who did an excellent job of editing the whole manuscript, to Judy McClard and Daphne Read who edited chapter 1, to Linda Biesenthal for copyediting, and to Liz Martin for handling production. Credit also goes to National Photography Collection, Public Archives, Canada (photograph on page 49); Manitoba Archives (pages 22, 28, 32, 78, 109, 122, 217); Paul Campbell (pgs. 10, 21, 42, 54, 75, 80, 86, 112, 141, 160, 170); Theresa Doga (p. 181); Meg Luxton (p. 146); Frank Rooney (p. 230); Roger Rolfe (p. 200); John Ruttner (p. 116).

Finally my housemates Paul Campbell, Jan Campbell-Luxton, Michelle Campbell-Luxton came through in unimaginable ways providing love, support, patience, criticism and experience. To everyone thank you.

CHAPTER ONE

INTRODUCTION

A man works from sun to sun;
A woman's work is never done.

Proverb

HOUSEWIVES make up one of the largest occupational groups in Canada. In 1980 more than half of the married women in Canada were working as full-time housewives. At the same time, in spite of the fact that the percentage of married women in the wage labour force has steadily increased since 1945, married women who work for pay have not relinquished their domestic responsibilities. Instead they have taken on a double day of work, labouring as both wage workers and domestic workers. Thus the vast majority of Canadian women perform domestic labour on a regular daily basis.[1]

For most wage workers there is a distinct separation between their workplace and home, between their coworkers and family, between their work and leisure. They leave their homes each workday to go off to their jobs and return at the end of the workday to rest and relax. For housewives, whose work is based on marriage and parenting, such distinctions do not exist. Housewives are not employed — they work for their husbands and children. Their work is unpaid and performed in their family home. It is therefore both private and unseen. Because their work is rooted in the intense and important relationships of the family, it seems to be a "labour of love". It appears that there are two distinct and unrelated spheres: the public world of work, based on economic relations, and the private world of the family household, based on love relations.[2]

Domestic labour seems to be invisible. It is neither understood nor recognized as work. For example, women are asked: "Do you work, or are you a housewife?" Women who do both wage labour and domestic labour are described as "working wives" or "working mothers," as if to deny that what they do in the home is also work. When women themselves are asked to describe what they do, they often have no name for it:

> I never really thought about it before. It's just what I do everyday. It's a bit startling to try and think about it as something more than just me living my life. But it is important to ask why I do things the way I do and especially how what I do is like what other women do.
>
> (Generation III, b. 1951)[3]

As a "labour of love," this work is not respected in the same way as wage work, partly because it is not directly supervised and because its standards and schedules seem to be determined by the women who do it. As a job it is full of contradictions. On the one hand, it is important, necessary and potentially satisfying. On the other hand, it has a low status and is often isolating and frustrating:

> It's looking after your family and what could be more important? You don't have anyone standing over you so you get to do what you want, sort of. But you don't get paid, so you're dependent on your husband, and you have to be there all the time, and there's always something needs doing. I feel so confused because it could be so good and it never is.
>
> (Generation II, b. 1930)

This book analyses the work that women do in the home. It is based on a case study of three generations of working-class housewives in Flin Flon, a mining town in northern Manitoba. Because the experiences of these housewives are typical for working-class women in general, their stories illustrate what it is to be a working-class wife and mother and what it means to run a home. The study describes the actual work that women do, shows how their work has changed over three generations and isolates the various forces that shape and change domestic labour. This analysis distinguishes between the way particular women organize their daily work and the patterns that are essential to the occupation of housewife.

Some Flin Flon women themselves recognized both the universal characteristics and the social importance of their work:

12

> When I think about what I do every day — I cook meals for my family, I make cereal for breakfast and sandwiches for lunch and meat and potatoes for supper. Nothing unusual about that. But when I think about all those thousands of other women all doing the same thing, then I realize I'm not just making porridge. I'm part of a whole army of women who are feeding the country.
>
> (Generation II, b. 1937)

By placing the specific, personal experiences of individual women in a larger social and economic framework, the book argues that women's work in the home is one of the most important and necessary labour processes of industrial capitalist society.

THE WORKING-CLASS HOUSEHOLD

In *The Origin of the Family, Private Property and the State,* a classic Marxist analysis of the family, Frederick Engels recognized as false the apparent separation of the family from other labour processes. He suggested a way to develop an integrated analysis:

> According to the materialist conception of history, the determining factor in history is, in the final instance, the production and reproduction of immediate life. This, again, is of a twofold character: on the one side, the production of the means of existence, of food, clothing, and shelter and the tools necessary for that production; on the other side, the production of human beings themselves, the production of the species. The social organization under which the people of a particular historical epoch and a particular country live is determined by both kinds of production: by the stage of development of labour on the one hand and of the family on the other.[4]

Unfortunately, the promise of Engels' statement — to deliver a balanced and comprehensive view of the total labour process — has been largely unfulfilled. From Marx onward, Marxists have tended to focus on the "production of the means of existence" and have left out of their analysis "the production of human beings themselves." This is particularly the case in studies of industrial capitalist society. Most Marxists have concentrated on the activities of wage workers engaged in industrial production, assuming that the eight-hour-shift experience is sufficient to explain capitalist labour processes.[5]

As feminists have pointed out, this concentration on industrial production ignores the fact that workers live a twenty-four-hour day. With such a limited view, it is virtually impossible either to analyse the sexual division of labour under capitalism or to explain what domestic labour actually is. If the perspective is expanded from a preoccupation with the eight or ten hours a day that wage workers spend in wage labour to a consideration of the complete twenty-four-hour cycle of daily life of the working class as a whole, then it becomes clear that domestic labour is one of the central labour processes of industrial capitalism. It is this particular and indispensable labour that converts the wages of the paid worker into the means of subsistence for the entire household and that replenishes the labour power of household members again and again so that it can be re-sold the next day, the next year and in the next generation.[6]

Domestic labour takes the form it does because one of the distinctive characteristics of capitalist society is that the production of commodities — items produced for sale in the market — becomes generalized, to the extent that even labour becomes a commodity. Under capitalism individual workers — proletarians — do not own the means of production, either land to grow their own food or machinery to produce goods to sell. Because they are divorced from these means of production, the first thing that workers must do in the daily cycle for survival is to go to the labour market and make a deal with an employer to sell the only commodity they possess, which is their capacity to work — their labour power — in exchange for wages. They do so freely, compelled only by their own needs. With their wages they can purchase housing, food and other consumer goods and services.

Once workers enter the employ of a boss, they become unfree in the sense that the employer determines what they do on the job. The employer's main objective is to extract as much work as possible from the workers. At the end of the work shift, they are worn out; their capacity to labour is exhausted. Because labour power is expended in the industrial production process it has been used up or consumed. If it is to be sold again, it must be regenerated or reproduced. When wage workers are hired, they sell the use of their labour capacity for a limited time period which means that workers retain ownership of their labour power.

Unlike slave or feudal societies where the owners of the means of production are at least partly responsible for the subsistence of their workers, the capitalist mode of production ruptures the relationship between the production of commodity goods and the production of human beings themselves. The production of commodities is taken over while workers remain free and thus responsible for their own survival. Because workers retain possession of their labour power, they, rather than their employers, are responsible for reproducing it.

Once workers leave their bosses' premises at the end of each shift, they are on their own. How they choose to live their lives is left almost entirely up to them. They are able to live because they are richer by one day's pay. Thus the nature of the wage worker/employer relationship is one that makes it possible for the working class to create a place — the private household — outside of capitalist production where they can live their daily lives. At the same time, it constantly reasserts the necessity of the private household where workers live and reproduce themselves.

While the wages they earn make it possible for workers to maintain themselves in their own households, money itself will not shelter or feed them. Instead further work must be expended to transform money into housing, food and other consumer goods and services. And so workers go to the consumer goods market to obtain the necessary means of subsistence. Once these have been purchased and the wages spent, the working-class household still cannot consume most commodities directly but must perform additional work, based on their residence, to put the means of subsistence in a directly consumable form. For example, the groceries have to be put away and the food cooked for supper. With these goods, household members meet their daily needs.

Simultaneously wage earners in the household rest and restore their energies — reproduce their labour power — so that the next day they are able to leave home once again to go to work. This completes the twenty-four-hour cycle of working-class subsistence and shows that the working class is formed, as a class, at two locations — on the job and at home — and its members are necessarily involved in two distinct labour processes in the course of a single day. This double day of work — wage labour and domestic labour — is necessary for the survival of all members of the working class.[8]

THE FAMILY HOUSEHOLD
AND THE SEXUAL DIVISION OF LABOUR

There are many different types of working-class households. Some people live alone, or with a friend of the same sex, or with a group of unrelated friends. But the most typical household form is based on the nuclear family, that is, a woman, a man and their children.[9] This nuclear family household is itself based on a division of labour. The man leaves the household regularly to earn money elsewhere. The women may or may not leave the household to work for money.

Whether or not the woman has a paid job, she is primarily responsible for domestic labour.[10] This involves producing goods and services for the family's use, such as cooked meals, clean clothes and a pleasant environment in the home. At the same time the work includes the preparation of labour power for sale. Thus women's work in the home has two dimensions: meeting household needs and producing labour power. Because household subsistence depends on wages; the production of labour power for exchange must always take precedence over production for family use. So, for example, the daily rhythms of family life — what time the family eats, gets up and goes to bed — are usually set by the schedules of the wage worker's job rather than by family preferences.

Domestic labour is also a production process that is conducted between two arenas of economic exchange — the labour or job market and the consumer goods market. The patterns of domestic labour are determined by the conditions of these two markets. For example, if the price of meat goes way up, women may learn to cook other foods, or if massive lay-offs occur in local industries, families may have to move in search of paid work. However, the working class is not passive in the cycle of capitalist production. While the working-class household is formed and limited by the system of capitalist development, it is also shaped by the working class as an expression of its needs and wants.[11] Women's labour in the home is one of the ways in which the working class adapts and modifies the effects that external market forces have on its households.

Through their work women are instrumental in creating the face that the household presents to the world.[12] By managing their homes skillfully and helping household members maintain comfortable relations with each other, women try to achieve the highest standard of living and the greatest degree of emotional and physical well-being possible. During periods of economic crisis, for example, women intensify different aspects of their labour in an effort to stretch the budget. They may shop more frugally, do more mending, or take on a paid job. In addition, they are expected to provide emotional support for members of the household who are unemployed, ill, retired, or under some other form of stress. This never-ending work is vitally important in making life tolerable for household members.

Although domestic labour, as a labour of subsistence for the working-class household, does not fall under the direct auspices of capitalist production, it is profoundly determined by capitalist production and functions at the heart of the social relations integral to the capitalist mode of production. One woman described her work this way:

> I send my husband off to work each day and my kids off to school. It's women like me keep the whole system running. Weren't for us, the men wouldn't work and there wouldn't be no kids to grow up, would there?
>
> (Generation II, b. 1927)

As the necessary complement of the wage labour/capital relationship, domestic labour is a central labour process of industrial capitalism.

WOMEN'S DOMESTIC LABOUR

Women experience domestic labour as a continuous series of activities, all geared to running their households and looking after their families. These daily activities consist of many intricately woven threads that together form the fabric of their work. In order to study domestic labour and to understand its effects on women's lives this fabric must be unravelled and each thread examined in turn, while at the same time showing how they are woven together into the whole that is domestic labour. Domestic labour actually consists of four related but distinct work processes, each composed of a variety of tasks and each having its own history, its own internal rhythms and pressures and its own particular pattern of change. The first two are directly involved with people, while the last two maintain the physical infrastructure of the household.

The woman's most immediate task involves looking after herself, her husband and other adult members of the household. Because the household depends for its existence on wages, the dominant requirement is that the labour power of the wage earner be reproduced on a daily basis. However, the household also depends on domestic labour, which makes the reproduction of this labour power on a daily basis similarly important.

The second component of domestic labour is childbearing and childrearing. For most working-class people, their expectation that they will have children is a major reason for marrying and setting up family-based households. Although people have children for a variety of personal reasons, the social effect is the production of labour power for the next generation.

The third component of domestic labour is housework. It includes all those activities, such as cooking, cleaning and washing clothes, that are necessary for maintaining the house and servicing household members.

The final component of domestic labour involves the transformation of wages into goods and services for the household's use. This process of "making ends meet" involves money management and shopping. Sometimes it also requires that women take on additional work to bring more money into the household.

Domestic labour is, however, not simply four distinct work processes going on simultaneously. Each component is affected by, and in turn affects, each of the others. Changes in one reverberate throughout the whole labour process, reorganizing its internal composition. The analysis of domestic labour must examine how these processes are interwoven to form the total fabric of women's work. It is important therefore to look at domestic labour in an historical context.

Throughout the twentieth century the development and expansion of industrial capitalism has reduced the range of production activities that go on in the household. Some activities, such as making clothes or preserving food, have been removed from the household and socialized in factories. Certain services, such as education and some health care, have also been taken out of the household. The modern household has been left with only one main productive function, the most fundamental and essential one — the production of labour power.

The labour that has remained in the household has also been profoundly affected by the technological revolution, and this has created another contradiction for the modern housewife.[13] Although new technological innovations (such as indoor plumbing, electricity, washing machines and other appliances) seem to be labour saving, modern women working in the home with up-to-date technology spend almost as much time at their work as their grandmothers did without using modern conveniences.[14]

Popular myth has it that modern housewives tend to make work for themselves. According to this myth, in the old days housewives really had to work hard doing everything at home by hand, while modern women can buy most of the things they need ready made as well as the conveniences to make their work easier. It seems then that running a home is no longer a full-time job and those women who do it full time are either inefficient, lazy or self-indulgent. This myth is a source of anxiety for some women:

> I know that I work hard all day. I don't think I'm inefficient either.
> But I keep thinking about how much easier things are for me than

19

they were for my mother. Everybody keeps telling me how with all the modern things I have, I shouldn't have to work very hard. Is there something wrong with me?

(Generation III, b. 1949)

But as another housewife pointed out, this myth is based on an inadequate understanding of what women's work actually involves:

Sure things are easier today. Modern houses are much easier to keep up. No one's denying that. But the same is true of mining. Mining today with power drills and trains and all that is much easier than mining was in my grandfather's day. But no one ever says that modern mining isn't work anymore. So the people who say housework isn't full-time, demanding, hard work are full of it. All that proves is they don't know what housework is really all about.

(Generation III, b. 1950)

What women do in the home is not just housework. It is domestic labour — the production of both family subsistence and labour power. As domestic labour has changed, certain tasks have either been eliminated or have become less onerous. But no matter what specific tasks they do, or do not do, women are always responsible for maintaining the household. To understand why such work is never ending, it is important to distinguish between two measures that are relevant to domestic labour: production time and labour time.[15] Production time measures the duration of a task from start to finish; labour time measures the specific period during which a worker is actually expending labour. For example, the production time involved in roasting meat may be as much as ten hours from the time the woman takes the meat out of the freezer until she puts it on the table ready to eat. The actual labour time may be as little as half an hour, and it includes the time involved in actually putting the meat in the oven, basting it and later removing it to a serving dish. Similarly, a woman may spend an hour putting her child to bed. Once the child is asleep, she is apparently free to do other things, including going to sleep herself. But she remains on duty, responsible for the care of her child all through the night.

20

Although labour time expended is only an hour, the production time is the duration of the night.

Both the production time and the labour time of specific aspects of domestic labour have been reduced considerably. Household technology has definitely eased the housewife's labour time in some specific tasks, such as washing and cleaning. However, the central task — the production of life itself — is an ongoing, endlessly recurring process. Its production time can never be reduced. Whereas wage workers sell their labour power for a specific, limited period of time, "from sun to sun," domestic labour is "never done."

CHAPTER TWO

DOMESTIC LABOUR IN FLIN FLON:
AN OVERVIEW OF THE STUDY[1]

The position of women rests, as everything in our complex society, on an economic base.

Eleanor Marx and Edward Aveling

FLIN Flon is a single industry, primary resource city of 10,000 people in northern Manitoba, more than five hundred miles north of Winnipeg. The highway winds across the Prairies to the Canadian Shield, then twists through a land of rolling, rock-ribbed forests, endless rivers, lakes and bogs. About ten miles out of town, the road curves up a hill and in the distance, the smokestack of Hudson Bay Mining and Smelting Company Limited is visible above the trees. From the outskirts of the town, the importance of the Company is obvious. Crowning the highest rock ridge, the grey smokestack, the red headframes of the mine, and the yellow and brown plant buildings dominate the town. Spread below the Company, across the rocky hills and around the lakes, are the small, brightly coloured houses — the homes of the Company's employees and their families.

In these homes I met the women. In their kitchens I drank endless cups of coffee and slowly unravelled the threads of what it is to be a wife and mother, what it means to run a home. Each story was unique and special; and each woman had her own experience to tell. But as I went from house to house and listened to the different stories, certain themes emerged, themes that reflect the shared experience of most women in industrial capitalist society.

Flin Flon housewives, particularly those who had lived elsewhere at various times, were unanimous in insisting that their experiences were no different from those of other women:

> My husband's a welder. He's worked in plants in more than half the cities and towns of this country. Being a welder's the same wherever you go. Same's true for me. I've been across this country; I've been a housewife everywhere; so I can tell you, being a housewife in Flin Flon ain't no different from being a housewife anywhere else.
>
> (Generation III, b. 1948)

Yet, while they assured me that what women do in their homes in Flin Flon is the same as what women do everywhere else, they also knew that there was something special about life in Flin Flon. As a small northern city, it is situated a long way from the large urban centres of Canada. And so they were puzzled. Why had I selected their city as a place to study housewives and their work? Or as one woman asked:

> I think it's great you're studying what women do, and it's sort of neat that you came here to do it, but housewives are housewives, whether we live here or in Winnipeg or Toronto or Vancouver. So why did you come here? Why are you doing a study of *Flin Flon* housewives?
>
> (Generation III, b. 1950)

FLIN FLON AS A CASE STUDY

I had two goals for this study. I wanted to locate domestic labour within the development of industrial capitalism in North America to show how it has changed throughout the period. I also wanted to illustrate the actual work process as women experience it to reveal the impact of those changes on women's lives. In a number of ways, Flin Flon proved to be a suitable place to achieve those objectives. In fact, some of the ways in which Flin Flon is unique enhance its value for a study of domestic labour.

Domestic labour in North America has undergone continuous change since the early nineteenth century, but much of the early part of this process is lost to us. In Flin Flon this evolution of domestic labour has been telescoped into a period of fifty years.

When it was first settled in the mid-1920s, Flin Flon was a cluster of tents and cabins in the northern bush. The transition from primitive to fully modern conditions of domestic labour has been part of the life experience of some of the older inhabitants of the city. By understanding their experience, it is possible to reconstruct the general trends that have transformed domestic labour over the last century.

From Flin Flon's history it is possible to observe the unfolding of distinct stages of capitalist development. Flin Flon is dependent on the Company for its existence. The direct relationship between the Company and the city and their rapid growth have resulted in the underdevelopment of many secondary or peripheral labour processes and services found in larger metropolitan areas.[2] Without these auxiliary labour processes, the core labours of the capitalist mode of production are found in a particularly pure form and the relationship of capital, wage labour and domestic labour is clarified.

The underdevelopment of secondary industry and social services also contributes to a rigid sexual division of labour within the community.[3] Because the Company refuses to hire them, women are excluded from most paid jobs. One of the only alternatives for them is to get married. Thus, the majority of households in Flin Flon is based on a single-income, two-generation nuclear family unit, in which the wife does domestic labour full time. As a primary resource community, Flin Flon imposes conditions on housewives that minimize the differences in the way they do their work. The city is small and isolated; it has limited variation in housing, shops and leisure activities. Most men in the city are employees of the Company. They are subject to similar pressures from their wage work, and they all earn about the same income. The result is a certain homogeneity of domestic labour that cuts across cultural, ethnic and personal differences.[4]

The Company and the Most Desirable Classes of Labour

Every day at 8:00 A.M., 4:00 P.M. and midnight, the Company disgorges one shift of workers into the community and swallows up another. For fifty years these demanding rhythms of the Company have reverberated through the life of the city. By now three generations of workers have sold their labour power to the Company. And three generations of women in their homes have helped those workers restore their ability to work by maintaining the family household. As mothers, these women have raised three generations of workers for the mines and the home.

The Company first located in Flin Flon in the 1920s. In 1927 it began construction on the mine, mill and smelter complex and a hydroelectric plant. In 1930 it started producing zinc, copper, gold, silver, cadmium, selenium and telerium from the rich ore deposits. To ensure the profitability of their investment, the Company directors drew on the lessons learned by other mining capitalists, particularly those in the Western United States and Central America.[5] The operation of their plant incorporated not only the most sophisticated scientific and technical knowledge available at the time but also the newly developed approaches to management-labour relations in production, including Taylor's scientific management theories for controlling the workforce. In addition, the directors had to consider the Company's relation to the town and to the living conditions of its labour force outside production. They developed a number of strategies by which they affected the character of the rapidly growing settlement.

The directors were not prepared to support a company town. Yet they envisioned the eventual development of a municipality with all the amenities of urban life. Such an environment, they reasoned, was necessary to attract and hold the kind of workers they wanted. Unlike industries in southern Canada which could draw their labour from the large populations of the larger cities, the Company had to lure people north.[6] This presented the managers with a challenge, which they met by offering the workers relatively high wages and other concessions. The managers also found themselves in the position of selecting their ideal workforce.

The Company directors wanted a workforce composed primarily of married men with families. The managers believed that the presence of women and children and the formation of stable family household units would provide a social basis for the growth of a stable workforce. They understood that if the workers made a social and material investment in Flin Flon their ties to the town and their willingness to stay on with the Company would be strengthened. In this sense, the managers not only were hiring workers but were seeking families to create a town.

The result of the Company's preferential hiring policy was the establishment of two strata of the industrial proletariat in Flin Flon: a core body of permanent workers who were mostly married men and a more transient group of single workers. The former was the labouring core of the Company's operation. These workers, because they had regular employment, were able to get married and with their wives establish stable family households. The more transient group of single workers were always coming and going. This peripheral, transient workforce was as essential to the Company as the permanent core. The Company could easily expand or contract its operations, according to the fluctuating market for its commodities, by hiring and laying off these single men without provoking the resistance of the settled working-class community of Flin Flon family households.

These two components of the Company's workforce live in different parts of the town. They spend their leisure time differently and spend their wages in different ways. Thus the Company's differential hiring policy has created an important cultural cleavage in the Flin Flon proletariat. To sustain its core labour force, the Company encouraged its workers to buy houses, build schools and community centres, to sink roots in the town. Such a view of Flin Flon was reflected in the report of a prospective manager, who envisioned:

> ... a town large enough to attract the most desirable classes of labour, i.e., men with families. The town will be large enough to support first-class schools, churches, amusements, and stores with first-class professional men and tradesmen in residence.[7]

The Company also provided many necessary services for the growing town. It made available cheap electrical power, contributed substantially to the schools and community centres, and provided free labour and materials for road construction. Throughout the fifty years of Flin Flon's history, the ever-present influence of the Company has, sometimes subtly and indirectly and other times explicitly, shaped and coloured the character of the town.

In 1977 the Company celebrated its fiftieth anniversary. As the managers congratulated themselves on the profitability of their operation, both city officials and local residents noted that Flin Flon had become a stable industrial city where people lived and worked, got married, had children, grew old and died. Retired miners had grandchildren working in the mine, and older women had young married granddaughters following in their footsteps. Flin Flon had become a city, and for many of the people who lived there it was also a community, a place they called home.

Main St., Flin Flon during strike — June 11, 1934.

At a party held at the community centre to celebrate the Company's fiftieth anniversary, one of the guests was a woman who arrived in 1926 when Flin Flon was still a bush camp. She was proud she had been part of the community from the beginning. She talked about what the town meant to her and about the central role of women in its development:

> I've seen this town grow from just some tents by the side of Flin Flon lake to a proper city it is today. It's the people what built this town, the people. We never got much help from the government. The Company helped some. But we built it. I'm proud of this town. I've seen it grow from nothing but muskeg and bush to a proper city.... Women were absolutely essential to this town. Without women this town would be nothing. Women organized the community centre, the schools, the hospital.... But most important, women were wives and mothers. They kept the house, raised the children right.... Women looked after the home and that's what makes this town great. It's a family town.
>
> (Generation I, b. 1905)

Settling In Flin Flon: The First Generation, 1927-1939

The first working people to settle in Flin Flon were drawn primarily from the agricultural region of the Prairies, particularly from southern Saskatchewan and Manitoba. Others came from across Canada and from Europe. Most families followed a similar pattern of migration. The men came first in search of wage work. When they got jobs, they found some kind of housing and sent for the rest of the family. The women settled the household affairs, packed up their belongings and, rarely knowing what to expect, shipped their possessions, the children and themselves north to Flin Flon:

> I got a letter from him saying he had a house; so I should come. I packed everything we had in two trunks and left one with my sister to send later. I put myself and the baby and the trunk on the train. When we got to Flin Flon it was July 1929. He met us and we moved into our new home. It was a one-room log shack and we lived there for forty years. Course we fixed it up some.
>
> (Generations I, 1896)

These women followed the same pattern as that of other members of the working class, locating not according to their own will but in accord with the movement of capital.[8]

Despite this basic similarity, women and men had very different experiences in starting work once they arrived. While the men could assume the conditions of their work were the same as those found anywhere else in the country, the women had to start from scratch. For the pioneer women of Flin Flon, this situation was starkly illustrated by what they confronted when they arrived. What they found initially was hardship:

> When I first got off that train, I couldn't see nothing but rocks and a few sparse trees and a couple of tumbledown shacks. On my first step I sank down into that mud right up to my knees. Took two men to pull me out and I lost my boot besides. That was Flin Flon when I first came — just rock and mud and a few trees.
>
> (Generation I, b. 1887)

The townsite did not offer many amenities. The houses were small, primitive and completely lacking in any of the facilities available in many working-class houses in the south.[9] One woman who arrived in the summer of 1930 described her house as "a small wooden shelter — not what you'd call a house really."

Another woman who arrived in Flin Flon in 1930, with three small children and another on the way, described what it was like to do domestic labour under such conditions:

> Dick was working in the mill when we came, long hours. I think he worked six days a week, so he was never around except to eat and sleep.... Then the children were babies — four of them all under six and all at home all the time. And home was just a two-room cabin with nothing much. I just went all day with never a break till evening.... It was hard work keeping house in those days. I didn't have any water. There was always dirt coming in from the roads. It wasn't safe for the children to play outside but the house wasn't safe for them either. And there wasn't much in the way of shops, so we had to make do with what we had. We managed. It was very rough. But there was a sense of adventure too. We knew we were building something. Being a housewife was hard, hard, but I was here and this was what there was, so I knew I just had to make the best of it and work hard to make it the best.
>
> (Generation I, b. 1895)

As soon as they arrived, women had to set up a home, making do with whatever was available. At the same time they began to improve their conditions of work by fixing up their houses.

By 1929 the influx of people into the area had created a chaotic situation. Sanitary conditions were terrible. Roads were muskeg bogs in the spring. The water supply was inadequate, and the whole settlement constituted a fire hazard. The number of accidents at the Company and in the town necessitated the opening of a hospital. With the increased migration of families into the area, there were numerous children needing schools. The residents began to demand various health and social services.

Women extended their domestic labour into the community. They acted collectively and politically to weave the fabric of social life in the town, lobbying for schools, sidewalks, more stores, community centres and recreational facilities:

> There was just so much to do. There weren't roads, just a few shops and that tiny little house. When I wasn't doing my housework at home I was out drumming up people to build the schools and make this a good place to live.
>
> (Generation I, b. 1897)

> It started when I realized how much we needed sidewalks. I was new and so was everyone else and I didn't know anyone, but I started going from house to house, talking up sidewalks, and pretty soon I knew lots of people and after a while, we had sidewalks too!
>
> (Generation I, b. 1899)

Gradually these problems were ironed out. All-weather roads were constructed. A hospital was built and schools were opened. In 1933 Flin Flon was incorporated as a municipal district and the first local government was elected. The separation of the Company from the formal governing structure of the town was complete.

During this period nearly everyone in the town was under forty and most of them were in their twenties. Most women's circumstances were the same, so there was a certain shared experience and sympathy. Some women formed solid friendships on that basis, which provided not only personal support but also help with their domestic labour:

> Me and Mary lived next door and we both had kids the same age so we used to help each other out — sometimes just with a chat, sometimes with a hand around the house.
>
> (Generation I, b. 1898)

But their youth and common interests were not always advantages. Some missed the advice of older women or the services of teenagers:

> Back in Bent River I had neighbours older than me who had done it already and I really relied on their advice. Here everyone was in the same state as me and they couldn't help much.
>
> (Generation I, b. 1896)

> It was all young families then and there weren't any teenagers available to help out with babysitting and such. I didn't like it much. I think it's better now with a real mix.
>
> (Generation I, b. 1898)

As these women became active in the town, they were instrumental in forming the social and personal networks that tied the town together as a community.

Water delivery, Flin Flon.

Growth and Development: The Second Generation, 1940-1959

The middle decades of Flin Flon's history were the most significant in terms of the changes that occurred in the conditions of domestic labour. During this time state and municipal services became widely available; the structure and layout of the house improved, making it a better place to work. These changes led to a restructuring of domestic labour, which in turn rearranged the social relations of the household. This was a period of rapid transformation from the primitive conditions of settlement to fully modernized domestic labour.

Gradually the children of the first generation of settlers came of age and began to set up households of their own. This process altered some of the social relations of domestic work for those women who had mothers or adult daughters living in Flin Flon.

For example, couples who were married during the early years of Flin Flon's history described their weddings as convivial parties which included all their friends. Their wedding photographs often showed a large group of people, all of them about the same age. These couples got married away from their natal families, and they took pleasure in sharing the event with their friends. Couples of the second generation frequently noted that their parents organized their weddings. This difference is reflected in the statements of a mother (married in Flin Flon in 1932) and her daughter (married in Flin Flon in 1957), each describing her own wedding:

> It was great. We all had a wonderful time. All our friends got together and they made such a party — there was dancing and singing and food. Everyone who was there was a good personal friend so it was a lovely way to start off being married, surrounded by all our friends.
>
> (Generation I, b. 1901)

> It was okay but it was really my mother's do and his mother's. They organized everything. They even decided what dress I wore and his mother made it. Most of the people at the wedding and the reception later we didn't know. They were friends of our parents. We had a celebration party with just our friends after.
>
> (Generation II, b. 1937)

33

By moving into a totally new community, Flin Flon residents of the first generation moved out from under the influence of their parent's generation. But once they had children, the standard pattern emerged and they subordinated the second and later generations to their authority. This relationship between generations became important for women organizing their domestic labour. While women of the first generation could not rely on their mothers for help, many of them shared their work with their adult daughters. Women of the second and third generations all indicated that their relationships with their mothers or their adult daughters were an important component of the way they organized their domestic labour.

By the end of the middle period, the modernization of Flin Flon was complete. Many families by this time consisted of three generations. There was a wide range of age groups and corresponding interest groups. The municipality was well organized and houses were equipped with modern services and technology.

Municipal Services

An offshoot of the consolidation of municipal government control was an improvement in the material conditions of domestic work. One of the first developments was a town plan that established a network of roads and house lots. In carrying out the plan, most of the existing houses had to be moved. One woman described what happened to her house when the town planners decided to put a street right through her living room:

> When they surveyed for the streets they had to move our house so we put it up on rollers and rearranged it so the back was now the front, and then we built on some more to make it fit in the new location.
>
> (Generation I, b. 1892)

Despite the problems, the construction of all-weather roads made transportation in the town easier and cut down on the amount of dust and mud that came into the house.

Municipal control also standardized house construction somewhat by legislating building codes. One woman recalled the impact of such changes:

34

Most houses were one room and when the men carried in the
stove it was heavy, so where they dropped it when it got too
heavy was where it stayed. Later they made a law that you had to
have brick chimneys so people had to rebuild their houses.

(Generation I, b. 1897)

Of more immediate significance to domestic work were the
changes brought about by the installation of electricity and the
construction of a water and sewage system, developments that
eliminated a great deal of drudgery from the household.

Electricity

The Company provided the town with relatively cheap power, so
most people had their houses hooked up to the power lines as
soon as they were built. Initially, however, they used electricity
only for lighting. They depended on wood-burning stoves for
heat. Most houses converted to electric stoves and oil- or gas-
burning furnaces only in the 1950s.

The introduction of electricity eliminated most of the dirty,
heavy labour involved in storing and transporting fuels,
maintaining lamps and stoves and cleaning out ashes. At the
same time it allowed women to use many electrical appliances
that dramatically altered housework.

An important result of the introduction of electricity was the
setting up of various communications systems. A telephone
network established in 1932 linked individual households to
others both within the community and around the world. A local
radio station began broadcasting in 1937. In 1962 the first
television channel became available and in 1976 two more
channels were added. These systems drew individual households
into community, national and international communications
systems.

Water and Sewage

The earliest settlers in Flin Flon obtained their water from the
lake or by collecting rain, ice or snow. In 1927 the Company
instituted a water delivery system, which was taken over by the
town in 1929. It was primitive and expensive. A horse-drawn

cart delivered water twice a week. Two men carried pails of water from the cart to the storage tanks of each house. Some of the houses were built on top of steep rocky hills, and the water carriers faced an arduous climb. The whole process of water delivery was inconvenient and messy and added to the housewife's work:

> They used to deliver water and put it in the big tank in the kitchen. The men who delivered it were sloppy, and so I used to tell them to let me take it into the house and put it in the tank. They used to grumble I was the worst old bitch. But I did it neater and it made less work.
>
> (Generation I, b. 1895)

Because the town lacked running water, every house had an outdoor privy. Under any circumstances privies are a health hazard and in the long Flin Flon winter they were unbearably cold.[10] Privies and the chamber pots that go with them involved considerable housework. As the town population grew rapidly, the inconvenience, poor drainage, unpleasant smells and threat of contagious diseases prompted the town to introduce indoor chemical toilets. By 1932 most privies had disappeared. By the 1950s, as new housing was built, it was linked to the municipal water system and older houses were gradually hooked up. Once there was running water, the town could install a sewage system. The construction of water and sewage systems allowed people to put in flush toilets, showers, bathtubs, and kitchen and laundry sinks.

In general the effect of electricity and water and sewage systems was to make the house cleaner and more comfortable and to make household labour more rational, efficient and less physically demanding. The labour required in various material-handling processes related to the distribution of water, waste and energy was taken over at the municipal level, relieving women of this kind of work.

House Construction and Design

Because the house is the central arena of domestic work and the general appearance of the family home is a public expression of the family's standard of living, its construction and design are important to the housewife. The first houses built in Flin Flon were small structures with two or three rooms:

> When we first moved there were three rooms. One had a sink and a stove in it and the other two were just big enough to put a bed in each. Out back was the wood pile and behind it the privy.
> (Generation I, b. 1894)

By the late 1950s, new houses being built in Flin Flon were typical of those found in any new working-class suburb of an urban area in the South. Of frame construction, they had a variety of rooms, central heating, running water and flush toilets:

> We got the plans for our house from a magazine on building your own house. It's two storey with a full basement. It has a built-in washer and dryer and dishwasher.
> (Generation III, b. 1951)

Stabilization: The Third Generation, 1960-1977

By the 1960s domestic labour in Flin Flon had entered its modern phase. A third generation of Flin Flon children was coming of age and setting up households. This was not a period of profound domestic change. The modernization of the house was basically finished and domestic labour had been reorganized in response to these changes. The organization of women's work has remained generally constant through the last two decades.

When Flin Flon was incorporated as a city in 1970, its transformation from a bush camp to an industrial city was formally complete. From a random scattering of tents and cabins, a city with all the amenities of most small urban centres had evolved. It was in this modern city setting that women of Flin Flon did their domestic labour. While in some ways domestic labour in Flin Flon was influenced by circumstances specific to a primary resource community in the Canadian north, the labour of Flin Flon housewives resembled the work of women in any industrial community.

DOING THE STUDY

In October 1976 I moved to Flin Flon and for the next fourteen months I tried as much as possible to live as the local people did. By sharing their experiences I began to know the complexity and richness of their daily life.[11]

As a neighbour and later as a friend, I took part in the daily life of women. I shared their work, doing my own shopping, cooking, cleaning and helping them with the same tasks. I babysat their children, and cared for my own when they came to visit for holidays. I socialized at the community centre, at the bar and at parties. We visited and talked, and I asked endless questions. By combining shared experience with constant observation, I gradually developed a sense of what work, and life, was like for Flin Flon women.

These day-to-day experiences formed the basis of my analysis of domestic labour. However, I did not want to use information told to me in friendship as the basis of this book. After about six months I began to develop a questionnaire with which to conduct formal interviews. To make up this questionnaire I took five different interview schedules that had been employed by other researchers investigating the family and women's work. I asked five women who had become my close friends to help me, and over the period of the next two months I interviewed each of them five times, each time using a different interview format.[12]

As we did these interviews, we evaluated the questions. Some were irrelevant to Flin Flon; others I felt too embarrassed to ask. A few seemed either silly or insulting. Simultaneously we tried to think of questions particularly relevant to Flin Flon and to the type of study I was doing. Out of this process, I derived an extensive questionnaire with which I subsequently interviewed one hundred women. In these interviews I asked questions that solicited both specific, detailed answers and open-ended responses on such topics as household composition, geneologies, household budgets, time budgets, the activities involved in housework, child care and general household management. I asked for information about female/male relationships, sexuality and generally how women felt about their lives.

One of the most crucial factors in how women experienced their work was the generation in which they settled in the town. Women established households in Flin Flon in one of two ways. In some cases, the women had been married and already had families when they moved to Flin Flon to set up new households. In other cases, the women married in Flin Flon and then set up households to accommodate their new families. I began by interviewing twenty women from each generation. Most women who had set up households in the 1920s were then over eighty years old. Since many of the original settlers had either moved away or died, I was only able to find five women who had set up households in the 1920s. Therefore I interviewed fifteen women who had set up households in the 1930s and ten women from each of the succeeding decades. This made a total of sixty interviews.

I wanted to find out how women learn domestic labour and how they teach it to their daughters and what patterns exist between mothers and daughters who are both doing this kind of work. I interviewed twenty women born in Flin Flon whose mothers were still living there. Their mothers were included in the initial sixty interviews. Of these daughters, eight established households in the second generation and twelve in the third generation.

Finally, because the period during which children are still the full-time responsibility of their parents is the most intense period in the cycle of domestic labour, I interviewed an additional twenty women who had at least one preschooler. All of these women established households in the third generation.

Almost all specific quotations and statistical observations cited throughout the book are drawn from this interview material. When citing such a reference, I have indicated the generation in which the speaker set up her household and the date of her birth. Names and exact occupations have been excluded or changed to protect the identity of the people concerned.

In addition to this general survey, I conducted several more specific studies, including detailed time budget studies of twenty households and complete financial budgets for eight households. I collected ten household inventories to determine what people actually kept in their houses. Wherever possible I also asked to see family photograph albums and other household memorabilia. [13]

During the latter part of my research, a close colleague moved to Flin Flon and started work as a miner for the Company. He provided valuable information about male social relations in the workplace. He shared his insights into the experiences and the attitudes and feelings of the men who lived with the women I worked with. Using the questionnaire, I also interviewed five men: one of the first generation, one of the second and three of the third. This small but very useful sample of men's responses highlighted and complemented the data I received from the women.

Each of the women interviewed was married and living with her husband, and each had at least one child. All of their husbands had worked or were still working for the Company. At the time of the study, twenty-three husbands were no longer working for the Company; instead they were working for hourly wages for some other local employer. Most of the women were still actively engaged as domestic labourers at the time they were interviewed. Of the hundred women interviewed, eighty-eight were still full-time housewives; twelve were retired. All five women who had established households in the 1920s were retired; they did little or no domestic labour and were no longer totally responsible for their own care. Their average age in 1976 was eighty-two. Of the fifteen women who had set up households in the 1930s, seven were retired. Their average age was seventy-nine.

During the process of assessing the data and writing up the conclusions, I sent each chapter to several of the people I worked with in Flin Flon and asked them to read and comment on it. Their responses acted as a check and a confirmation. Even where we disagreed, their observations and comments were helpful in formulating the final version of this work. This is a relatively under-utilized technique in the social sciences. It could be employed more regularly as one way of giving the people involved in the study some input into what is being written about them.

After she had finished reading the completed manuscript, one woman commented:

> You be sure and tell it like it is. A book about what women do at home would be good. It's true that most people ignore housework. They tend to think housewives are a bit not all there. You write all this down, what I'm telling you and make sure you know what being a housewife is really like.

(Generation II, b. 1932)

CHAPTER THREE

WIVES AND HUSBANDS

I [woman] take thee [man]
To my wedded husband
To have and to hold
From this day forward
For better for worse
For richer for poorer
In sickness and in health
To love, cherish and to obey
Till death do us part.

Solemnization of Matrimony

IN her marriage vows, a woman promises "to love, cherish and to obey" her husband. While couples appear to marry on the basis of free choice and love, their dependence on the wage imposes structural imperatives which undermine their freedom and love. The daily requirements of household survival mean that both adults must subject themselves and each other to dictates which, for the most part, are beyond their control and which are not particularly in their interests.

Consequently, marriage is indeed "for better for worse." While some aspects of marriage are good and women often mention the pleasure and happiness they derive from their marriages, the underlying imperatives create all sorts of tensions which diminish the marital relationship, binding people to each other not by choice based on love but by dependency and a lack of alternatives.[1]

WAGE LABOUR AND DOMESTIC LABOUR

For many working-class women, supporting themselves independently by wage labour is not an inevitable or even a realistic alternative. The sex segregation of the labour market restricts women to the lowest paid, least secure and most monotonous jobs. Women's wages are so low that it is virtually impossible, especially if they have children, for women to survive.[2] Often in periods of high unemployment or in small towns like Flin Flon, there are simply not enough jobs available for those women who want to work. For these women marriage becomes a primary option — it appears to be the only viable life strategy available to them.

In this way there is a basic economic compulsion to marriage and women's low wages help to keep the nuclear family together. Though women marry on the basis of free choice, they have very few real alternatives because of how those alternatives are structured. By associating themselves with men who are earning relatively higher wages, women probably have a higher standard of living than they might have if they depended on their own wage labour.

This economic dependency permeates and threatens female/male relationships. For family households to survive, the husband must sell his labour power in exchange for wages to an employer on an ongoing, regular basis. Once the men enter the bosses' employ, they are no longer free but come under the direct control of their employer.

The employer's primary objective is to extract from his employees as much of their ability to work as possible, to maximize the product of their labour by the end of the shift. Once workers are employees, they become part of capitalist production and how they work depends on how the capitalist organizes production — his control over his labour force, his capacity to co-ordinate and rationalize the various operations of his enterprise — in other words, his capacity to harness labour in the production process and to utilize his workers' labour power to the hilt.

Marx described this type of labour, showing vividly its implications for the (male) worker's state of being:

> Labour is external to the worker — that is, it is not part of his nature — and that the worker does not affirm himself in his work but denies himself, feels miserable and unhappy, develops no free physical and mental energy but mortifies his flesh and ruins his

mind. The worker therefore feels at ease only outside work, and during work he is outside himself.... The external nature of work for the worker appears in the fact that it is not his own but another person's, that in work he does not belong to himself but to someone else.[3]

From the perspective of the worker, the labour process is not for the satisfaction of needs. Rather it demands the denial of needs. Time spent at work is segregated from "real life"; it is time spent for, controlled by, and at the service of another. The man returning after a day of work comes home tired. His capacity to labour has been consumed, so he is spent and depleted. He considers his time off work to be his own, to do with as he pleases. He demands the right to spend his time away from wage work in voluntary activities.

But the experiences of wage work are not so easily shaken. His experiences at work usually leave him tired, frustrated and irritable. The worker bears the social residue of this alienating labour process and of the oppressive social relations of capitalist production. He needs to find ways of releasing those feelings of tension, of assuaging the dissatisfaction. He wants his leisure time to be free of conflict and to be refreshing, restful and personally satisfying. He needs the opportunity and the means to re-energize — to reproduce his labour power — before he goes back to work the next day.

A miner who had worked for the Company for forty-one years explained how he experienced this process:

> I work hard, see. And it's not great work. And when I gets home I'm tired and fed up and I want to just rest till I feel better. I come home feeling sort of worn down and I need to loosen up and feel human again. At work there is always someone standing over me telling me I have to do this or that. Well, I don't want any more of that at home. I want to do what I want for a change. I want a chance to live when I'm off work.
>
> (Generation II, b. 1920)

Despite the social relations of production, or perhaps because of them, a man is usually proud of his skill, strength and intelligence in performing his job. This pride focuses on the wages he receives; a good wage is an expression of his ability as a worker.

For the man the importance of the wage is represented by his home, for it is his wage that buys the house he lives in and provides for his needs and those of his wife and children. A male worker measures his worth by his ability to provide for his family. He is proud to be able to support a wife who can devote all her time and energy to maintaining their household. His self-esteem is derived from his ability to provide and maintain his side of the sexual division of labour. This helps motivate him to continue working. And for his labour he expects that the home will be his castle. For the man there is a distinct separation between his workplace and his home, between work time and leisure time. He usually assumes that his wage labour fulfills his obligations within the division of labour of the family household. When a man comes home he is finished work:

> He is at home when he is not working and when he is working he is not at home. His work, therefore, is not voluntary, but co-erced, forced labour. It is not the satisfaction of a need but only a means to satisfy other needs. Its alien character is obvious from the fact that as soon as no physical or other pressure exists, labour is avoided like the plague.[4]

No such separation exists for the woman. Her workplace is her home, and for her, work time and leisure time are indistinguishable. She discharges her obligations within the division of labour by doing all those things that are necessary to ensure that the adult members of the household are available for work everyday — able and relatively willing to work. In this way she ensures, as far as possible, the regular continuance of the wage on which she depends in order to meet her own physical and social needs. Because the labour power of her husband is exchanged for a wage, while hers is not, the needs of the husband and the requirements of his wage labour always take precedence over other household considerations. Part of the woman's work includes caring for her husband, creating a well-ordered and restorative home for him to come back to. In the process her work becomes less visible and its importance is less acknowledged. The wife is subordinated to the husband.

The sexual division of labour, although inherently hierarchical, makes the participants mutually dependent. While the dependency of women is greater economically and socially, men are dependent on their wives not only for the physical aspect of domestic labour but also for important psycho-emotional support. Within the household division of labour, it falls to the woman to provide for the immediate needs of the wage worker. All aspects of women's work, from its schedules and rhythms to the most subtle personal interactions, are touched and coloured by the type of wage work the men are doing, by the particular ways in which their labour power is consumed by capital.

If the man is engaged in shift work, the household then operates around two, or sometimes three, often contradictory schedules. It is the woman's task to service each routine and to prevent each of them from coming into conflict. This process is well illustrated by one housewife's day. The woman gets up at 7:00 A.M., feeds the baby, then gets the three older children up, fed and off to school by 8:45 A.M. Meanwhile, her husband who is on the graveyard shift (midnight to 8:00 A.M.) comes in from work and wants a meal, so once the children are fed she prepares his dinner. Then he goes to bed and sleeps until about 6:00 P.M. During the day she must care for the toddler, do her housework, feed and visit with the older children who come home for lunch from noon to 1:30 P.M. and return again at 4:00 P.M. All of this occurs while "daddy is sleeping" and the noise level must be controlled to prevent him from being disturbed. At 5:00 P.M. she makes supper for the children and at 6:00 P.M. she makes breakfast for him. By 8:30 P.M., when the children are in bed, he is rested and ready to socialize while she is tired and ready to sleep. Another woman in a similar position described it this way:

> It totally disrupts my life, his shift work. I have to keep the kids quiet — I'm forever telling them to shut up — and I can't do my work because the noise wakes him. It makes my life very difficult.
> (Generation II, b. 1941)

The impact of shift work on family life is subtle and difficult to pin down. Workers on weekly rotating shifts cannot sleep properly and their eating patterns are disrupted. The result is general irritability, headaches, constipation and a host of other physical ailments. The social and psychic effects are more elusive.[5] Flin Flon women generally maintained that the graveyard shift was the hardest for them. Some of them did not like being alone with small children at night. Others said they never had time with their husbands, who went to bed as the women were getting up:

> Those changing shifts are awful. It's a constant reminder that his work comes first, over any other needs this family might have. We can never get ourselves organized into any regular pattern because our lives are always being turned upside down.
>
> (Generation III, b. 1947)

The requirements of the husband's wage work affect the women's work in a variety of other ways. Women usually have to pack a lunch for their husbands. They may have to wash and repair work clothes. Most significantly, they have to organize their time around their husband's time. All of the women interviewed said that they got up before their husbands in the morning because it was their responsibility to wake them and get their breakfast ready in time for them to leave for work.

A song from a play about mining towns illustrates how women have to organize their time around the Company's schedules:

"Who says we don't work to the whistle?
With us it just don't show.
We got to have dinner on the table before that whistle blow." [6]

Or, as a Flin Flon housewife described it:

> Lots of people say what a housewife does isn't work. Well, it is work, and it's just like men's work only it isn't paid and it isn't supervised. But I have things I have to do at certain times. The main difference is, my work is regulated by his work. And whatever I have to do is somehow always overshadowed by the requirements of his work.
>
> (Generation II, b. 1934)

Beyond doing these immediate tasks, the housewife must enter into a far more complex and profound relationship with her husband, for she must also ensure his general psycho-emotional well-being.

The types of demands placed on domestic labour in trying to meet the husband's needs are partly a function of the specific way in which the husband's labour power has been consumed by capital. For example, levels of mental or physical fatigue vary according to the job as do the types of stress, kinds of injuries, size of appetite, and so on. What restoring his ability to work

48

actually involves depends to a large extent on the personality and personal preferences of the individuals in the marriage. These various constraints and possibilities account for some of the differences between households.

In many cases the men develop their own ways of dealing with their work-related tensions. Their wives simply have to recognize their patterns and allow them to do what they want. Some men want to be left alone for a while when they get home. Others insist on going to the pub for a few drinks before coming home. Three of the women interviewed said their husbands insisted that supper be on the table when they walked in the door. These men refused to talk to anyone until they had eaten.[7] In some households the wife and the children had to be home waiting for him when he arrived home from work:

Bill likes to play with the kids when he comes in, so I always make sure we're home and the kids are washed and changed.
(Generation III, b. 1955)

In others the children had to be neither seen nor heard when their fathers first returned from work:

When Mike comes in he likes a quiet time with a beer and no kids, so I have to make sure the kids keep quiet and don't bug him in any way.
(Generation III, b. 1950)

Men who do heavy physical labour such as shovelling muck (broken rock) or very noisy work, such as drilling, may need a quiet time alone to relax when they first get off work. Those working under the direct supervision of a boss may choose to release the tensions generated by drinking, playing with their children or yelling at their families. Some men like to spend their free time at home watching television. Others like to go visiting or to have friends over. Some prefer to go off with their male friends to the bush for hunting or fishing or to the pub for drinking. Others like to be very active in voluntary organizations, municipal politics, union politics or other activities that take them out of the home and away from their families. Whatever their choice, the women's task is to facilitate it.

This is a subtle process. Though the tendency for women is to do things "his way" women are not powerless within marriage. They do have a certain amount of leeway and considerable influence, and they regularly exercise discretion about how much they let their husbands' needs structure their lives. When the man is not present, the housewife can do things "her way." She can sometimes expand and alter his tastes. Depending on the quality of their relationship, she can even get him to do things her way.

If the relationship is poor, the wife may do all she can to make her husband's life miserable by regularly asserting her own will in deliberate opposition to his. When there is no conflict between them, she may do things his way because she loves him and wants to make him happy. Finally, many women will say that they do things their husband's way because they believe that is the way a household should function. In fact, the events they

50

describe suggest that what is often designated "his way" is often really "their way."

On some level all of the woman's work takes into account her husband's preferences. This was reflected repeatedly in the decisions Flin Flon women made about what to buy, what to cook, what to wear. When asked why they prepared the foods they did, most women replied that they made what their husbands' liked. Often women mentioned that they liked certain foods or were interested in trying a different type of cooking but they refrained because their husbands' tastes had priority. They also bought clothes with their husbands' tastes in mind. A friend and I were shopping for shoes. She tried on a pair that she liked very much. After much indecision she rejected them because "Henry just wouldn't like them." In another instance a woman spent several hours preparing her dress and getting ready for a formal party. When her husband came in he took one look at her and commented that he had never liked that dress. She immediately went to change her clothes.

An older woman recalled moving into a new house from a two-room cabin in 1940. The new house was completely modern, and they had enough money to furnish it as they liked:

> We settled in slowly. We did one room at a time. We would sit down and discuss the room and what we wanted to do with it. We would talk it out together, then I would go and buy the things we needed and set it up. I always did it the way he wanted. After all, it was his money what bought it and he should have his house as he likes.
>
> (Generation II, b. 1915)

This woman described a co-operative process of decision making and then, without mentioning any conflict or deferral, she said it was his way. How much this suggests that her preferences are guided by him and how much it reflects her notion of how things should be is impossible to determine.

LOVE AND AFFECTION

All of these types of interactions have an impact on the social relations of marriage. One of the striking features of marital relations in Flin Flon over the last three generations is that, as soon as limitations imposed by their working conditions were modified, Flin Flon residents altered their marital arrangements. Love, affection and caring have changed considerably over the last fifty years. Largely because of their respective work patterns, women and men in the early period had little time to spend socializing together. Sometimes men had to work away from home for months at a time. Even when they lived at home, they often worked for twelve and fourteen hours each day six days a week. The woman's housework required long, uninterrupted days.

Older women described their expectations of marriage as "making a family." For them the sexual division of labour was explicitly embodied in their interpersonal relations as well. A couple co-operated to form a household and to have children. They recognized very distinct women's and men's spheres in their leisure activities. As working time decreased for both women and men, the quality of their relationships changed. The shortened work week and the improvements in housework meant that men could be at home more often and that women had more opportunities to take a few hours "off."[8]

Younger women described their marriages as "partnerships." While they adhered to the traditional division of labour based on work, they seemed to share more activities with their husbands and they expected to be "friends" with them. Over the last fifty years wives and husbands have increasingly spent more time together. Couples seem to expect more demonstrated affection, intimacy and friendship from each other. A young woman described how her marriage differed from her mother's:

> They didn't seem to expect much of each other. They lived together and I know they cared, but they each went their own ways. I don't think that's right. I want to have more closeness with my husband. I think husbands and wives should be each other's best friends.
>
> (Generation III, b. 1952)

Comparing observations of an older woman recalling her past and a young woman describing her present confirms this changed perspective:

When we was married [1926] and moved here we knew we each had our own harness to pull. Jake worked for the railway and later for the Company and he worked long hours for most of the week I recollect he worked twelve to fourteen hours each day Monday to Saturday and on Sunday he slept or went out for a drink with his mates. He brought home the wages; that were his job. Me, I looked after the house and took care of the kids and made sure his clothes were clean and his meals were on the table. That were my job.

(Generation I, b. 1895)

Jim's my best friend in the world. I don't like to do anything unless he can too. Well, he works for the Company, eh, and I take care of the house and the kids but all the time he's home we do things together.

(Generation III, b. 1949)

Besides changing work patterns other social forces, such as the increasing isolation of the family, have affected marital relationships. In the early period in Flin Flon social life involved regular collective activities. Large groups of people held dances, floating card games, berry-picking outings and socials organized by groups of individuals who came together for a specific event. Women were central to organizing these get-togethers.

Over the years there has been a shift from community-based entertainment to smaller family events. The number of communal activities has decreased and are organized either by businesses or formal organizations. Women are still active, but the scope of their decision making and authority has been reduced. Where women once organized for both the community and their families, they now organize primarily for their families.

This shift has reduced women's social horizons and increased their orientation toward the family. An older woman described her experience:

When we first come here the town was small and there weren't no Trout Festival Association or Rotary or whatnot to organize things. So we did it. Oh I remember lovely times, big dances and lots of fun. The men were all working odd hours so we women would do it and everybody would go.... Now it seems everything is done for us. There's this or that event, all organized in advance for you, and families go to them or not. It's not the same somehow.

(Generation I, b. 1901)

As she suggests, this change is partly a result of the growth of the municipal infrastructure. However, other factors have also contributed to the changing social patterns.

Before people in Flin Flon owned cars, groups of people sometimes got rides in horse-drawn wagons into the bush to collect berries or to go hunting, picnicking or exploring:

Before we had the car we often used to go in groups for a wagon ride somewhere. Now we just all go off separately in our own cars.

(Generation II, b. 1923)

Another source of major social change was the development of television:

Before the TV come we used to have a regular, floating card game with the people on the street. We'd go from house to house playing cards and having a whale of a time.

(Generation I, b. 1898)

54

Used to be, we'd go visiting. Folks would go out for a walk and drop in and chat, have a beer. Nowadays we just all stay home and watch telly.

(Generation II, b. 1931)

The result of these changes is that families have become more dependent on their own internal resources for planning and organizing leisure activities. When female and male spheres were quite separate, women were less concerned with entertaining their husbands and more involved with the community at large. Their increased isolation within the family, coupled with the modern expectation of friendship and companionship, has meant that wives and husbands are more dependent on each other and therefore more vulnerable to personal whim:

I don't like to go out visiting without Mike. It just doesn't seem right. We like to do things together. But he hasn't been feeling like going out since he started working night shift, so I haven't been going out either. I miss it.

(Generation III, b. 1951)

SEXUALITY

I don't know what sex is all about. Sometimes I wish you could just do it cause it feels good. But of course you can't. You're not supposed to do it till you're married. You might get pregnant. He wants it and you don't. There's all these different things happening all at once. And you don't know what's right or wrong or why it's all happening. Oh sex! Who would have thought anything so simple could be so complex?

(Generation III, b. 1950)

The "long arm of the job" stretches from the workplace into the bedroom and exerts its grip on the most intimate part of marriage. Sexuality is so complex that it operates on many levels and has different meanings in different situations. In some ways it is an expression of human need, of pleasure and of the social togetherness of lovers. In other ways it is an oppressive and repressive relationship which grinds the tenderness and love out of people, leaving behind the frustration, bitterness and violence. From the perspective of domestic labour, there is an aspect of sexuality that is work. On one level marriage can be understood as an exchange between wife and husband — her domestic work, including sexual access, for his economic support.[9]

This underlying exchange becomes apparent in the prelude to marriage, the period in which women are recruited for domestic labour. The process of dating — of selecting a mate for marriage — is, of course, not experienced as an exchange by the people participating in it. The economic necessity for women and the sexual motivation for men are hidden under massive layers of ideology, propaganda and confusion. People date and marry for many reasons, often because "that is the way things work." They are usually so caught up in the process that they do not have time to reflect on it. Although very few Flin Flon women and men had analysed the forces that underpin their lives, they did experience the power of those forces. In dating practices, for example, women generally dated men their own age or older. Men rarely dated older women. While a couple may have agreed to share the costs on a date, men were generally expected to pay. Most significantly, women were not supposed to initiate a relationship. They had to wait until a suitable man approached them.

This means that the balance of forces in any female/male relationship is likely to be unequal. Men tend to have the advantage of being older, having economic power and social authority. Women rarely have access to as much money and they cannot act forthrightly. They are forced to manipulate and insinuate — to set things up so that men will ask them out and, ultimately, ask them to marry.

This inequality permeates sexual activities. Whatever their real feelings (and often they do not know what their real feelings are), both women and men get involved in the process of serious dating where women trade sexual "favours" for a "good time" and economic rewards. On some level the participants are aware of this underlying exchange.

The women know that if they hold out too long, they risk losing the man to someone who is less resistant. Three young women were evaluating their relationships with their current steady boyfriends. All three men were working. One woman,

age sixteen, had been out with her seventeen-year-old boyfriend six times. She commented:

Tomorrow will be our seventh date. Last time he really wanted
me to neck with him but I wouldn't. I only let him kiss me
goodnight when he took me home. I don't think I can get away
with that again this date. I'm going to have to let him go further or
he'll never take me out again.

Her boyfriend had been working for the Company for two years.
He owned a car and had sizeable savings. He had also stated
publicly that when he married, as a wedding present he would
give his wife the downpayment for the house of her choice.
Because of his resources he was considered a "good catch:"

Her fifteen-year-old friend replied:

Yeh, John [age sixteen] and me were necking last weekend and we
got real close. He wants to go all the way but I said no way. Not till
I get married. But he laughed and said I'd be an old maid if I never
made out till then. I'm afraid that if I give in, I'll get pregnant, but
if I don't, then I'll lose him.

The third woman, sixteen years old, agreed:

Yeh! Boys always expect you to go all the way. And if you won't,
then they go find someone else who will. Andy [her eighteen-
year-old boyfriend of six months] said that it wasn't worth his
while taking me out all the time, spending his money on me, if I
didn't come across.

The men had a similar understanding. One seventeen-year-old
man returned from a date in a foul mood. He complained bitterly
that he had had a "lousy time" because:

Jesus, I took her out for supper and we went to a show, and when I
took her home she would do nothing but peck my face and say,
"Thank you for the nice time." I spent all that money on her, and
was real nice to her too and that's all the thanks I get.

Men try to cajole and coerce women "to go all the way."
Women resist, give in a bit, resist some more. Everyone knows
the risks involved and when a woman finally "gives in" and
"allows" the man to go all the way, two related but opposed social
expectations come into play. The first is the assumption that
pregnancy is the woman's responsibility. If she does not take
precautions to prevent conception, she must face the consequences alone. The second is that men do have responsibilities.

If a couple have sexual relations and the woman gets pregnant, they will probably marry.

Once a woman is pregnant, the man is not bound by the same constraints in the situation. Unlike the woman, he can decide or choose whether or not to accept some of the responsibility for her pregnancy. If he does not accept it, then she has been "knocked up" and as a single woman she is subject to material and social hardships. If the man does accept some responsibility, they get married. For the woman this is clearly the preferred choice. It indicates to her as well as to others that he thinks enough of her to want to marry. It makes her a "good woman." However, her dependency on him establishes yet another tension in their relationship.

Many Flin Flon women expressed feelings of gratitude because their husbands had married them. Some spoke of feeling indebted to men who offered to marry them:

> Bob is my honey. When I told him I was pregnant he didn't give me no hassle. He just said right off, "Why then we'll get us married and I'll be a daddy." He was so good to me.
>
> (Generation III, b. 1955)

> I owe him so much. You know, I got that way and I wasn't going to tell him, only my sister said she would if I didn't. At first he was mad. But he agreed we'd get married.
>
> (Generation III, b. 1956)

Many women expressed anxiety that their husbands had married them only because they were pregnant. These women talked about how they and their children were burdens that the man had "nobly" taken on. One woman, married for over thirty years and the mother of five children, described her fears:

> I think maybe he hates me deep down. We had to get married and then I had four more after that one. So he didn't want to marry me. I don't think he ever loved me. But he stuck with us. It was a sort of noble gesture on his part back then. I don't think he knew what it would mean.
>
> (Generation II, b. 1924)

After the first child is born couples are confronted with a series of problems and decisions that focus on sex, children and domestic work. Here, more than anywhere else perhaps, the different interests of women and men are illuminated. For men the issue seems relatively straightforward. They have an acknowledged and socially recognized desire for sexual inter course. They tend to assume both that birth control is the responsibility of the woman and that having children is part of marriage. They also generally favour having several children.

For women the question is far more complex. While a few women have come to terms with their sexuality and have apparently satisfying and active sex lives, most young women find sexuality problematic. They say that they rarely enjoy sex except as an indication that their husbands still love them. They are ignorant about their own sexual needs and are terrified of getting pregnant. A standard complaint raised by women of all ages was that their husbands wanted sex "too often:"

> He's forever wanting it. Never a weekend goes by but he isn't after me to sleep with him. I don't understand why men want it so often.
>
> (Generation II, b. 1929)

This discrepancy between the experiences of women and men is reflected in interactions between friends or cohorts of the same sex. Men at work joke about making it or "scoring" with their wives on a regular basis. Older men comment regularly on younger men's work patterns by assuring them that the reputed laziness of the younger men occurs because they have such active sex lives. Older men caution younger men to wait until they have been married for ten years; then they will not have sex so often and will be able to get a good day's work done.

Women regulary console each other for having "over-sexed" husbands who constantly make demands on them. Older women reassure younger women that after they have been married for ten years or so their husbands will not want sex so much. It will then happen only a couple of times a year and the younger women will not have to worry any more. A young woman who had been married for three years commented:

> My husband wants sex too much. I think he is oversexed. If he had his way, we'd make out every day!
>
> (Generation III, b. 1950)

Her older neighbour reassured her:

> My man used to be that way too, but he got over it. Just wait a few
> more years and yours will slow down too. It's hard on you now,
> but it gets better.
>
> (Generation II, b. 1925)

While the primary reason women give for avoiding sex is the
fear of pregnancy, the contradictions they experience are
compounded by the fact that their work is continuous and tiring.
When a man gets home from work he expects to relax. For a
woman home *is* work and she can rarely relax. Relaxing and
concentrating on sex may be almost impossible for the woman if
she is listening for the children, or has just finished cleaning up
and is trying to organize herself for the next day:

> Then he wants to make out, but I just can't. My head is racing,
> thinking of all the stuff to be done tomorrow morning, and I'm
> tired and just want to collapse asleep. And part of me is always
> listening for the baby.
>
> (Generation III, b. 1954)

In general, their tension about pregnancy and the nature of
their work combine to make women reluctant sexually. Just as
patterns of love, affection and caring have changed over the last
fifty years, so too have patterns of sexuality. In her analysis of
"the marriage bed," Lillian Rubin found that in the last fifty
years American sexual practices have changed tremendously.
"The revolution in American sexual behavior is profound."[10] She
also found that while working-class couples were having sex
more frequently and with greater variation, it was at the man's
initiative. The women felt great ambivalence and insecurity
about sex.

In Flin Flon it also appears that women of the third generation
experienced greater confusion, bewilderment and pressure
about sexuality than their mothers and grandmothers did before
them. One explanation is that as sexuality is increasingly
identified with leisure activities, popularity and personal
expression, it acquires increased significance for both women
and men. Another explanation emerges from an analysis
developed by Michael Schneider regarding the dynamic between
wage work and male sexuality.[11] Schneider notes the oppressive

characteristics of wage work, where the work processes and the machines take over the worker. The body of the worker moves in response to predetermined patterns. His mind has to obey the logic of work processes determined by someone else. Fundamentally, he is denied his humanity.

One area that capitalism does not directly control at work is his sexuality. Because this is one area left to the man, it becomes an important one for him to develop and express. Schneider also notes that as labour has been steadily degraded by capitalism, sex has become increasingly important as a focus of survival for the individual. In sex male workers have increasingly sought solace and release and an assertion of power, which means there is now more sexual pressure on women.

Older Flin Flon women described sex as a duty a woman is obliged to provide for her man. Because they believed that male sexual needs are direct and urgent, they said it was the responsibility of women to meet them. They rarely referred to any sexual drive on the part of women:

> A woman doesn't need that like a man. Men need it regular or they go a bit nutty. So women have to give it to them. You just leave it up to them; just let them do what they want.
> (Generation I, b. 1894)

These women received no direct sexual education. Instead they received extremely contradictory messages. Sex was "not nice" and something to be avoided. Sex was a duty that a woman performed willingly and passively for her husband. They learned to repress and deny their sexual feelings while submitting to men. Older Flin Flon women said that their usual sexual experience was limited to the missionary position, which maximizes the passivity of women. Younger women described a considerably wider range of sexual activities. The sexual revolution of the 1960s expanded knowledge about sexual physiology and sexual practices. As various studies have shown, more people are practising more variations in their sexual behaviour now than in the 1940s.[12]

Rubin found that men were interested in changing their sexual behaviour and pushed women to experiment. She also found that women viewed men's attitudes, including their concern for female orgasm and gratification, as a mixed blessing. She concluded:

> As long as women's sexuality is subjected to capricious demands and treated as if regulated by an "on-off" switch, expected to surge forth vigorously at the flick of the "on" switch or to subside at the flick of the "off," most women will continue to seek the safest path and remain quietly some place between "on" and "off."[13]

"Quietly somewhere between on and off" is an apt description of the way most younger Flin Flon women talked about their sexuality:

> Sometimes I get real excited and I really want it but what we do doesn't really do it to me so then I feel frustrated and irritable. So it's better if I never get turned on.
>
> (Generation III, b. 1952)
>
> I usually don't get turned on very much but sometimes he's just so nice and he loves me so much that I feel sort of like it.
>
> (Generation III, b. 1951)
>
> Mostly I don't think about sex, but if I get too turned off then it's awful when he wants it, so I can't shut myself off completely.
>
> (Generation III, b. 1954)

The passive lover is a natural extension of the "good girl." Women who for years learned to deny their sexual needs cannot suddenly reverse those years and "turn on." But for younger men sexuality is an important part of the way they have learned to express their feelings. As one man explained:

> I love her and I want her to know how deeply I feel and I can't understand why she won't let me show her [by having sex].
>
> (Generation III, b. 1945)

His bewilderment was genuine; so was his affection. Rubin describes the uncertainty that women and men experience when they confront each other's sexual expectations:

> The cry for understanding from both men and women is real. Each wishes to make the other understand, yet, given the widely different socialization practices around male and female sexuality, the wish is fantasy. As a result, he asks; she gives. And neither is satisfied.[14]

For women the recent sexual patterns that men have introduced are bound up in contradictions. Men want women to be more active, to participate more energetically in sex, to initiate it more often. They want greater variety, particularly oral sex. They also want to feel that women are enjoying sex. But women and men have not generally learned how to share mutual pleasure. Instead men tend to exert even more pressure on women and then appropriate women's pleasure for themselves.

So women become more active, take the initiative and either have orgasms or fake them, still mostly to satisfy the men:

> He keeps telling me he wishes I'd start things off sometimes. But when I do he's always busy or too tired or I'm interrupting him. I think he wants me to start things when he wants them to start.
> (Generation III, b. 1945)

For some women sex is still a duty, but a duty that now includes being active:

> He wants me to be real turned on and excited. He sort of likes it when I pant and moan and wiggle around.
> (Generation III, b.1941)

Some women do what their husbands want out of resignation or fear:

> I don't care any more. I just let him do what he wants, and if he wants me to do something I do it. So what?
> (Generation III, b. 1946)

> When he wants it he has to get it or he gets mad and beats me up, so I always do as he wants.
> (Generation III, b. 1957)

Just as women are afraid when dating that if they hold back they may lose the men, some wives are afraid that if they do not participate in sex, they will lose their husbands to other women, to the pub or to male friends:

> I do it whenever he wants. Otherwise I figure he'll run off with other women — ladies of the night types.
> (Generation III, b. 1945)

> I try to act real interested and sexy just as he's leaving for work so he'll be interested and come straight home after work.
> (Generation II, b. 1935)

> I always seduce him just before we go to a party. That way I figure he won't be interested in other women. He'll be too pooped.
> (Generation III, b. 1946)

For some women sexual co-operation is a way of inducing or rewarding good behaviour. Some even recognize the sexual-economic exchange that underlies marriage:

If I want something, I just get all sexy and loving, and after I tell him what I want.

(Generation III, b. 1956)

If he does something really nice, like help me with the dishes or take me out somewhere to something special, then I always try to make love to him so he'll know I liked what he did.

(Generation II, b. 1933)

When I want something for the house, like a new washing machine or something, then I just make love like crazy for a while and then stop. Then I tell him what I want and say that if he wants more loving he has to buy it.

(Generation III, b. 1949)

For many other women, however, sex is a way of expressing their feelings of affection and caring. For them "making love" is literally that. Sex both expresses and reinforces the love they feel for their husbands:

I love that guy. So I try to show him.

(Generation III, b. 1947)

He's a sweetie. I love him so I make love with him lots.

(Generation III, b. 1948)

He's a wonderful man. I love him. It's the best way I can let him know.

(Generation III, b. 1953)

Love and affection can hold women back sexually. Some women decide that there is no percentage in "turning on." To turn on is to assert one's own needs. Sex traditionally revolves around the man's advances, his schedules, his rhythms, his climax — *his* needs. For a woman to be turned on seems to contest this one-sidedness. Women often subordinate their needs and wants to ensure family harmony. Sublimating their sexuality to their husbands' may be an expression of this pattern, an attempt on the part of the wife to express her love for her husband:

Sometimes I'd like to say stop when he is pounding away at me. Then I'd tell him to slow down, to touch me the way I dream about. And I imagine us making love beautifully. And I like it and I

love him. But if I did, I know he'd feel hurt. It's important to him
that he thinks I like the way he makes love. If I started suggesting
things he'd feel bad. So I don't.

(Generation III, b. 1948)

The sublimation of sexuality, in the interests of marital
harmony may be one reason sexual activity apparently decreases
as the marriage ages. Sixty of the women interviewed reported
that as their marriages progressed, their level of sexual activity
decreased. It may be that, faced with their inability to resolve all
the contradictions that surround sexuality, many couples give
up. They minimize their sexual activities rather than continue to
confront the tensions:

> When we were first married, sex was really difficult. I never liked
> it and he knew that and it made him feel bad. Gradually it just
> didn't seem worth it to go on. So we don't do it much any more.
>
> (Generation II, b. 1931)

FAMILY VIOLENCE IS A HATEFUL THING

Men and women come to marriage from very different
positions and their experiences of work and marriage create
different understandings. At best these contrary positions are
barriers which must be struggled against. For most couples they
become sources of tension and all too frequently the tension
leads to hostility and conflict.

At work men are powerless, so in their leisure time they want
to have a feeling that they control their own lives. Because they
are responsible for the household's subsistence, men often feel
that they have the right to control the arrangements of the
household and the people who live there. As the wage *earner*, the
man is the wage *owner*. He is the property owner in the family; his
power is rooted in real property relations. This property
prerogative is the basis of the unequal relations of the family.

Structured into household relations therefore is a "petty
tyranny" which allows the man to dominate his wife and
children. Such male domination derives partly from the fact that
domestic labour is predicated on wage labour and therefore
caters to the needs of the wage worker. It is reinforced partly by

societal norms of male dominance and superiority. Male chauvinism easily flourishes in such a setting. Some men exercise their "petty tyranny" by demanding that their wives be at home when they get off work. The reason men give for making this demand is partly a reflection of their desire to assert their authority:

> She's my wife and she should be there when I get off.
>
> (Generation II, b. 1919)
>
> You [to wife] be home when I get off. That's where you belong.
>
> (Generation III, b. 1946)

Knowing that they can demand that their wives be at home waiting for them is a mechanism for releasing some of the feelings of powerlessness the wage work engenders:

> It makes me feel good to know she is at home waiting for me, like there's a place where I'm a man. I think about that when I'm at work.
>
> (Generation III, b. 1953)

One result of the economic relationship between women and their husbands is to bind the men to their jobs. While divorce from the means of production structurally compels men to do wage work, once a man has a dependent wife and children he incurs responsibilities and debts, which means that he cannot afford to stop working. While a single man can choose to quit a particular job when it becomes too unpleasant, a married man cannot. Objectively the woman becomes a force in keeping the man tied to his job. From her position of economic dependency, a wife adds more pressure to the structural compulsion to work.

Historically the Company has hired married men precisely because they create a more stable workforce. Sometimes women themselves recognize this aspect of their relationship:

> I know he hates his job. It's a terrible job. But he can't quit 'cause of me and the kids. We need his wages.
>
> (Generation III, b. 1953)

Subjectively women act as pressure to keep their husbands not only at work but working regularly and responsibly. Many men deal with their dislike of work by quitting periodically, or less drastically, by going late, taking time off or slacking on the job. Such behaviour is directly threatening to the household standard of living as it affects the amount of money the men bring home. It is in the women's interests to try to prevent the men from taking time off. When a man considers doing so, his wife may point out that they are in debt and need his money. Thus some men see their wives as constantly nagging, forcing them to work when they hate it. This induces tensions between the needs of women as domestic workers and the response of the men to wage work, tensions which are often expressed as hostilities between the sexes. A woman whose husband regularly skipped shifts expressed her sense of frustration and anger at men:

> Men. They're just no good. They are lazy and irresponsible and selfish. Look at Jim, he just skipped another shift and how are we going to make do?

> (Generation II, b. 1929)

On the other hand, the responsibility of being bread winners generates in men all sorts of pressure and fear, which in turn are often projected onto women.[15] This hostility is reinforced by women's work as tension managers for their husbands.

When men express their work-related tensions, anxieties and hostilities at work, it is economically threatening to the employer. When their protest is collectively expressed, for example in a general strike, the results are politically threatening to the capitalist state. Therefore, both employers and the state employ sophisticated means to minimize this potential. The threat of firing is the most significant means of repressing outbursts in the workplace. Labour legislation, especially laws against wildcat strikes, and the armed force of the police protect the interests of the state.

On the other hand, family violence is not directed against either employers or the state. While in recent years, primarily because of pressures from the women's liberation movement, family violence has gradually come to be considered socially deviant, it is still not recognized as a major social problem. Very little is done by either employers or the state to prevent family violence.

If no mechanisms are available by which workers can channel their work-related tensions into forms of struggle at the workplace, they carry those tensions and angers home with them. Part of reproducing the worker's labour power must therefore include ways of displacing those work-related fears and hostilities:

> When he comes home from work, I really think it's up to me to help him relax and feel good. If he's grumpy and tired, I cheer him up.
>
> (Generation II, b. 1926)

This part of women's work in reproducing labour power is the most hidden and profound. It is also of vital importance for her work and her life. While part of this tension management is done for the sake of the man, another part is for herself and the children. Women do not want to live with fights and the threat of violence everyday. They defuse tension, refrain from a certain argument, or protect their husbands from things that will upset them in order to maintain peace:

> I remember how I always used to try and meet him at the door with a cup of tea. He liked his tea. If I made him feel better after work, then our home was a happy one.
>
> (Generation I, b. 1900)

In some instances, women are the recipients of overt anger and rage. Some examples will illustrate what this means in practice. A thirty-two-year-old man had worked for the Company for sixteen years. His current supervisor did not like him and they had regular clashes at work. He came home almost every night tense and irritable. His wife described what happened at night:

> We go to sleep and then sometimes in the middle of the night I wake up because he is groaning and punching me and crying out angry stuff at his boss. Sometimes he punches me real hard and once he broke my nose. Course he didn't mean to and it wasn't me he was mad at. It was his boss, but still. So I get out of bed and go make tea and wake him up and talk to him, then he settles down and we go back to sleep. It happens maybe two or three times a week.
>
> (Generation III, b. 1949)

The wife received the brunt of the rage and violence that her husband bottled up and repressed at work. She considered it her duty to get up and make him tea and comfort him, even though she had an infant to feed at 6:00 A.M. She was constantly tired and sometimes dozed off in the middle of a conversation. She apologized for doing so by explaining:

See Joe has a hard time at work so I have to get up with him in the night, so I don't get too much sleep these days.

In another case, a twenty-eight-year-old man had worked for the Company for twelve years. He too had a supervisor with whom he fought regularly. His solution to his work-related tensions was to get drunk or stoned on marijuana every night after work. His wife was concerned for his health and worried that he drank or smoked "all that hard-earned cash." When he was "ripped" he tended to think that she was the hated boss and he lashed out at her:

Once he came at me with the kitchen knife saying I was [the boss] and he wasn't going to take no more shit from me. Another time he took a swipe at me and broke my glasses. Usually though he just yells at me that I can take my fucking job and shove it or something like that. I just keep out of reach till he calms down.

(Generation III, b. 1951)

Growing out of the various power struggles that occur between men and their work and between wives and husbands is sex-based hostility where male contempt for women is expressed through physical violence.

Wife beating is one of the hidden crimes in this society. In recent years the women's liberation movement has pointed out how widespread it is. The few studies that have been done show unequivocally that wife beating is a phenomenon that occurs with equal frequency among families of all classes.[16] It is part of the larger problem of generalized violence against women and must be understood in that context. For working-class families, it is compounded by the pressures and dependency generated by the proletarian condition:

My husband beats me, usually on pay day. He gets mad and hates me. His violence is a really hateful thing.

(Generation II, b. 1935)

Why do women put up with such treatment? They do so partly because there are no resources to give them the support necessary to deal with the abuse. Flin Flon has no hostels for women; the police will not interfere in what they term "domestic squabbles" and economically the women have no resources to leave. Equally important is the fact that most women feel it is their responsibility to "stick it out" because marriage is "till death do us part" and tension managing is part of their work. Of the hundred women interviewed, only three were divorced. Most women, when male violence erupts, "just keep out of reach" until it subsides.

One woman who was beaten regularly by her husband was recovering after a particularly bad attack in which her arm was broken. What she said explains in part why so many women accept the abuse they receive from their husbands:

> He puts up with shit every day at work and he only works because he has me and the kids to support. Weren't for us he'd be off trapping on his own, with no boss breathing down his neck. He hates his job. He's got all that mad locked up inside with nowhere for it to go. So sometimes he takes it out on me and the kids. Well I sort of don't blame him I guess.
>
> (Generation II, b. 1935)

Thus a terrible but logical and extreme extension of their roles as tension managers is for women, as the victims, to blame themselves and to feel guilty for having induced male hostility and aggression.

MEETING WOMEN'S NEEDS

Domestic violence is the most extreme form of women's oppression within the family. However, in a myriad of other less obvious ways the subordinate character of domestic labour denies women their full humanity.

Domestic labour is responsible for reproducing the labour power of all the adults of the household. In other words, the women is responsible for reproducing not only her husband's capacity to work each day but her own as well. In some ways, domestic labour is similar to wage work. It is frequently physically and mentally exhausting and monotonous. While it is not alienated in the sense that wage labour is alienated, it is the epitome of self-sacrificing labour. Because it is unpaid, women can justify it as reasonable and honourable work only by considering it a "labour of love." This definition reinforces its self-sacrificing quality and encourages women themselves to underplay the extent to which it is much more than a labour of love. In daily life this means that women's needs are not always met

When household resources are scarce, it is the women who cut back their consumption first. There is a working-class tradition of women eating less than their husbands and children, denying themselves sustenance they badly need so that other household members can have more.[17]

In many Flin Flon households, on the day before payday there was very little food in the house. A number of women regularly did not eat that day because there was only enough for one or two people.

> He's got to eat or he can't do his work and the baby needs food to grow, but it won't hurt me to skip a meal for once.
>
> (Generation III, b. 1958)

Women's sleeping time is also vulnerable to demands from other household members. In some households where men worked the night shift, their wives got up at 3:00 A.M. either to greet them coming off shift or to send them off to work. When those women had school-aged children, they also had to get up at 7:30 A.M. so their sleep was disrupted and inadequate. When other household members were sick or frightened or simply unable to sleep at night, the women got up with them to comfort, feed and care for them. A number of women talked about how tired they felt all the time. They attributed this "housewife's fatigue" to regularly interrupted sleep.

Even when women were ill, they had to carry on with their work. Those women who were actively engaged in domestic labour reported that their husbands were sick enough to stay in bed an average of four days each year. Their husbands went to bed when they got sick, and the women took care of them in addition to doing their regular work. The women themselves were sick enough to warrant staying in bed an average of eight days each year. However, they unanimously agreed that, no matter how sick they were, they could not take time off to go to bed. They continued with their regular work despite their illness. In every case, women took time off work only when they were hospitalized — for a major illness or having a baby. Women said they enjoyed their stays in hospital when their babies were born. They relished the rest and being catered to.

The twenty-two women who were retired said that a similar pattern continued even when the couple was older and nearing retirement. In older people, illness was compounded by the fact that many of the men had work-related injuries or illnesses, which meant they required constant nursing. Even though the women were also often ill or crippled by age-related diseases, such as arthritis and rheumatism, they still continued to nurse the men. A number of women said that dealing with an ill spouse finally forced them to retire:

> I kept on managing my house for twenty years after my husband retired. He had bad lungs [from working underground] and at last he took to bed and needed regular nursing. Well I kept at it for about a year, but I wasn't strong enough so I finally had to give it up.
>
> (Generation I, b. 1888)

Reproducing labour power also involves ensuring that workers have a chance to recuperate, relax and engage in leisure activities that are not related to their regular work. For domestic workers, especially with young children, meeting this need is almost impossible. There is no time when the woman is totally free from work-related responsibilities. Even when she is relaxing, she is on call. Women recognize that their situation differs from their husbands:

> I guess I have to take care of all of them and then I have to take care of myself too.
>
> (Generation III, b. 1955)

> How come there's no one to take care of me?
>
> (Generation II, b. 1934)

> When they are tired, or can't find something or they want something, I do it for them. When I want something I get it for myself.
>
> (Generation III, b. 1945)

When women described their activities during a typical day, they frequently mentioned periods when they took time "off" to visit with friends, watch TV or just sit down for a cup of tea and a cigarette. However, even during these breaks, those with young children must be alert to their activities. And all too often, women described their breaks as time not only to relax but also to "do a bit of mending or sewing."

The responsibility of constantly caring for the needs of others means that it is often difficult for women to determine what their own needs are:

> When I wake up early I like to lie in bed and have a think about my life. It's the only time I have to myself and what I need, you know, to get me through my day. Like I know what he needs — his lunch box and a hot supper — and what they need — clean clothes and their lunch. And they all need love I guess. But what do I need?
>
> (Generation II, b. 1936)

Sometimes the work women do becomes so merged with their identity that they have trouble distinguishing them. They confuse their own needs with those of their families. This confusion is reflected in the way women sometimes describe family needs. A woman buying a jacket for her six-year-old child remarked: "I need this jacket. It's getting cold these days."

The lack of clarity that women have about their own needs as domestic workers begins with marriage when most couples set up households and the women establish the social relations of their work based on inexperience and lack of knowledge. The first few years of household formation are critical, for it is during this period that patterns of work, personal interactions and the particular expression of the division of labour within the household are established. Once established they are extremely difficult to change.

A woman with three children under ten years of age observed that when her first baby was born she was so interested and excited by the new baby that she wanted to take care of it herself. She never asked her husband to help out with child care. When the second and third children were born, the novelty had worn off, her energy was dissipated and she wanted him to become involved:

> But he just wouldn't. He said he'd never changed a nappy and he wasn't about to start. In fact, he used to point out regularly that I had insisted on doing it all alone with the first one and why had I suddenly changed my tune now?
>
> (Generation III, b. 1948)

Because of their initial inexperience and lack of knowledge, women frequently flounder around for several years trying to understand what is happening to them and trying to get some control over the situation.

At the same time, they are caught up in the demands of young children, keeping a house and relating to their husbands. Many of them end up in the same situation as the Red Queen in Lewis Carroll's *Through the Looking Glass,* having to run as fast as they can simply to stay in one place.[18] An older woman recalled her feelings of bewilderment and confusion during this early period of her marriage:

> I never quite got on top of things. I kept thinking that if I could just get a week of peace I could think things through and then I'd be okay. But everything was always rushing here and there and I didn't ever catch up. Now I sort of have a routine and a pattern of work. But I never chose it. It just happened by default.
>
> (Generation I, b. 1907)

Most women are not deliberate martyrs; they make a concerted effort to ensure that their own needs for relaxation and support are met at some level. They develop strategies, such as organizing their workplace and the social relations of their work in the most convenient and convivial ways possible. This means that women are interested in adopting any new developments in household technology, in the organization of their work or in new products and materials.

Another strategy involves organizing their work so that they can assert themselves as they choose when their husbands are not around. Most women organize this part of their time around their own interests:

> When he's not here I do things how I want. I scrub my floors or do my wash or go visit or play with the kids — whatever I want to do and how I want to do it. When he gets off, I have to make sure I'm on time for work, I have to be at home waiting for him and I do what he wants while he's there. That way he feels good, we have a good time together and I get my own time too.
>
> (Generation III, b. 1947)

As a third strategy women establish and maintain networks of coworkers, friends and neighbours to provide a milieu in which they can pool their knowledge about their work and share information, goods and services. All of the women interviewed described these networks as vitally important to them. On an average women spent three to four hours each day visiting, either in person or on the phone, with friends and neighbours. During these visits women combine a number of activities. They enjoy each other's company while exchanging information about their work and their lives. Simultaneously they care for their children and continue doing some aspect of their housework, such as ironing or cooking:

> I try to visit with my friends as often as possible. It helps me get through my day. We sit and chat about this and that. We watch the kids. I help do the laundry or whatever.
>
> (Generation III, b. 1949)

They also rely a great deal on assistance and support from female relatives. Of the twenty women interviewed who had mothers living in Flin Flon, nineteen said they saw their mothers at least twice a week. Of the eighty-eight active domestic workers interviewed, seventy-two said they relied on a close female relative, mother, mother-in-law, daughter, or sister to help out in crisis situations. Women in sixty-three households said they visited with a close female relative at least once each week and that those women provided assistance, information and affection:

> My sister and my husband's mother are just always there when I need them. If I want to pop out to the store, one of them will mind the baby. If I'm feeling low, I go for a visit.
>
> (Generation III, b. 1951)

Through their women friends and relatives, housewives can improve the social relations of their work and meet some of their own needs for work-related tension managing. Even women who considered their husbands to be their best friends asserted that women friends were special and important:

> Well, my husband, he's my husband and I love him, and he knows me better than anyone and he's my best friend. But Sarah is something else. I see her everyday and we chat and when I'm down she cheers me up and when I'm in a muddle she sorts me out and when things aren't good with my husband, she hugs me.
>
> (Generation III, b. 1948)

Frequently, several women got together to do some part of their work collectively. Two or three women went shopping in one car, and as they shopped they pooled ideas about good deals and menu suggestions. They looked out for each other's children and borrowed money from each other. On occasion, several women assembled in one house to spend the day cooking. They usually did this when the food such as pierogies, cabbage rolls or preserves required lots of chopping or a long cooking time and constant watching. The women prepared a large quantity of food to be shared among all of them. I participated in two collective cooking activities. One day three of us worked from 9:00 A.M. to 5:30 P.M. and made 435 pierogies. On another day, four of us worked from 10:30 A.M. to 4:30 P.M. and made 193 cabbage rolls. Working together turned an onerous job into an interesting social occasion.

Most of the women interviewed said that periodically when their children were young they arranged with another woman to exchange child care services. Two women with children of similar ages took turns looking after each other's children for a number of hours each week. This gave each of the mothers some time "off" to spend as they wished.

Because individual women work most of the time in the isolation of their own home, these relations with other women combine both the need for coworkers with whom to share information and advice and the need for friends with common interests. It is these relationships that provide much of the tension managing that domestic workers need. Women pointed out that their husbands rarely did domestic work and consistently undervalued both its difficulty and its worth. Other women, who from their own experience understood the requirements and rigours of the work, were more helpful in providing support, reassurance and comfort for work-related problems:

> Sometimes I feel so tired and out of sorts with my family. I can't really talk to David about it. He tries but he really doesn't understand, and anyway sometimes he's part of the problem, if you know what I mean. My mother or my sister or my neighbour next door, I just go and have a good cry with them and then I feel better.
>
> (Generation III, b. 1942)

Women's efforts to improve the conditions of their work, and their families' lives, and all the contradictions inherent in that, have an impact beyond their immediate household and friendship networks.

The tension between women's short- and long-term interests as domestic labourers and as members of their class was illustrated during the period of contract negotiations between the union and the Company in 1976. A number of women noted that the negotiations directly affected them and their ability to do their work. One woman pointed out the contradiction between the immediate objective conditions of her work, the long-term interests of that work, and her subjective understanding of her class interests. Her immediate interests were the regularity of the wage, ensuring that money kept coming into the household purse. Her long-term interests as a domestic labourer were concerned with the magnitude of the wage and its increase. As a member of her class she had to grapple with the short-term/long-term trade-offs that are always part of class struggle:

> I don't want a strike because I can't live on strike pay. I just can't feed my kids on strike pay. But I think we should strike because that company makes so much money off those men and it thinks it can get away with murder. We need to stand up to the Company

Flin Flon Strike, 1971 — Marching Women Call for Action.

and show them that they can't go on trashing us workers any more.

(Generation II, b. 1926)

There is a long tradition of miners' wives acting militantly in support of the miners in class-struggle situations.[19] In both strikes in Flin Flon, in 1934 and 1971, the wives of strikers played an important role in the union struggles. They organized strike support committees, went on the picket lines and regularly indicated both their support for the men and their own interests in winning the strike.

A woman who was active in the 1971 strike described her experiences and noted the connections between her work in the home and her husband's wage work:

The men were on strike and their families were hurting. A bunch of us women were talking. Some of them wanted to end the strike — they were scared and just wanted life to be normal again. But others understood better that it was our strike too. We needed more money and better conditions for our men, [and this] meant better conditions at home. Miserable angry workers make rotten husbands.... So we went on the picket line and did what we could.

(Generation II, b. 1929)

78

By seizing the initiative, women begin to gain some control over their working conditions and their lives. This gives them strength to struggle against the inequalities of their marriages. It undermines their subordination and helps to make better, rather than worse, the position of wife in industrial capitalist society.

CHAPTER FOUR

MOTHERS AND CHILDREN

In some ways it is the ultimate alienation of our society that the ability to give birth has been transformed into a liability.

Eleanor Leacock

FUNDAMENTAL to marriage is an assumption that the couple will have children:

Having kids and looking after them. That's what it's really all about, isn't it?

(Generation III, b. 1948)

For Flin Flon women, as for the vast majority of women in advanced capitalist countries, the two aspects of having children — bearing them and raising them — are inseparably linked. It is important to note that such association is by no means natural. It is fostered by a lack of alternatives and by a powerful social belief that having children is "natural" for women, that the essential responsibility for bearing and rearing children is located within the nuclear family, and that mothers make the best rearers of their children.[1]

Flin Flon women reflect these beliefs when they acknowledge that one of the primary reasons for getting married is that the woman is pregnant or that the couple want to have children. Because women place such a high value on children, the work of mothering is extremely important to them. Women say that their work with children makes the other aspects of domestic labour "all worthwhile." On a deeper level, the work of childbearing and childrearing is also part of the reproduction of labour power. People do not have children with any intention of providing future workers for capitalist industry. They have children for a variety of reasons and that is clearly not one of them. And while households cannot survive without the daily reproduction of the labour power of the adult members, they can survive very well without children. However, the continued existence of the working class, as a class, and hence of the capitalist mode of production itself, is in part dependent on generational reproduction, and so this labour too is one of the underlying essentials of the capitalist economy.

CHANGES IN MOTHERWORK

Child care, particularly when children are young, is demanding, constant work. Unlike all other components of domestic work, its "production time" is twenty-four hours a day, seven days a week. Even when children are asleep or playing away from home, the mother is always responsible for them. Such a commitment of attention and awareness can never be contracted or made more flexible.

While the time involved in caring for any one child cannot be reduced, with each generation, women are having fewer children; they are having them closer together, and the chances of their infants surviving is now significantly higher. As the average life span increases, the proportion of women's lives actually spent bearing children has decreased.

Flin Flon women of the first generation had an average of 4 children who survived infancy; women of the second generation had an average of 3.5 children and women of the third generation averaged 2.3 children. Although women of the third generation are still fertile and may yet bear more children, Flin Flon women generally indicated that they thought family size was decreasing. Women of the current generation said they intended to have fewer children than their mothers had:

> Families used to be a lot larger didn't they? My mother had four and I don't want that many. I want to have two and then stop.
> (Generation III, b. 1950)

While the social relationship between a mother and her children lasts for a lifetime, the *work* of mothering basically ends when the last child leaves home. Considering that the age of leaving varies, a mother's work lasts a minimum of sixteen years, if she has one child. Of the twenty women of the first generation, sixteen had been active working mothers for over forty years. One woman had her first child in 1923 when she was seventeen and her last one twenty-four years later when she was forty-one. This last child lived at home until he was twenty-one. Her work life as a mother lasted fifty years.

Most younger women insisted that they wanted to have all their children close together so that they could "get it all over with quickly." It seems reasonable to estimate then that for most Flin Flon women of the current generation mothering will be an active occupation for twenty to thirty years. While this is less than the number of years spent in the earlier period, it is still a very significant proportion of their lives.

Because she has fewer children the potential exists for the mother's relationship with her children to increase in intensity. Having fewer siblings to interact with, the child becomes more dependent on the mother:

> As the family has become smaller, each child has become more important; the actual act of reproduction occupies less and less time and the socializing and nurturance process increase commensurately in significance.... Thus the mother's reproductive role has retreated as her socializing role has increased.[2]

The intensification of the relationship between mothers and their children has emerged as a result of two developments outside of the home. First, improvements in the consumer goods sector have altered housework, freeing a certain amount of women's labour time. Simultaneously, various scientific advances, particularly the persuasive Freudian insight that the first five years of life are critical to the development of a child's character, called for a reassessment of the necessary qualities of people who care for children:

> One of the great revolutions of modern psychology has been the discovery of the decisive specific weight of infancy in the course of an individual life.... The preconditions for the later stability and integration demand an extraordinary degree of care and intelligence on the part of the adult who is socializing the child.[3]

As women have learned of new developments in the scientific understanding of human development and as they have inculcated the resulting theories about mothering, the time and energy they have spent in caring for their young children has increased.

While women intensified their involvement with their young children, they lost some of their control over the socialization of their older children. Because children now spend almost half of their waking hours in school, the school system has taken over a major portion of socialization, considerably reducing the parent's influence. School attendance subjects children to the philosophies of the educational system and the personal idiosyncracies of particular teachers, both of which may conflict with the socialization process occurring in the household. Schoolage children are not readily available to help with domestic work, especially the care of younger siblings. They are less able to learn from their mothers how to do this work. School attendance also introduces children to membership in a peer group, whose influence becomes increasingly strong as the children grow and whose interests and demands frequently run counter to those of the parents.

Television has introduced into the home a range of ideas, values and cultural traditions that often conflicts with those of the older generation. Both school and television are forces beyond the mother's control that affect the child's socialization. In the case of television, the mother can minimize its impact by refusing to have a television in the house or by strictly monitoring the programs her children watch. But, other children who are not similarly restricted can introduce her children to the ideas, attitudes and concepts from the shows they watch. Through the peer group, children who do not have access to television in their own homes can still be affected indirectly by TV culture.

The importance of school, the peer group and television have all increased for children over the last three generations. These external forces are frequently at odds with what the mother is trying to do. Women find themselves in an increasingly contradictory position. Their relationships with their children.

are more intense, and their work as mothers is increasingly recognized as important not only for children but for society. At the same time, mothers are experiencing a loss of control over the socialization of their children as various forces outside the home play an increasingly significant role. Despite the impact of such forces, mothers are primarily responsible for their children. If as their children grow they exhibit any signs of deviance, the full social blame for this "failure" falls on the mothers' shoulders. Increasingly women have internalized a sense of personal responsibility for the development of their children.

This change was vividly demonstrated by women's responses to infant mortality. Of the twenty first generation women interviewed, six had lost one child in infancy and one had lost two children. First generation women attributed infant mortality to a variety of causes beyond their control. They suggested that the babies died because of "God's will," illness and inadequate medicine, or just because babies are frail and likely to die. Of the eighty women of the second and third generations, only two had lost a child in infancy. Both of these women blamed themselves:

> I lost my second one. It might have been that crib death. But I can't help feeling I did something wrong — like gave him the wrong foods or left him alone so he choked or something.
>
> (Generation II, b. 1937)

> My first baby died when she was three months old. I think it was because I didn't know what to do with babies.
>
> (Generation III, b. 1948)

The general drop in infant mortality and the intensification of motherwork means that now if a child dies in infancy, the mother considers it a testament to her negligence.

As children grow up, the situation becomes more complex. Women continue to accept responsibility for their children even when external influences have more weight in their children's lives. The type of people their children are likely to be is profoundly affected by the work mothers do and by the nature of their relationships with their children. All of this puts tremendous pressure on mothers and generates significant and unresolvable contradictions in the work of mothering.

THE CONTRADICTIONS OF MOTHERING

Children must learn consciously and internalize unconsciously the social values, attitudes and behaviours appropriate to their culture, class, race, sex and age.[4] As the future owners of labour power, they must also learn the various attitudes and skills they will need to become workers. Mothers experience a major contradiction between the social relations of mother and child and the work of child care. Children are people but they are also objects of labour. The process of bearing and raising children is profoundly creative. In a world where women often feel impotent, motherhood generates a form of creative power. Children are living beings women can shape. Caring for children involves intense interpersonal relations and some of the most significant and potentially loving relationships. Women usually enjoy the warmth and intimacy of the relationship. However, while children are young, child care is also full-time work, which can be frustrating and onerous. Women frequently resent and dislike the work involved.

Because the two aspects are not differentiated, women often experience mixed feelings that usually focus on the child. Hence, the typical response of one mother of four children:

I look at them sometimes and I wonder. I love them more than life itself and I wish they'd go away forever.

(Generation III, b. 1940)

This blurring of social relations and work leads women to deny or minimize the work aspect of mothering:

Oh, how can you call bringing up your children work? Taking care of your children isn't work. It's such a pleasure.

(Generation III, b. 1938)

This contradiction is intensified by the demands placed on women to produce future workers. Immediately, Flin Flon mothers confront a double bind. Advanced capitalist society is not monolithic. Internally, it generates different and sometimes contradictory requirements as it expands and develops. Therefore, its imperatives are constantly changing, and those changes occur unevenly. The competitive and unplanned nature of the economy creates a built-in uncertainty. Women can never know what they are preparing their children for. They are socializing their children for an unknown future in a world outside the home over which they have virtually no control.

As they engage in their work, mothers draw on their childhood experiences. Since their experiences are at least twenty years old, women often try to raise their children in ways that are no longer suitable. When they turn for advice to their mothers and other female kin, the guidance is likewise distorted. The traditional sources of female training are not very helpful, and women find themselves drawing on an irrelevant past.

Tensions generated by this situation are expressed through conflicts between mothers and their children. The inherent conservatism of socialization, seeking to reproduce or duplicate past social relations, conflicts with the changing social environment that makes duplication impossible. This conservatizing aspect of the work reinforces the image of women as traditional and repressive. The difference between the values with which women set out to rear their children and the circumstances that those growing children encounter can engender in children a contempt for their "old-fashioned" mothers. Women rarely understand

87

the source of this conflict, although they are sensitive to its expression within their families. One mother of three children under fourteen explained it this way:

> I spend most of my day trying to teach the children to be good people, to teach them so they will grow up to be the kind of people that other people respect. But what thanks do I get? They argue with me all the time, saying that things just aren't done my way anymore, that I'm square and out of it. And when I insist, they don't understand that I'm doing it for their own good. They think I'm just mean.
>
> (Generation III, b. 1940)

There is often a tension between the future that women raise their children for and the actual situation that those children encounter when they grow up. A number of women whose children were born in the late 1940s or early 1950s pointed out that when their children were young it was popularly believed that if children got a university education they would be guaranteed a good job on graduation. Some parents encouraged their children to get an education. When those children graduated in the early 1970s with B.A.s, they discovered that circumstances had changed and their degrees did not guarantee any job, much less a good job:

> When the children were small we decided that we wanted them to have something better in life so we saved really hard. We lived really frugally so we could pay for them both to go to university and we always encouraged them at school and told them to work hard and we'd see they went to university and then they could get good jobs. Well, they went and just look, the only job Peter could get was with the Company like his dad and, Shirley, she works in the bank. Well if I'd known that would happen, I wouldn't have scrimped so hard when they were little.
>
> (Generation II, b. 1937)

Depending upon their own strength, sensitivity and class consciousness, women as mothers experience their work as difficult and contradictory. One mother commented as her oldest of five children began to work for the Company:

> I watch him go off to work for the Company just like his dad. Eighteen years I've raised that lad. I cared for him; I taught him.

I don't feel very good about doing all that just so he can go work for the Company and kill himself like his dad is.

(Generation II, b. 1931)

Another woman described similar contradictory feelings and how she dealt with them:

When John [her middle child of three] went to work for the Company I told him plain, "I raised you good, son. Now you are growed and off to work, and you know how to be a good worker, we taught you that. But you have to know how to be a fighting worker. You get into that union and you make sure it looks out for your interests, working folks' interests, not the Company's. I didn't teach you all that just so the Company can make a profit off you. You stand up for your rights."

(Generation II, b. 1940)

A third woman noted the discomfort some women felt about watching their sons go off to work and commented that a similar process occurs with daughters:

I complain about my son having to work but it's true for her, too. I want for her to be happy and I'm glad she's married, but I see her doing just what I had to do all my life, keeping house, raising kids, caring for her husband — and I wonder if that's really what I raised her for.

(Generation II, b. 1931)

While some women express concern about raising their children to face lives of oppression and exploitation, the children themselves often rebel against the conditions of their upbringing. Frequently their anger and resentment is directed at the immediate agent of their socialization, their mother. Whether or not women understand the underlying causes of this anger, their children's rage is profoundly disturbing. Two mothers, one with a fifteen-year-old daughter and the other with a fourteen-year-old son, had different responses to their children's rage:

She's really rebellious right now, really angry and I can't blame her. What's she got to look forward to I ask you? When I tell her she has to go to school on time, study hard and so on she screams at me that I'm ruining her life always nagging her and I think she's got a point. Why should she have to learn when all she'll get is a job in a shop or a bunch of babies. Still I feel it's my duty to teach her responsibility. It makes me really unhappy when she screams at me.

(Generation II, b. 1930)

I don't know where I went wrong, how I failed. He's so angry and he does bad things. Like him and his friends hang out and break things and he won't do what I tell him and he says he hates me. My own son says he hates me.

(Generation II, b. 1943)

The problem of drawing on an irrelevant past to prepare for an unknown future in a situation where the mother has very little control is even further complicated by the fact that no coherent, generally agreed upon pattern of childrearing exists. Motherhood imposes upon individual women a bewildering and frequently contradictory set of conditions and interpretations within which they do their work. Women in Flin Flon sometimes described themselves as unsure of the appropriate ways to raise their children:

In the old days you knew what was what. Women did what their mothers did. You knew what the rules were. Now the rules are always changing and you never know where you are at.

(Generation II, b. 1931)

This uncertainty leaves domestic labour susceptible to outside intervention. There are external institutions to guide women in their work and women work in conformity with them — school, church and neighbourhood friendship networks.

Throughout the twentieth century, the social sciences have developed as a distinct and prestigious body of knowledge, which has been transformed by mass popularizations into the folk wisdom of the late twentieth century. "Experts" in childrearing help to modernize the women's mothering activities, bringing them more in line with the needs of the current situation and thereby minimizing generational tensions.

Women seek out what expert advice is available and discuss among themselves the various theories currently in vogue. A constant theme in the conversations between women in Flin Flon was the latest information about child care practices. The following conversation was typical of many. The three women all had children under seven:

90

> There was a show on TV last night about teenagers in this society. This man is a doctor and he says that parents should let their children make most of their own decisions like about whether they want to go to school or not. It was really interesting but I don't know if he is right or not.
>
> (Generation III, b. 1947)

> But then other people tell you kids need more discipline and that they want parents to tell them what to do.... There was this article in *Chatelaine* last month that said...
>
> (Generation III, b. 1943)

> There was another show on TV where these three experts on children were talking and they said.... But I never know what all that means for me.
>
> (Generation III, b. 1950)

The contradictions inherent in child care are irresolvable, and experts do not agree on how to moderate them. Flin Flon women had to manoeuvre their way through the confusions and pressures that surround child care:

> Having children is really a difficult thing to do. I never realized it until I had kids but it's all so confusing. You never know if what you're doing is right. Everybody tells you to do something different and it all happens so fast anyway.
>
> (Generation II, b. 1924)

> I used to think having a baby was just natural. I mean women have done it for thousands of years, right? But now, every time I go to do something, I have to think about it. Is this the right thing or not? It makes me very anxious.
>
> (Generation III, b. 1947)

This already difficult situation is complicated by the fact that the work of bearing and rearing children is often incompatible with the other aspects of domestic labour. Women noted that the birth of their first child diminished their ability to cater to the needs of their husbands:

> I used to be able to pay attention to my husband whenever he wanted me. Now with the baby I just can't. The baby takes up so much time.
>
> (Generation III, b. 1951)

They also noted that their work as mothers frequently interfered with their work as wives:

He likes me to sit down with him when he comes home from work
and just chat about the day. I try to whenever I can but with four
small children about the house, I often just can't.

(Generation III, b. 1949)

He wants to make love sometimes during the day, especially when
he works night shift. But I am always afraid the children will come
in looking for me so I won't do it.

(Generation II, b. 1935)

Sometimes I feel torn in two. He's got hold of one arm, wanting
me to do something and the kids are on the other and they're all
pulling in opposite directions and I think one day I'm going to
split apart.

(Generation II, b. 1939)

Sometimes in their dual roles of wife and mother, as tension
managers women have to mediate between their husbands and
their children:

Jake is always yelling at the children about something and they
come running to me all crying and then I have to go and tell him to
cool it and I have to make them feel better.

(Generation III, b. 1947)

My oldest son [fifteen] and his dad are always at each other about
this or that. Sometimes I'm afraid of a punch out. So I just make
sure they don't get in each other's hair too much.

(Generation II, b. 1929)

Child care is also largely incompatible with good housekeeping. In her study, Ann Oakley noted that "children are directly
antithetical to the demands of the housewife role."[5] Good housekeeping involves keeping the house clean and tidy. Children
automatically mess things up for "the child is the foe of waxed
floors."[6]

This incompatibility can generate all kinds of tensions
between women and their children. Women who worked hard to
clean the house got angry when their children rushed through
and made it untidy and dirty:

I spend hours cleaning up and then the kids come home and in no
time it's all messed up again. It makes me furious.

(Generation II, b. 1931)

But many women also wanted their children to feel comfortable
in the home and they did not want their housework to interfere

with their relations with their children. To accomplish this, they had to compromise their housekeeping:

I don't want to think that a clean house is more important than happy kids. I try not to let it get to me. If I clean the house and they mess it up, well, I know it was clean once. I don't like a messy house but I don't like to yell at my kids either. So what can you do? So we live in a mess and it's awful and I hate it.

(Generation III, b. 1941)

All the problems of mothering were summed up by one Flin Flon mother of four children:

It's the perfect Catch 22. You get married cause you're having kids. And you set up house to care for your kids. But once you got kids, you got no time for your marriage and you can't keep a nice house. And you have those kids, God knows why, and there is no knowing how to raise them right. And you work and work and they grow up awful and lippy and you're embarrassed as hell that anyone might think they were your kids. And you fight with them and can't wait till they're gone and then you miss them like hell. My kids are the most important thing in my life.

(Generation II, 1932)

FROM CRADLE TO EMPTY NEST: THE RHYTHMS OF MOTHERWORK

The rhythms of mothering are based on children's biological development. However, the manifestations of the work and the form that it takes is social and depends on the social relations at the time. There are two aspects to child bearing. The first centres on the woman and has to do with procreation — conception, pregnancy and child birth. The second centres on the newly born child who is incapable of caring for its own needs.

Conception

For the most part, Flin Flon women said they wanted to have children. However, women of all three generations wished they could have more control over how many children they had and

93

when those children were born. A dominant complaint was that they could not control their own fertility.

If women cannot plan when or how often they have children, they cannot plan their lives. Because unexpected pregnancies create major disruptions in their life strategies, their lack of control over fertility spontaneously structures their destinies. Therefore, fertility control — birth control, abortion and sterilization — were definite work-related issues that women took very seriously.

Women of all three generations maintained that both their information about and access to birth control were inadequate:

> I knew I didn't want to get pregnant but I didn't know how to stop it.
>
> (Generation I, b. 1900)
>
> I didn't want this baby now but I couldn't find out about birth control.
>
> (Generation III, b. 1953)

Many women explained that their first child was unexpected. They complained that they became pregnant sooner than they wished, which had forced them into marriage earlier than they had intended, or into marriage with men they were not sure they really wanted to marry:

> I knew I was taking a risk but we were doing it and we got caught so we had to get married but I was only nineteen and I didn't want to marry then and I wouldn't have married John if I hadn't had to. I wish I could have had a few more years to meet some other men first before I had kids and settled down.
>
> (Generation I, b. 1899)
>
> I never thought it would happen to me. I didn't want kids then. I wasn't ready. But when I realized I was that way [pregnant] then I was trapped.
>
> (Generation II, b. 1923)
>
> I wouldn't have married Mike if we hadn't got caught. He was fun to date for a while but not to marry. But we got stuck and here we are.
>
> (Generation III, b. 1948)

A number of women described birth control techniques they had learned from other women, some which they had tried with varying degrees of success. Three women had tried using rags soaked in vinegar. Another three had tried supernatural technique such as prayer and astrology.

Nonprescription birth control, such as condoms and foam, have long been available from the drug stores, but until the 1970s they were kept behind the counter and had to be asked for. The embarrassment induced by this situation prevented many women from obtaining birth control even when they knew about it:

> When I was sixteen I started sleeping with Jim and I decided to use birth control so I knew about douches and foam so I went into the drug store to get something. I stood and looked at the stuff for ages but I was too embarrassed to ask anyone for help and I couldn't figure out what all the stuff was for so I finally gave up.
> (Generations III, b. 1950)

More effective birth control techniques, such as diaphrams, IUDs and the birth control pill, require a doctor's attention. Flin Flon doctors have consistently refused to provide birth control to unmarried women. In 1976 doctors at the clinic told a young woman who was engaged to be married in two months that she could not have birth control until her marriage. She was told to make an appointment the day before her wedding.

The majority of women interviewed (fifty-two out of one hundred) did not use birth control prior to their first pregnancy. Once they had had their first child, their access to birth control was made easier. At the same time, they became less reluctant to get pregnant:

> I didn't want the first baby but no one would give me anything to stop it. So I got married and now that it's easier to have more kids, my doctor will give me the pill. It's crazy.
> (Generation II, b. 1931)

There are at least three other ways of avoiding pregnancy: abstention, abortion and sterilization. Abstention becomes a real option for Flin Flon women when their husbands spend periods of time during their work life away from home, fulfilling apprenticeship requirements, earning high wages on northern construction, searching for wage work. A number of women referred to this time as "one of the best in my marriage" precisely because "if he ain't here, he can't knock me up." Another woman expressed pleasure at her husband's apprenticeship program because "he'll be away so I don't have to be on the pill." Other women tried to avoid having sexual relations to prevent pregnancy. But this forced abstention threatened their relationships with their husbands. And its effect on the sexuality of the women and on their self-esteem was personally destructive.

The sterilization option has really been available only in the last ten or fifteen years. Of the women interviewed, only six had been sterilized and of these, two had had hysterectomies for reasons unrelated to birth control. Seven men (out of a hundred) had had vasectomies. All of the women in the third generation said they had thought about sterilization but their decision making was complicated by the types of sterilization procedures available and the sexual tensions of their marriages.

Sterilization for men, vasectomy, requires a simple operation which reportedly has no after effects and does not impair any kind of future activity, including sex. Vasectomies are available in Flin Flon and take about half-an-hour in the doctor's office. Sterilization for women is more complex. Despite the fact that two simpler and less dangerous operations have been practised for years, the only female sterilization offered in Flin Flon was the tubal ligation, colloquially known among women as the "hack and slash job." This is major surgery which cuts the stomach muscles. Especially if women have young children whose care requires regular lifting, which involves frequent use of the stomach muscles, they are reluctant to have this done. Less drastic procedures are available in Winnipeg, but because the health care program will not pay for the expenses involved, no one can afford them. Women talk frequently with each other about vasectomies, wishing their husbands would volunteer. They are, however, often reluctant to ask their husbands directly and many men when asked refuse to even consider the idea.

> I just can't have any more kids. I can't handle it. But I'm terrified I'll get pregnant. I've begged him to get a vasectomy but he won't. And I'm afraid there's no way I can get anyone to look after the kids while I'm in hospital having my tubes tied. And you know how after it takes weeks to get better. I have three little kids. I'm always lifting them up. So I told him that no more sex til the kids are old enough that I can get the operation.
>
> (Generation III, b. 1943)

96

For Flin Flon women, a legal, medical abortion is not really an option. Although medical abortions that are adequately safe have existed since the early twentieth century, the issue of abortion is subject to intense struggles between women who want abortions or people who defend a woman's right to choose and the medical profession, anti-abortion groups and the state. The hospital in Flin Flon does not perform abortions; nor will the Manitoba health care program pay the expenses for obtaining an abortion in Winnipeg.

Nonmedical techniques for inducing abortions involve self-inflicting injury, such as falling down stairs, jumping off tables, consuming massive doses of alcohol, laxatives or laundry starch, or inserting objects into the uterus hoping to destroy the fetus. They are all dangerous and their efficacy is questionable.

Eight of the woman interviewed said they had had abortions. Two of them were legal abortions performed in other cities, which the woman paid for themselves. Four illegal abortions were performed outside Flin Flon; and two women successfully induced their own abortions.

Pregnancy and Childbirth

The degree to which pregnancy affects the work women do depends upon their response to it. The attitudes toward and the experiences surrounding pregnancy and childbirth vary a great deal. A woman's response to the realization that she is pregnant depends on a whole range of factors — her feelings about herself and her body, her current relationship with the baby's father, her financial situation, and the response of her family and friends.

Whatever her response, pregnancy profoundly alters a woman's life. The physical effects which last for almost a year, impair her ability to do housework and child care. It also results, finally, in a new household member. So most women consider pregnancy a "double whammy:"

> It's two strikes against you at once. You're pregnant so you feel tired and can't work as much; then you've got a new kid to look after which is even more work but you're even more tired and unable to do the work.
>
> (Generation III, b. 1941)

If a woman is single and decides as a result of her pregnancy to get married, then being pregnant is the means by which she is recruited to domestic work. For a woman already at home, pregnancy may interfere very little with her work or, if she is ill or tired, it can impose severe constraints on her.

One of the striking differences between women's experiences of pregnancy in the early period in Flin Flon and those of the last twenty years is the extent to which husbands have increased their participation and involvement. Older women were unanimous in noting that their husbands, while often excited by the prospect of having children, did very little to help during the pregnancy or after the child was born. Younger women, especially in the last five or six years, seem more willing to insist that their husbands help.

In a conversation with five women, three of whom were in their fifties and two in their twenties, one of the older women noted that in her time men never helped around the house with young children. She turned to one of the younger pregnant women and congratulated her on how frequently her husband helped her during her pregnancy. The younger woman replied:

> He'd better help. After all it's his kid too that I'm having. So he can jolly well help out. After all, being pregnant and nursing a baby is my share; he can't do that part so he can do other stuff like wash the dishes and take care of me when I'm tired.
>
> (Generation III, b. 1953)

The older woman responded, and her contemporaries nodded their agreement:

> Well I agree and I just wish in my day I could have said the same but somehow in those days having a baby was women's work and men wouldn't be bothered by it.
>
> (Generation II, b. 1926)

Although these women observed that involvement of men had increased, they assumed that domestic work, particularly bearing and rearing children, was women's work. They described men's involvement as "helping out" and not as assuming equal responsibility. Even among younger families, men tended to remain on the sidelines during pregnancy and childbirth. The rare husband who really did take on more work to relieve a pregnant wife was admired and described as wonderful but unusual.

A number of men responded with impatience to their wives' fatigue or illness. One older woman recalled her pregnancy in 1929, noting that she was ill and tired for about six months. Although her doctor told her to rest in bed, her husband insisted that she was "not ill" and should continue to do her work as before. In 1975 two men, talking together in a pub about their pregnant wives, commiserated (with each other) about how women use being pregnant as "an excuse" to slack off. When challenged by three women who had children, they backed down reluctantly and admitted that "maybe" their wives were not slacking. Several months after the baby was born, one of these men had to stay home to look after three children while his wife was in hospital. He recalled the conversation ruefully and admitted that he had not realized how much work his wife had to do:

> Jesus, I'm not even pregnant and I get wiped out doing the housework and looking after the kids. Being pregnant must have really made her job harder.
>
> (Generation III, b. 1946)

Another striking difference between the experience of first- and second-generation women and those of the third generation was the amount of preparation for a new baby. Older women recalled months of sewing clothes, bedding and diapers for their babies. Inexpensive prefabricated baby clothes were not readily available until the 1960s, and women who washed by hand and dried on a clothes line required large numbers of every item simply to ensure a regular supply of dry clothing. A woman whose children were born during the 1940s said that for each infant she needed twenty nightgowns and one hundred diapers because in the winter everything took two days to dry. Younger women purchase ready-made infant clothing and diapers, and those with washers and dryers reduce the number of garments they need by increasing the amount of laundry they do. One mother with two infants in diapers had fifty cloth diapers for both children. She washed and dried them every day.

Women's childbirth experiences also varied, not according to decade but according to their proximity to hospitals. Many Flin

Flon women gave birth to their babies while living on farms in isolated rural area. Some of the older women gave birth under the rugged pioneer conditions of early northern settlement. These children were born at home, often without professional medical assistance. Women who lived near hospitals had their children with full medical procedures.

Women of all ages were concerned with the relative merits of home versus hospital births. There was a general agreement that hospital births were probably safer, but some women complained about the treatment they received in hospitals, particularly the loss of control they experienced. Whatever their opinions, women unanimously noted one major advantage that hospital births have over home births. It is socially acceptable for a woman giving birth to spend four or five days in hospital where she is not responsible for anything. Women considered their hospital stays as vacations or holidays. They were waited on. Someone else made meals and cared for the baby. Someone else, usually husbands or parents, took over the domestic labour at home. The stay in hospital acted as a breather, a chance to unwind and prepare for the new period of hard work and social adjustment that follows the birth of a new child.

Once the woman has had a few days to rest and recover, she and the baby return home to begin a whole new phase in her work life. The physiological component of the work of generational reproduction starts after the baby is born and continues until the child is able to take responsibility for its own physical needs. The mother's tasks are to feed, clean, clothe and protect the children and, at the same time, to teach them to do those things for themselves. These tasks overlap and correspond to the second aspect of generational reproduction, that is, socialization.

Infancy

Children are wholly dependent on others from birth until they are walking and beginning to talk. Their dependency and particular needs impose certain restrictions on women. Their schedules are usually at variance with the schedules of other household members, and their care creates a great deal more housework. Because they are so totally dependent, women are often anxious about caring for them. Infants are often considered to be highly suspectible to disease and vulnerable to injury. Their presence substantially increases women's workloads and alters all the rest of women's work because the unique needs of an infant take priority over all other household responsibilities:

> Each new infant adds to, and modifies, the existing pattern, not by doubling work, but by changing all components of the mother role.[7]

Feeding

Babies can obtain all the food they need during their infancy from breast milk. However, breast feeding in Canadian society is surrounded by taboos, social sanctions and even legal prohibitions, which tend to fluctuate and change. For a while nursing became all the rage; then it went out of style and became unusual. One reason for this is that manufacturers of processed baby foods launched periodic attacks on breast feeding. In these campaigns there was often an element of collusion between food manufacturers and the medical profession. The result is that many women are confused about the relative merits of breast milk and processed foods.[8] They do know that bottle feeding and processed foods increase both their labour and their costs.

For those women of Flin Flon who gave birth to children in remote areas, on farms or in northern bush camps, where processed foods and bottles were not available, there was no choice. They nursed their babies for at least a year or two. Women who lived in more developed areas had to choose whether or not to breast feed, at what age to introduce solids, whether to use processed baby foods or to make their own. Since it was almost impossible for women to obtain accurate information about the advantages and disadvantages of various infant foods, they often experienced frustration and anxiety. Their decision could not be made rationally. Therefore, they weighed what they thought was best for the child, the relative cost of different processes, and the amount of time and energy they had available:

It's hard to know what is best. Some people say it's best to nurse for a long time; others say that's bad because it makes the baby dependent. Some people say the store-bought baby food is good, but it's expensive. Others say it is bad for the baby because it has too many chemicals and too much salt and sugar. For a while I made my own baby food but it took so long. I'm not sure what I'm going to try next.

(Generation III, b. 1955)

While many women nursed their children for the first few weeks, and some continued for a few months, most weaned their babies by the age of six or seven months. A few continued to nurse longer, but by the time the child was a year old the mothers were told that the child was too old to be still nursing. At least two women nursed their children longer, but they did so in private because the social criticism was so severe.

One important factor in a woman's decision to nurse or not is that breast feeding is socially unacceptable to many people, and it is apparently illegal to nurse in public. Flin Flon women cited at least three instances from their experience in the 1970s where women who were breast feeding their babies in public washrooms were threatened with charges of indecent exposure by the police! Although no charges were laid, the threat acted as a deterrent for many women. Many women felt that nursing would isolate them from other people, whereas bottle feeding allowed them to remain socially active while feeding the child. Some women, especially those active in and supported by the local branch of La Leche League, disregarded social prohibitions and nursed publicly.

The age at which babies were first introduced to solids also varied. Some children were fed pablum in their third month. By six months most babies were on a regular schedule of three meals a day supplemented by a bottle after meals and at bedtime. Children's meals were either processed baby food, which required little labour because it could be heated and served in its containers, or homemade meals, prepared by cooking food until very soft, forcing it through a sieve or mushing it in a blender. Older women noted that processed baby foods were not available until the late 1940s so they tended to nurse their children longer as "straining food was such a bother." Women whose children were babies in the 1940s and 1950s made their own baby food because "it was the thing to do."

The way women make choices about feeding their infants indicates that reducing their own labour is only one consideration. Breast feeding requires no preparation at all, but the social constraints frequently motivate women to use other food sources that require a considerable amount of work and added expense. Similar patterns appear in other areas of infant care.

Toilet Training

It is in a woman's interest to have her children toilet trained as quickly as possible. Just changing a diaper takes from five to fifteen minutes and diapers are usually changed six to eight times a day. Diapering one child requires from thirty minutes to two hours each day. Soiled diapers require soaking and rinsing before they can be washed. Having one child in diapers increases the average amount of laundry by three loads each week. Since soiled diapers frequently soak through to the child's clothing, the amount of baby clothes to be washed increases as well.

Changing diapers is generally unpleasant and messy. It is the one task associated with infant care that men consistently refuse to do. The women of Flin Flon considered the time their children were in diapers as one of the worst periods of childrearing, and they were relieved when the diaper period ended.

A whole set of social factors affect a woman's decision about when to begin toilet training. Beginning to toilet train before children are ready can be a tedious, frustrating experience for parents and children. Prolonged training makes a lot of work for the mother. So toilet training practices vary.

In Flin Flon the burden imposed by endless diaper washing was a powerful motivation for early training. Women who had to wash diapers by hand were more inclined to train their children earlier:

> I was washing diapers all the time. There were always diapers hanging up everywhere and I went nuts so I trained those kids to the potty real quick. I was never so glad to quit washing diapers.
>
> (Generation II, b. 1933)

Women who had washers and dryers and used disposable diapers as a backup were more inclined to prolong the pretraining period.

> Well, it's true diapers are a pain. I don't like changing her pants but still I figure she'll learn when she's ready so I leave her alone.
>
> (Generation III, b. 1952)

Some women were embarrassed to have toddlers still in diapers so they tried to train them early and quickly. Others maintained that early toilet training has adverse effects on the development of personality and refused to start training until the children initiated it. The majority of women assumed that toilet training should begin once a child can walk. By two-and-a-half years most children were trained at least during the day, and by three years children were expected to be able to get through the night as well.

Social Relations

It is in the social relations aspect of child care that the most striking changes have occurred. A Flin Flon great-grandmother, reflecting on three generations of childrearing, commented on the changing patterns she had observed:

> Well, babies, they're a bit tough to figure. When mine were wee we figured all they needed was feeding and a bit of loving now and again. I left mine to sleep most of the time for the first year. But my daughter, her babies were born in the 1940s and she was all modern and they were on a schedule so she fed them when the book said, and she took them for a walk when the book said, and bathed them and talked and played with them, all when the book said. She spent more time with them than I did but it seemed odd to me. And now my granddaughter has a wee one and she thinks it needs all sorts of attention. She says babies need talking to and music and she has her sit on the table with her and that baby's never alone except at night. And the baby seems to thrive on it but her mother's never alone and gets no peace.
>
> (Generation I, b. 1893)

In the early period infants were excluded from many social activities because they were expected to sleep in their beds for the greater part of the day. In the second and third generations infants were included in many more activities and expected to be more active. This changing pattern of child care is illustrated more clearly in the childrearing practices for slightly older children.

Preschoolers

From the time children learn to walk and talk until they are ready to start school, they have to be supervised all the time. During this period they learn a variety of essential social skills, such as talking, getting dressed, eating and amusing themselves. As the changes in the patterns of child care flow out of changes in the physical and social environment of the household, the level of municipal development and household technology are significant factors in the organization of motherwork.

Women who moved to Flin Flon during the period of settlement encountered numerous problems with childrearing under primitive conditions. One woman who moved to a bush camp in 1926 lived in a tent for the first five years. For four consecutive winters she gave birth to a baby in her tent (ten by fourteen feet) in temperatures that stayed around minus forty-five degrees. She recalled the last winter she lived in the tent:

> It was the winter of 1930 and we were still in that tent and I had the fourth baby and then there were four wee ones and me cooped up in that tent. Well I tell you I did what some Indian women used to do. I tied the babies up in a papoose. It kept them warm and safe and out of mischief. You know when we moved into the house we built and I could let them crawl around, well at first they was so used to staying put that they was afraid to go far. But well, I couldn't risk them running loose in that tent now. When I think of how we lived, me with four babies! Well!!
>
> (Generation I, b. 1894)

Because small children must be supervised, mothers frequently become victims of the "captive wife" syndrome[9] by finding themselves housebound and socially isolated. In the early period in Flin Flon this isolation was compounded by the primitive conditions of life in the new town. Husbands worked long hours six or seven days each week, and initially there were no support networks of kin or friends to help out or exchange child care services. Women were also physically isolated. The streets were simply cleared spaces between the buildings — muskeg that froze into rough uneven surfaces in winter and thawed into oozing mud in the spring. Only Main Street, and a few side streets off Main, had sidewalks, initially made of wooden planks. The open sewer ran alongside the boardwalk. Dogs ran in packs and mingled with the teams of huskies brought in by the trappers. Crowds of rowdy men gathered on the sidewalks and quarrels and fights were frequent.

These conditions made it difficult for women with small children to move about the town, especially if they did not live on Main Street. If a woman had more than one small child, it was almost impossible for her to get out of the house. Several older women recalled the hardships imposed upon them by the inadequate streets and sidewalks. One remembered her first five months in Flin Flon in 1930:

> I arrived here in this house in August of 1930 and I never saw Main Street [which is one block away] until Christmas time in December. I was five months never outside that house. But he was working sixteen hours six days each week and there was mud all around so I never went out. I never ever had a babysitter — weren't no one around to do it. When things froze he built a sleigh and I put the three kids on it and went uptown to see the Christmas stuff in the store.
> (Generation I, b. 1894)

Generally the rugged housing conditions of the early period made child care difficult. Sometimes they created bizarre and unusual incidents:

> I remember when we first came north and were living in our cabin — the first place we lived. There was just one wood stove and the cabin was cold that winter. One day I set the baby on the floor while I had to do something else. She peed and her diaper froze, stuck to the floor.
> (Generation I, b. 1897)

The premechanized household was often hazardous for children, especially, the range, which was constantly hot, the open water cisterns into which children occasionally fell, and the wood floors which splintered easily. Chamber pots, water pots and indoor wood piles were tempting play things. A mother of three children under ten in 1931 described her house:

Seems like there was always some trouble happening with those kids. Billy were burnt something fierce on that stove once; then he learnt never to go near it again but the others, they just never learnt though they never got hurt so bad. We kept the tweezers on a nail by the sink 'cause someone always had a sliver somewhere what needed taking out. Then when I wasn't afraid of them getting into the water cistern and drowning, they was making a mess in the wood pile.

(Generation I, b. 1898)

Most women recalled childrearing in early Flin Flon as totally incompatible with the requirements of housework! One woman said:

I just couldn't do both you know. Either I looked after them kids or I did my housework.

(Generation I, b. 1891)

But the same woman pointed out that however incompatible they might be, she still had to do both:

But I didn't have that choice you know. The kids were there and I had to look after them and the housework sure never left, so I learned to do both. And at the same time too.

The tensions between the requirements of the two jobs made domestic labour unpleasant. It also motivated women to try to change the circumstances of their work. One solution to this dilemma was for women to put their children outside while they did the housework. In 1930 a woman with infant twins wrapped the children up warmly and left them outside in their pram all day, only bringing them in to feed them:

Every morning after I nursed them I'd just wrap them up and pop them outside in the carriage while I did my work. People said they would freeze but they never.

(Generation I, b. 1895)

For those mothers with infants who stayed put, this solution frequently eased the situation. For those with mobile youngsters who required supervision, it was no solution:

When the kids were little, three or four, I used to go nuts with them around my feet while I was doing housework so I'd put them outside but all the time I'd worry for fear they'd fall down on rocks into the lake and drown or slip on the ice in winter and crack themselves on the rock so all the while I'd be straining to hear them and then I'd get so's I couldn't stand the tension so I'd bring them in, then I'd be afraid they'd hurt themselves in the house. It was just awful.

(Generation I, b. 1900)

In large cities it has become difficult to leave small children unsupervised because the traffic, strangers and the vastness of the city threaten young children. This is less true of Flin Flon, where the traffic is neither as dense nor as fast, and where even in the uptown area someone is likely to know where a particular child lives. As Flin Flon developed, roads were laid, sidewalks installed and parks created. It gradually became a safer place for children alone. One mother described the impact of sidewalks:

We lived on Hill Street [one block east of Main] and Sue [age seven] went to the school in the hospital parking lot [one block west of Main and three blocks from her house]. Well the mud was so bad I used to get up every morning and dress the baby and I'd walk with the baby and Sue down to Main Street till she got to the sidewalk. Then me and the baby would come back home. When my husband and a neighbour got some boards they laid a walk from our house to the Main Street sidewalk. Then I didn't need to go with her and I could let the baby sleep longer. It made things easier.

(Generation I, b. 1898)

Another woman commented on the changes that occurred in her work when a playground was built near her house:

Well you've no idea what a relief that playground was when they put it in. Before that the children played on the rocks and I worried for fear one of them would drown but after the park went in, I just told them they were to play in the park and nowhere else and then I knew they were safe and I could find them when I wanted to.

(Generation I, b. 1902)

As the municipal infrastructure developed, women with small children found it easier to move about the town using push carts or sleds. This helped to break down the isolation many of them experienced. The safer physical environment meant small children could play outside. Neither of these changes, however, resolved the problem of time-consuming, labour-intensive housework.

A solution for those who could afford the expense was to expand and improve the house. One woman described changes made to her house around 1930:

> That house had two bedrooms and a medium-sized other room. But with three small children who soon began learning to walk it was impossible. So we built a kitchen onto our house so I could put the children to play in the living room and block the door into the kitchen with a door so I could wash and get it as wet as I liked and not have to worry about those children getting into everything.
>
> (Generation I, b. 1899)

Other women who had older children, especially girls, sometimes made them responsible for the younger children. Although classes started for schoolaged children soon after the first families moved to Flin Flon, formal schooling was not well established until the early 1930s, and even then some women kept their children at home:

When the last one was born I had three little ones at home with me and the four older ones at school. So I told Sally [then aged ten] that she could stay home and help out. She stayed home for two years till all but the baby were ready for school. Sally were a big help to me.

(Generation I, b. 1895)

Whatever solutions women attempted, the fact was that the demands of housework under primitive conditions meant that there wasn't a great deal of time available for child care. Women organized the care of their children so that they could have long periods of uninterrupted time to do housework. With the increase and reorganization of space in the household, women could do housework in one area while children played in another. Decreasing household hazards also enabled children to play inside but away from immediate observation:

Once we'd extended the house the children had their own rooms so they could play there while I did my housework. Sometimes I'd even run out to the store leaving them for a few minutes all alone. Sometimes I worried but it seemed safe enough what with the new stove and all.

(Generation II, b. 1931)

As housework gradually became less demanding women were able to incorporate the care of young children into their housework and also to take time out from housework to spend with their children. One woman, born in 1929, had three children in the 1940s. Twenty years later she had a "second family," two children born in 1967 and 1969. When the first children were born, she lived in a primitive three-room house with an electric stove but no running water. By the 1960s her house was fully modernized. She compared these two experiences and noted how her changed material circumstances had affected her child care:

With the first three I had so much work to do around my house I barely spent time with them during the day, just at night I'd play with them. But now with these two, my housework wasn't so demanding so I spent lots more time with them especially when they were babies — talking to them, teaching them. You wouldn't think that having an electric stove and modern kitchen would affect the way you treat your babies would you? But it sure does.

(Generation II, b. 1929)

Women who had infants in the 1970s frequently sat their babies on the kitchen counter or table while they worked. The child was at eye level with events and other people. While they cleaned or cooked, mothers chatted with their babies. High chairs, jolly jumpers, walkers, portable playpens and plastic infant seats, all geared to different stages of development in the young child, facilitated combining close observation of young children with housework.

These changing patterns of child care are reflected in two aspects of the ideology of motherwork: the changing theories that women have about young children and the changing ideas they have about what mothering should include. In the early period women generally assumed that all their young children required was care and lots of love. Otherwise, the babies could be left alone and they would flourish:

> Children need care and guidance and love. Then they grow up and learn at their own pace.
>
> (Generation I, b. 1900)

Compatible with that was a theory of mothering which held that while mothers should care for and love their small children their responsibility did not include teaching. Now women assume that even very small babies need regular emotional, sensual and intellectual stimulation and they believe that it is primarily their responsibility to provide this. Young mothers frequently agonized over whether or not they were "doing a good job" with their small children. They spend a great deal of time with their preschool children, playing, talking, reading, and generally worrying over them.

The impact of these changes on women's work has been to bind women even more tightly to their young children. When asked how much time they spent with their young children, women unanimously responded with "twenty-four hours each day every day." When groups of mothers with young children got together, their discussion inevitably revolved around their ambivalent feelings about their work as mothers. They liked their children, enjoyed their company and delighted in watching and helping them grow. Yet they felt trapped by the complete dependency of their children and by their own sense of total responsibility.

Their conversations were full of comments that reflected the intensity of their work. Numerous activities ceased when children were born, not to be resumed until the children reached school age:

> I used to work at the bank full time and I did sports and all sorts of social activities. Since I had the kids I haven't done anything. I just stay home with them all the time.
>
> (Generation III, b. 1950)

> I know that when my children are small they need me. But sometimes I think I'll go nuts if I don't get out of this house and meet some grown-ups. I find I'm starting to talk like a three year old all the time now.
>
> (Generation III, b. 1952)

Their conversations also reflected the tensions of the work:

> I feel like I'm going mad, stuck with these kids. I mean I really love them and I'm glad we have them but I'll be glad when they're off to school.
>
> (Generation III, b. 1954)

This period of childrearing is tolerable because women know that once the children begin school the intensity decreases, and they will be freer to resume a more independent and active life style:

> It's hell now but I know it will only last two more years. As soon as the youngest starts school, I'm going to go back to work.
>
> (Generation III, b. 1960)

Schoolaged Children

Legally children must begin school when they are six and continue until they are sixteen. During those ten years, the mother's work is transformed from physical caring to managing interpersonal relations. It becomes less physically demanding but in many ways, more emotionally and psychologically demanding.

Mothers of all generations agreed that it was during this period that their children had to learn to behave properly, although "properly" was vague and undefined. Because these values were often unconscious and implicit, it was hard for women to give their children clear messages and explanations. This introduced a certain authoritarianism into childrearing practices. Children were told that certain behaviours are "done" or "not done" "because I say so." Such arbitrariness caused a great deal of conflict because children regularly responded by challenging the authority of their elders. The potential for this form of conflict increased as the children grew up and began to consider themselves old enough to make their own decisions.

The ways in which children learn the appropriate behaviour are extremely complex. From the perspective of the women doing motherwork, this process involves tension managing, mediating between the demands of the household and the larger social milieu and the demands and needs of her children. It is the women's task, for example, to ensure that their children get up and leave in time for school; that they go to school dressed appropriately and prepared for classes. It is their task to referee the conflicts that occur between siblings or between their children and their husbands, or between their children and people outside their households.

The question of authority relations is two sided. Women want to minimize their children's conflict with the external world. They know that if children have a power conflict with people in authority (teachers, truant officers, police), the children will lose. From the mother's perspective, the only element over which she has any control is the child. Therefore she exercises her power over her children to try to minimize conflict between them and others. At the same time, she is held responsible if her children behave inappropriately. Her children have the capacity to embarrass her and to bring down social and legal sanctions on her. She becomes an agent by which the authority relations of the whole society are transmitted to her children.

At some point her children begin to leave home and eventually the last child leaves for good. Some women watch their children leave with pleasure. They feel satisfied with a job well-done and they consider their children's new found independence to be a measure of their own success as parents. They talk with pride and delight of their children's achievements and it is obvious that they give themselves credit as well. For some women this period is the first time in their adult lives that they are able to concentrate on themselves.

However, because childbearing and childrearing are such intense and all-consuming activities, when motherwork ends many women experience a period of profound shock, which has been referred to as "the empty nest syndrome."[10] Given the strength of the motherhood myth in women's lives their self-identity — often their main reason for existing — is bound up in their children. When the children leave, the women often feel great pain and loneliness; their lives feel futile and meaningless. The other aspects of their domestic labour seem somehow irrelevant:

> I used to work and clean for eight of us and now there's only two so what's the point? It was the children who made my work worthwhile.
>
> (Generation II, B. 1925)

In many ways this period in a woman's life is comparable to retirement for men. Everything she has done on a daily basis for at least sixteen years suddenly changes. Because mothering is not generally recognized as work, there is little social recognition that the retirement period is problematic and there is actually no support for women going through this difficult time. What distinguishes women's domestic work from men's wage work is that, in fact, she does not retire. While the component of domestic labour that involves childbearing and childrearing comes to an end, the rest of it continues.

CHAPTER FIVE

HOUSEWIVES AND HOUSEWORK

> *Every time I turn around*
> *There's something else to do,*
> *It's cook a meal, or mend a sock,*
> *Or sweep a floor or two.*
>
> Peggy Seeger
> "I'm Going to be an Engineer"

HOUSEWORK involves all those activities that maintain the house and service its members — planning and preparing meals, cleaning and maintaining the house and its contents, and obtaining the materials and supplies needed for that work. By creating the material conditions of life, housework structures and underlies all the other aspects of domestic work.

Because the house is the living space for the housewife and her family, the services provided by her labour directly affect the well-being of household members. Housework, the most tangible daily "product" of her labour, provides evidence of both her skill as a worker and her affection for her family. A clean house and well-cooked meal become expressions of her worth and caring.

Housework is the one component of domestic labour that has been recognized consistently as work,[1] although the "job title" assigned to it reflects the extent to which housework is intimately connected with the social, emotional and psychological aspects of the rest of domestic work. The worker who does housework is a "housewife," a term rich in implication — and inherently ambiguous.

Since the nineteenth century housework has changed significantly. The transformation began as early as the 1830s and progressed gradually until the 1880s. During the next fifty years the rate of change accelerated, finally slowing in the late

1920s. By the 1950s the modern structure of housework had emerged. In Flin Flon this transformation process was telescoped into a shorter period. From the time of settlement in the late 1920s until the 1940s, housework in Flin Flon corresponded to housework of the late eighteenth and nineteenth centuries in North America. By the late 1950s housework in Flin Flon was generally the same as it was in most other urban areas.[2]

Most significant in the analysis of the forces that have transformed housework is the fact that changes did not emerge directly out of the needs arising from within the household. Instead, the major developments, both technical and scientific, that transformed housework flowed from the requirements and concerns of capitalist production. This pattern is reflected most clearly in two critical trends in industry. One was the emergence of a secondary manufacturing sector that processed raw materials; the second, the scientific and technical advances within production. Thus there was the drive to sell more, and new products derived from new processes, materials and technology.

As the range of commodities produced by industry expanded, certain work shifted from the home to the sphere of commodity goods production. While eliminating some work, this shift also created new types of work. Women no longer grew their own food or made their own textiles and clothing. Food and clothing were mass produced, and the housewife's task increasingly involved shopping for these commodities and then transforming them into usable items for her household. Simultaneously a variety of commodities, processes and technical developments were introduced into the home, drastically altering housework.

SCHEDULES AND PLANS: THE RHYTHMS OF HOUSEWORK

The organization of housework requires a set of priorities, sequences and time allocations for its various components. Domestic scientists and home economists in the early nineteenth century, before technological developments had had much impact on the household, were quite rigid about what should be done each day of the week. They urged housewives to plan and stick to schedules. Later authors, particulary after the 1920s when the impact of technology was being felt in housework, tended to allow greater spontaneity.

Most nineteenth-century writers agreed on the sequence of daily activities. The work week began on Monday, which was usually washday. Tuesday was devoted to ironing and putting away clothes and linens. Wednesday was baking day, and Thursday was a time for sorting and mending clothes and linens. Friday was for washing the floors, checking food supplies and preparing for the weekend. Saturday and Sunday were days during which most household members were at home and friends dropped in to visit. Thus, housework during the week concentrated on the material needs of household members. On the weekend housework centred on their social needs.

Although each day was devoted to a different job, certain tasks, such as preparing meals, washing dishes and tidying up, had to be done each day. So the authors outlined daily routines which incorporated these repetitive tasks into the major daily job. Books written after 1900 do not often distinguish between weekly and daily schedules. Instead, they allocate several hours each day to an "optional occupation" like laundry, baking, ironing or mending.[3]

This changing pattern of scheduling is reflected in the work rhythms of Flin Flon women. Two 1929 diaries described an almost identical distribution of tasks through the week and on a daily basis. All the women of the first generation described a similar pattern (see Tables 5:1 and 5:2).

In the fifty-two interviews of third-generation women no such clear pattern of work scheduling emerged. While all women do basically the same tasks, the way they organized them varied. Some women followed a regular daily plan; others blitzed for a few days so they could take the following days "off." Some did all their work in the morning and used the afternoon for social events; others used the morning for major projects, such as baking or sewing, and did the rest of their work mainly in the evening. Some women said they did not follow any particular pattern of work.

TABLE 5:1

Weekly Schedule For 1929 In Flin Flon*

Monday	Washday. Washing takes the best part of the day from 4:30 A.M. to 7:00 P.M.
Tuesday	Ironing. All washed items are ironed and put away, which takes from 6:30 A.M. to 4:30-5:00 P.M.
Wednesday	Baking and sewing. While one batch of bread, cakes, pies or cookies is either rising or baking, she "takes time out" to sew or mend from 6:30 A.M. to 5:30 P.M.
Thursday	Sewing and shopping (for major supplies) from 6:30 A.M. to 5:30 P.M.

TABLE 5:2

Daily Schedule For 1929 In Flin Flon*

5:30 A.M.	(4:30 on Monday) Get up and start fire in stove, cook breakfast and wake and feed family, wash breakfast dishes, make beds.
6:30 A.M.	Begin work of the day (see Weekly Schedule).
11:30 A.M.	Prepare lunch. Wash lunch dishes.
12:30 P.M.	Resume work of the day.
4:00 P.M.	Begin supper preparations.
5:00 P.M.	Finish work of the day and tidy up.
5:30 P.M.	Prepare supper and serve it. Wash supper dishes.
7:00 P.M.	Put children to bed.
8:30 P.M.	Spend about half-an-hour tidying up the house and preparing materials for next day's work.
9:00 P.M.	Relax for an hour and either visit, play cards or *do a bit of mending or sewing* (my emphasis).
10:00 P.M.	Stoke up fire and go to bed.

* Both schedules are from the diary of a woman born in 1903, who had three children born in the 1920s.

Housework schedules and plans have changed because it has been possible to rationalize and mechanize the various work processes involved. This flexibility allows women to fit their housework around the demands of the other aspects of their domestic work.

One element of housework planning involves ensuring that all the equipment and supplies needed for particular tasks are available. This was one element of their work which a number of women considered to be onerous. In comparing their work situations with those of their husbands, many women referred to precisely this point. They argued that when a man goes to work, he is expected to do only the work assigned to him. It is up to the employer to ensure that the worker has the tools necessary for his work. If he does not have them, the worker simply waits to begin work until the needed items appear. Not so with housework, where part of the housewife's work is to ensure the availability of her own supplies:

> When he goes to work, he just does his job and that's it. If he doesn't have something he needs then he just waits till it comes. But if I'm in the middle of my work and I run out of something, well it's my fault and I have to stop and go get it. Like if I'm making a cake and I realize there is no butter then I have to run quick to the store to get some.
>
> (Generation III, b. 1948)

PROCURING HOUSEWORK SUPPLIES

Since part of housework involves acquiring the materials necessary for the household, it is in this context that the housewife enters into a direct relationship with the economy through the commodity goods market. At the beginning of the nineteenth century, most North American households procured some of their supplies through hunting, fishing, gathering, or domestic crafts. Throughout the century, the growth of industrial production removed from the home much of the domestic craft work and eliminated the possibilities of hunting, fishing and gathering. New types of manufacture, the growth of transportation networks and the introduction of new technology resulted in a reorganization and growth of commodity distribution. Mass communications and advertising helped spread information about new commodities. Urban households became increasingly dependent on the market to supply their needs.

Many of the Flin Flon women interviewed had lived for some period of their lives in rural areas where domestic production supplied some of their material needs, especially food and clothing.[4] When they moved to Flin Flon in the late 1920s, they had the knowledge and equipment needed for hunting, fishing, gathering and domestic crafts. The bush was nearby and full of game, fish, lumber and berries. Under these conditions, foraging provided a regular source of supplies for Flin Flon households. Such activities have continued to the present day because they are challenging and offer an interesting way to spend time. Their product adds variety to the household and supplements wages during periods of depression or unemployment.

Hunting, Fishing and Gathering

Hunting, open-water fishing and ice fishing are popular, predominantly male activites, although some women do participate. Hunting and fishing have been economically

Flin Flon, 1939.

122

significant for households at various times. During the Depression of the 1930s, and again in the recession following 1973-74, foraging activities increased. During the six month strike in 1971, when many households had little or no income and the men had time, many families ate freshly caught fish nearly every day. In the precontract negotiations of 1976, many households stocked up on fish and game "just in case." Among the people I interviewed, those in four households bought no meat at all during 1975 and 1976. They ate moose meat regularly. One moose fed a four- to five-member household for about a year.

Gathering is predominantly a female activity which Flin Flon women did alone, with their children, or with groups of women and children. Occasionally men accompanied their wives. At least six types of fruits and berries were gathered regularly (strawberries, raspberries, bog berries, blueberries, cranberries, and rose hips.) A few women knew about other edible wild plants, such as fiddleheads, nettles and birch leaves for tea.

Women of the first generation described their gathering activities in the early period as contributing significantly to the household diet:

> Every year I picked in season and I made jams and jellies and pies and I canned fruit — all from stuff I picked myself. We never bought desserts — but I made something every night.
> (Generation I, b. 1897)

The growth of the town reduced the quantity of fruit nearby, so that some berries, especially strawberries, were increasingly hard to find. While more than half of the women in the second and third generations still gathered some fruits, their dependence on gathered produce declined. Another potential source of non-market produce in some urban centres is gardening. In Flin Flon the lots are small and mostly rocky so gardening generally did not contribute much to subsistence. However, in 1976-77, when money was tight, a number of households began converting their small lots into garden plots just to grow a few things to "help stretch our food budget."

Another non-market source of supply was available to some households that had links to prairie farms. One household of five people never bought meat in the eight years of its existence. The wife's parents had a farm in southern Manitoba and every year they provided their daughter with a butchered cow, a pig, several sheep and some chickens. Members of another household regularly killed a moose, which they exchanged for a cow with the husband's uncle in Saskatchewan. Other households had irregular but still significant access to farm produce. On visits to farm relatives they received not only meat but vegetables, fruits, honey, cream and cheese.

Domestic Crafts

Activities such as carpentry, woodworking, preserving, pickling, baking, sewing, knitting, crocheting and other crafts were all popular among Flin Flon residents. Most households had at least one member skilled in at least one of these domestic crafts and who contributed regularly to the household. The extent to which such activities supplemented household expenditures varied tremendously and was difficult to evaluate. It ranged from the situation in one household, where both adults insisted that they never did anything, to another, where the man built the whole house and its furnishings himself, or one where the woman made all the clothing worn by household members. But, despite the significance of such non-market sources, the majority of supplies were purchased at local stores.

Shopping

A housewife must decide what she needs to buy, determine where she can find the best deal, go get it, transport it home and put it away. While each step is potentially varied and complex, certain patterns emerge.

The rhythm of household purchases is determined by the level and frequency of the wage. The Company's pay day was every other Friday. The majority of households shopped that day or the next. Of the twenty-three households where the wages were earned from different employers, twenty shopped on the day they received their pay.

It is interesting that the variation in the amount of money spent on food and dry goods each month did not appear to correspond to household size or income. While the average household size was five, and the average household income was $11,000 per year, households spent between $200 and $400 per month on food — approximately one-quarter to one-half of household income.

Purchases of other items, such as clothing and household furnishings, were made less frequently. Most housewives said that their household members combined spent from about $100 to $200 per year on clothing. While this seems low, people did not appear to have large wardrobes. Women passed on children's clothing, and men wore heavy-duty work clothes most of the time.

Major household purchases were also made from time to time. Because people could not accumulate enough money to pay cash for large items, they bought on credit. The availability of credit to the working class has increased dramatically in recent years. People of the first generation in Flin Flon were less able to acquire the range of material goods that are normally found in households of the current generation. Almost every active household owed money to a creditor for their house and their car. In addition, many had, at various times, debts of several thousand dollars to various stores, the credit union, or Visa.

The increasing diversity of choice in stores, goods and services forces housewives to develop shopping skills. Because the skills required for hunting, fishing and gathering and for domestic crafts are very different from those necessary for purchasing, they cannot be readily transferred. Home economists at the turn of the century recognized the growing importance of shopping skills and were concerned with the problems housewives encountered.[5] Writers, like Ellen Richards and Christine Fredericks, gave their readers explicit directions to facilitate "wise shopping." This trend continues in women's magazines, such as *Chatelaine*, which is widely read in Flin Flon, and which regularly provides "shoppers' guides" or "advice to prospective buyers."

Since 1930 there have been stores in Flin Flon selling a wide range of items. While there are now more stores than there were in the 1930s and 1940s, Flin Flon housewives have always had potential access to a variety of consumer goods. There are small grocery and butcher stores selling fruit, vegetables, dairy products, meat and dry goods. There are stores selling hardware and household appliances, textiles, clothing and furniture. The Eaton's catalogue service was available from 1927 to 1976 and a number of national chain stores such as The Bay, Woolworths and the Co-op provide shoppers in Flin Flon with items that are typically available across North America. What is not available are the speciality shops of larger cities, and women complained about the lack of variety and the scarcity of certain items like books, health foods and the latest fashions.[6]

In major urban centres the range of outlets and products available results in a relatively high level of competition. Large-scale buying patterns can force business to take into account household and, therefore, women's purchasing patterns. In a small town like Flin Flon, however, with its limited number of stores, consumers are less able to play stores off against each other.

Flin Flon stores do compete with each other and Flin Flon women "shops around" for the best buy. However, prices do not vary widely and the range of commodities available is not great. Flin Flon housewives agreed that for "real bargains" they had to leave Flin Flon to shop in larger centres like Winnipeg or Edmonton.

Because Flin Flon is a small city, it has what Helena Lopata calls "the traditional city store," one which caters to a "small and steady clientele with whom almost primary relations" are maintained.[7] Flin Flon women said that they usually enjoyed shopping, partly because it gave them a chance to get out of the house and meet people. Ann Oakley found a similar sentiment in England where women enjoyed the chance to get outside, window shop, meet with friends. However, both Oakley's informants and Flin Flon women agreed that shopping with time pressures and money constraints, or with small children, was not pleasant. Instead, it became another chore.[8]

The social aspect of shopping, the fact that it occurs outside the house, distinguishes it from other housework tasks and is perhaps the reason men regularly get involved in shopping. Lonata found that two-thirds of the husbands in her study assisted in some way with purchasing. Similarly, Dulic, Darh and Berheide noted that "errands are ... the one type of housework discussed ... for which the husband seems to make a substantial contribution."[10] In Flin Flon wives and husbands regularly shopped together in sixty-two out of eighty-eight households. Women in nineteen households said their husbands helped them occasionally. Men did all the shopping in four households and none at all in three households.

The amount of time women spent shopping varied according to the distance from home to the shops; whether or not the shoppers used a car; the number and ages of the children they had to take with them; the amount of shopping they had to do; and the money they had available to spend. Women estimated that they spent a half-an-hour to two hours each week shopping for groceries.

The skills required for shopping range from physical strength to mathematical competence. The need for strength was vividly illustrated when I watched a friend walk home from the Co-op carrying four bags of groceries and her one-year-old child. She walked nearly a mile with the four bags which we later weighed, finding they totalled thirty-seven pounds. The child weighed twenty-three pounds, and he complicated the procedures by wiggling and pulling groceries out of the bags and dropping them on the ground.

Most of the women I knew were aware of the prices of all their regular purchases and could, off the top of their heads, list comparative prices in each store and evaluate the extent to which something was a bargain. This is a very subtle and essential skill that involves estimating how much to spend on which items to ensure that the household eats as well as possible within the available resources. A skilled housewife can "stretch" the household income by shopping carefully, by cooking innovatively, by sewing and mending. In other words, she can juggle household needs and household income by intensifying her labour.

Flin Flon women were conscious of doing this. One woman recalled the Depression and its impact on her work:

Things were tight. His wages weren't enough. So I took in boarders and stopped buying anything but essentials. Course, it meant I had to work a lot harder.

(Generation I, b. 1913)

A younger woman commented on the impact of inflation on her work:

When things cost more and we haven't enough money, I just work harder, that's all.

(Generation III, b. 1950)

This ability to stretch the income or make ends meet is one of the socially necessary features of domestic labour under capitalism; it is also one of the criteria by which women evaluate their skills as housewives.

TECHNICAL CHANGE AND THE ORGANIZATION OF LABOUR

The transformation of housework over the last 150 years is the result of technical changes and the corresponding reorganization of the housewife's labour. While technical change is the product of developments made outside the home, the reorganization is the housewife's response to these changes. But the interaction between technical change and housework is not necessarily direct. It is often mediated, in the sense that manufacturers of new technology, home economists and domestic scientists inform women of the new products and urge women to buy them.

In the early nineteenth century, housework was a labour intensive "craft". There were no machines and the housewife performed every operation by hand, using tools when needed. The quality of the product, such as dinner or a clean house, depended on the worker's skill; its completion, on her willingness to finish the task. Domestic output, a measure of the total work done during the day, was limited only by the psychological and physiological stamina of the housewife, not by the technical limits of machines.

Since no other individual or machine contributed to the domestic product, a clear relationship existed between the product and the woman's labour. Thus, the potential existed for the housewife to derive pride, satisfaction and self-esteem from her work:

> I remember when I made all the children's clothes by hand. They looked so nice. I'd look at them and feel so good about myself.
>
> (Generation I, b. 1908)

Nevertheless, this kind of work was often onerous and fatiguing, requiring long periods of uninterrupted time. This combination of factors was sufficient motivation for women, along with other members of their households, to adopt new technical developments as they became available.

From the late nineteenth century on, housewives began using new machines, such as electric stoves, refrigerators, washing machines, dryers and vacuum cleaners, which mechanized a number of domestic tasks. In addition to these mechanical changes, new materials simplified their work and new house designs resulted in the reorganization of their workplaces. When housewives decided to invest in a new item of domestic technology, they had to take into account the effect of that expense on their household finances. Many women of Flin Flon felt that the acquisition of most of the new technology was worth the burden of the investment. While cost was a serious consideration, it was rarely decisive. The needs of the household members and the requirements of domestic labour made the purchase of new machines and materials a necessary expense:

> Even when money was tight, we usually bought new things. It always seemed worth it somehow, to have the new things that made life easier.
>
> (Generation II, b. 1923)

When a housewife goes to the market to purchase a new household item, she faces the product of another person's ingenuity. The new product is based not on her design but on that of an engineer working for a manufacturing company, whose major concern is to make more profits — not to solve the problems of domestic labour. Based on what she knows about the choices available to her, a housewife makes decisions about what new technology she adopts. While these new acquisitions present a housewife with the means to alleviate specific burdens, they also create new problems. What a housewife cannot predict is the long-term, cumulative impact of new machines and materials on her work.

In the development of technology, multi-purpose tools became progressively specialized. These new tools were the basis for machines, initially powered by human labour. In industry, this process led to the formation of integrated continuous production. It also drew together many workers in one location. The result was an integrated system of socialized production where further technology was developed to produce a profit.

Housework has not been socialized. Instead, it remains fixed in individual, isolated household units, each too small to permit the integration of specific work processes through mechanization. The housewife buys domestic technology for household use. In addition, the household is mechanized only in specific areas, particularly in those involving heavy labour. Material handling processes (for example, carrying the laundry to the washing machine, placing it in the dryer and then carrying it upstairs again) are not. The housewife must still do the transporting. No work process has developed that is completely mechanized from start to finish. Housework remains fragmented, with the labour of the housewife as the integrating component.

Another result of the technical changes in housework is the increasing loss of control the housewife has over the means of her labour. The technology is a product not of the household but of industrial capitalism. Its workings are unfamiliar and the housewife often lacks the scientific knowledge to modify or repair it. When it breaks down, she must rely on outside help.

The problem, however, is not limited to periodic malfunctions of domestic technology. The household, as a technical unity, is dependent on external sources for a constant supply of energy, water and the removal of sewage. For Flin Flon housewives, the impact of this dependency was brought home when heavy snows damaged the town's main power lines. For twenty-four hours every house was without electricity, and thus without heat, cooking facilities, hot water and lights. And there was nothing housewives could do about the situation.[11]

The increased dependence on machinery has also resulted in the "deskilling" of housework. As the techniques of cooking, cleaning and laundry are incorporated into machines housewives lose the traditional skills that become irrelevant. The new skills women acquire are less complex and demanding. Shopping is the sole exception to this trend. Women have learned new and sophisticated skills in the consumer marketplace. But the results of this labour are frequently defined negatively or not noticed at all. The economy and thrift that women practise, their ability to get a good deal, are not socially valued in the same way that the production of something tangible is valued and respected.

While modern housework is still labour intensive, the housewife often needs only to set a machine in motion and then stop the process. Her labour is no longer required for those specific operations which are now taken over by machinery. As the amount of labour time actually involved in any one process of housework is reduced, the work day gets divided into smaller, less integrated segments of time. This makes housework more flexible, since it can be manipulated to fit in with the demands of the other aspects of domestic work. The result of all these changes is that housework has become "despecialized," and that it tends to be part time, dull and repetitive. This has contributed to the low esteem that many people have for domestic labour and, consequently, for the women who do it.

The fragmentation of the work means that the sequence and impact of technical change varies with each operation, depending on the degree of mechanization and the particular circumstances of the work. So, for example, technical developments in laundry followed a logical sequence in that each development superceded pre-existing forms. The washboard and mangle were replaced first by the wringer washer and later by the automatic washer. That process did not occur in either food preparation or cleaning where more recent technology coexists with preceding forms. When women bought vacuum cleaners they did not throw out their brooms.

To understand the impact of specific technical changes as well as the overall effect of the new technology on housework, it is necessary to examine each of the specific labour processes involved in housework, considering what the process involves;

what changes have occurred; and how these developments have affected the housewife and her labour.

Food Preparation

Food preparation includes transforming materials obtained from the bush, the garden or the store into meals for household members, and after the meal, cleaning up and putting leftovers away. In the tool-based period, food preparation was time consuming. Most foods had to be prepared from scratch. All the food preparation had to be done by hand. The housewife worked over a stove that was designed not only for cooking but also for heating the house. Literally, she "toiled over a hot stove."

By the 1970s working conditions, materials and some techniques had changed dramatically. Food production required less physical output and a different kind of planning. The most notable change was that, while the physical environment of the kitchen improved immeasurably, the social environment became more restricted. Now the housewife is isolated from contact with other household members.

In the tool-based household, the kitchen was frequently the place where people gathered to work, to visit and to relax around the warmth of the stove. It was furnished with a free-standing dresser or cabinet for storing dishes and cutlery. Food was stored in bins and jars and preserved mainly by canning, pickling or, in the case of fish and meat, by smoking or salting. Water was kept in buckets or pails and thrown outside when it was dirty. A long trestle-table served both as a surface for food preparation and as a dining table.

As early as 1869 domestic scientist Catherine Beecher advocated eliminating the free-standing dresser and table and substituting built-in cupboards, counters and a sink with a drain, thus combining storage, preparation and cleaning in a single, integrated centre.[12] These organizational concerns were adopted by household architects in the 1920s, who introduced the "well-planned" kitchen modelled on the compact Pullman dining-car galley.[13] By the mid-1930s the "streamlined" kitchen was common in North America. The kitchen had become a separate room. Manufacturers began to sell standardized, matching units of cupboards, countertops, recessed sinks, stoves and refrigerators as well as floor tiles, wallpaper and kitchen tables and chairs to match.

The advantages of the streamlined kitchen were reported to be the integration of work areas, continuous work surfaces and the compact arrangement that brought together all kitchen work in a small space, thereby eliminating a lot of walking. The main disadvantage was that control of kitchen layout and the organization of the work process was taken totally out of the control of individual workers by architects and builders. The streamlined kitchen could not be rearranged to suit the needs of individual households. The compact size was designed for one worker, who was thus isolated from other centres of household activity.

Flin Flon women were quick to adopt the new kitchen layout. They felt it rationalized their work. As cabins were renovated, the kitchen was frequently the first room to be modernized. One woman recalled her feelings when her kitchen was remodelled in the late 1930s:

> There was lots of storage space — just so much room and countertops to work on and a real sink with hot and cold running water whenever I wanted. It made my housework so much easier.
>
> (Generation I, b. 1900)

This is an example of the contradictory effects of changes in domestic layout and technology. Women accepted changes because they simplified the physical aspects of their work. What they were unaware of, at least at the time, was the impact of change on the social relations of their work, for example, the effects of isolation. Some of the older women in Flin Flon recalled with regret the loss of the communalism and sociability of the old-style kitchen:

> Used to be we'd all gather round the stove and while I worked at getting supper ready, the men would chat, the children played on the floor and it was real cosy. Now they are all off elsewhere and I'm stuck here in the kitchen doing my work alone. When they were all around they used to help out a bit more too. Now I end up doing it all by myself.
>
> (Generation II, b. 1919)

The separation of the kitchen as a room to itself and its transformation into the modern kitchen depended on the development of the stove.

The Stove

For many years stoves served three functions. They were used for cooking, for heating water, and for heating the house. Gradually, with the development of hot-water heaters and furnaces, these three functions were separated and stoves could be made more efficient for cooking.

Although electric stoves and inexpensive electricity were available at the time Flin Flon was first settled, most households first used multiple-function castiron ranges. One retired housewife recalled working with a wood-burning range in the early 1930s:

> It was a big dirty thing that dominated the whole room and it was too hot in summer by half.
>
> (Generation I, b. 1880)

The use of such stoves required a steady supply of fuel. Flin Flon residents obtained their fuel either by cutting their own firewood from the bush surrounding the town or by purchasing wood or coal which was delivered by wagon.

The main supply of household fuel had to be stored near the house and a smaller supply kept inside near the stove. The jobs of chopping wood for kindling and keeping the interior supply well stocked was frequently assigned to children, especially boys. The first person to get up each morning, usually the housewife, cleaned the ashes out of the grate into a bucket and took them outside to the garbage. Then the early riser laid and lit a new fire for warming the house, heating water and cooking breakfast.

At regular intervals throughout the day someone had to add fuel to maintain the fire. It took a certain amount of expertise to know how much fuel would produce what temperature. A woman who now has an electric stove described temperature regulation on her wood stove:

> Once I had a bed of coals I knew that it took four quarter logs to hot it up enough to bake bread. It only took a crumpled paper and a stick or two of kindling to boil the kettle though. If you wanted

to cook muffins you stoked up the fire then stuck your hand in and started counting. If you got to eight before it got too hot to stand it, it was right for muffins. Bread was six and pies were ten.

(Generation II, b. 1902)

The fire, which had to be sustained all day, provided pleasant heat in winter but it was stifling in summer. Because the stove was constantly hot, it was free-standing and took up a lot of space. Such ranges were smoky, so the house was frequently dusty and dirty. Since the stove was always hot, there was a potential risk of fire and injury. A number of women mentioned that while playing their children had bumped into the stove and burned themselves.

During the 1930s many households used small electrical appliances, such as hot plates or electric kettles, for making tea or cooking small amounts of food and used the range only for major cooking or water heating. By the 1950s most houses in Flin Flon had electric stoves. One woman recalled her feelings when her new electric stove was hooked up:

It was wonderful — just wonderful. No mess, no bother — just turn a knob and there's heat — easy to clean — it was wonderful.

(Generation II, b. 1925)

Another woman said that her electric stove transformed her working conditions:

It completely changed my life. No more chopping wood, messy ashes. It was so efficient.

(Generation II, b. 1927)

Until the mid-1970s, electric stove designs changed very little. During the pre-Christmas period of 1976 microwave oven manufacturers launched a massive sales campaign throughout Manitoba. While a number of women were interested in the new technology and several attended microwave cooking demonstrations in local stores, no one I knew was considering purchase. The sales manager for the local department store confirmed that while interest in the technique was high, there were few sales. This was probably due to the fact that microwave ovens in 1976 retailed for about five hundred dollars. Because they reduce only cooking time, not cooking labour, for full-time housewives the expense is too great for the amount of labour saved. Microwave

ovens will probably be slow to achieve popularity among housewives, at least until the price drops. However, for those women
doing wage work as well as domestic work, they may prove to be
more useful.

When asked if they had suggestions for improving stove
designs, most of the women interviewed indicated that they considered their stoves adequate and efficient. The satisfaction they
expressed with the types of stoves available to them contrasts
with the fact that cleaning the stove was one of the least
favourite tasks. This contrast suggests that women are inclined
to accept what is available because they lack both mechanisms
for influencing manufacturers and access to the science behind
inventions; thus, they can neither demand nor create new technology.

The Refrigerator and Freezer

The other major appliance which has affected food production is
the refrigerator.[14] Refrigerators were not widely owned in Flin
Flon until the late 1940s. Before then domestic food cooling
varied with the season. From late November or December until
March the outside temperature remained below freezing, so for
four months nature provided a freezer for foods stored outside
the house and a coolant for foods stored in unheated porches.
During summer months, some people had ice boxes and bought
ice from the butcher. Others constructed ingenious storage-
cum-cooling places. One household by Ross Lake cooled food by
storing it in jars in the the lake. Another household dug a partial
cellar into the cool bedrock under their house. Two women said
they never had any cool storage place in the summer; they simply
did their shopping every day. By 1976, every house surveyed had
small integrated freezers. Seventy-two households also had
chest freezers. Women unanimously listed refrigerators as one
of the most essential household items.

The effects of the development of refrigeration on household
labour were indirect. Some of the key changes took place outside
the household in the area of food production, distribution and
marketing. The types of food available to the housewife
changed, thus altering dietary preferences and food preparation.

The introduction of refrigerators and freezers made it possible to have food on hand and allowed women to cut back on canning and preserving. These altered patterns of food storage affected shopping habits and meal planning.

While stoves and refrigerators were universally acknowledged to be useful machines which improved the lot of the housewife, other technical developments related to food preparation had a somewhat different effect.

Tools and Appliances

In the early nineteenth century a wide range of hand powered mechanical utensils, such as apple-parers and -corers, eggbeaters and lemon-squeezers, were available. Domestic scientists joined with manufacturers in encouraging the use of such tools on the grounds that they were more efficient, required less skill to operate and were more economical.[15] Many books addressed to housewives recommended lists of over 150 tools that the authors considered necessary for the "typical" kitchen.[16] Two diaries from the 1930s contain lists of kitchen tools and appliances that housewives brought with them to Flin Flon; one includes 162 items, the other includes 157. Because shipping goods by train to Flin Flon was expensive, these two women must have considered all the tools necessary for their housework.

As industry took over major aspects of food preparation with the development of processed foods, much of a housewife's food preparation work was eliminated and many specialized tools were no longer needed. However, modern Flin Flon households all have a number of generalized tools and appliances, both hand powered and electrically powered, which vary in usefulness. When they listed the utensils they had, several women commented that they rarely used certain items, or that some are more bother than they are worth. Often this is because the appliance does not save time or energy when maintenance and cleaning are considered. One woman cited an electric carving knife as an example. Her analysis of why such things are produced has a certain validity:

Seems to me that things like this are made just so they can be sold so someone can make a lot of money. It sure isn't useful but it's the kind of thing that will sell 'cause it makes a good gift. Some manufacturer is making a fortune off this silly thing!

(Generation III, b. 1951)

Other appliances were considered more useful and were used regularly. All households but one had a toaster; all but two had an electric kettle and an electric mixer. In each case the appliance was easy to maintain and clean, and required less human energy to perform its task of boiling water, making toast or mixing batters. Excluding dishes and cutlery for cooking and eating, the number of additional hand powered tools and pots ranged from thirty-five in one household to over two hundred in another. The average was eighty-seven items of kitchen tools and appliances.

Food

In addition to making tools and appliances available, technical developments have also changed the materials that women use when preparing food. The development of adulterated processed or "convenience" foods has made it possible for women to eliminate much preparation and cooking. What was interesting was the fact that even with the availability of a wide variety of foods, not only did most people in Flin Flon eat standardized meals every day with only minor variation, but the type of food eaten changed very little in fifty years. The major change was an increasing use of convenience foods such as frozen vegetables or cake mixes.

Breakfast typically consisted of cereal with milk and sugar or bacon and eggs and toast with butter or margarine. Lunch included soup and sandwiches of peanut butter, cheese or some other filling. Supper was almost always "meat 'n' potatoes" — meat or fish, mashed or baked potatoes, a cooked vegetable and a dessert. Although the type of food remained very much the same, the quality changed a great deal and the amount of preparation time and energy expended by the housewife decreased.

The Labour Process

These changes were reflected in the way women described the work process. Women of the first and second generations talked about how they used to "cook" breakfast, using grain cereals which commonly required boiling. Women of the third generation talked about "serving" precooked dried cereals. One of the effects of the use of processed foods was that women increasingly depended on them and no longer cooked, or even knew how to cook, certain foods. Another off-shoot of the switch to processed foods was the standardization of recipes, which meant that many women lost the ability to improvise when preparing certain recipes.

There was an apparent contradiction between the extensive use of processed foods, particularly mixes for baked goods, and the frequently articulated preference for goods made "from scratch." Women valued the skill and energy represented in a homemade item and had ready praise for women who baked regularly. But most of the time they depended on store-bought, ready-made items or on mixes. In a conversation between two women, the seventy-two-year-old mother was urging her twenty-nine-year-old daughter to make an angel food cake for an approaching party. The daughter was agreeing until they realized that the mother was suggesting that she make it from scratch: "I'll lend you my recipe for it," and the daughter was intending to use a mix; "I have a mix already in the cupboard." When the mother expressed disdain for mixes, the daughter defended herself by noting:

> The mix cost $1.35 and a dozen eggs cost $1.05 so just on eggs alone the mix is almost cheaper. Making an angel cake from scratch is chancy — you don't know for sure that it will turn out and if it doesn't then you've wasted all the ingredients and you have to start over. Anyway, I have a mix here so I know I can make the cake anytime and if I use your recipe then I have to make sure I have all the right supplies and I don't really like to have all that stuff around because I don't use it often. I know your recipe tastes much better but a mix is just so much easier.
>
> (Generation III, b. 1947)

Nowadays women use processed foods because they are frequently cheaper, easier to prepare, require fewer supplies and eliminate the risk of failure. The actual work of food preparation includes a number of smaller tasks[17]: planning meals, setting the table, preparing and cooking the food, serving the food, clearing the food and dishes from the table, putting leftover food away, washing dishes or loading the dishwasher, drying dishes or unloading the dishwasher, putting dishes away, cleaning counters and stove, wiping the table and sweeping the kitchen floor. These tasks vary in complexity, and it is with them that women draw other people into the work of food preparation. All women in Flin Flon said they were responsible for food preparation, but when discussing who did which tasks they noted that certain jobs were frequently done by others.

One task that consistently falls to the housewife is the responsibility for planning meals. Because meals occur several times each day, "thinking what to eat" is, as Oakley noted, "an endless duty."[18] Oakley goes on to quote one of her informants:

> I find it so exhausting just trying to think of what to eat: that's why I get so fed up with cooking. It's not the actual cooking itself. To make things work out well, one needs to plan ahead and be very well organized.[19]

The same sentiment was expressed by several women in Flin Flon, one of whom almost echoed the preceding statement:

> I get just weary thinking up what to eat. I wouldn't mind doing the work — I like cooking actually, but it's always endlessly having to think up what to eat that gets me down.
>
> (Generation II, b. 1931)

Of all the tasks, women unanimously listed cooking as one of their favourite jobs. They considered cooking to be the most potentially creative of all their tasks. However, they qualified their responses by noting that cooking could only be creative when the cook had sufficient time and resources. Flin Flon women echoed Oakley's observation that "limitations of time and money act as brakes on the enjoyment of cooking."[20] Oakley also noted that housewives rarely have time to cook without other demands of their domestic work encroaching.

> Cooking ... recognized as a potentially creative activity by the majority of housewives, often is not, because husbands and child-

ren demand certain sorts of meals at particular times during the day, and the housewife also has to meet a mass of other demands on her time.[21]

Men and older children frequently helped out with cooking. Fifty-eight percent of the women interviewed said that their husbands helped out with cooking at least once a week and sixty-four percent said that their older children helped out at least once a week. The participation of husbands and children in other food preparation tasks was less regular. While forty-three percent of the women said that they insisted that their children help with setting the table and washing the dishes, only thirty percent said that their husbands helped on any regular basis.

Flin Flon women said that they did all of the tasks involved in food preparation at least once a day. On a weekly basis eighty-five per cent of the tasks were usually done by housewives, while husbands contributed to twenty-two percent of the tasks and children contributed to thirty-two percent of the tasks. These results are similar to those of Berke, Berke and Berheide's study

of domestic labour in Evanston, Illinois, which used the same list of tasks.[22] They also compare with a study by Martin Meissner of dual income families in Vancouver where the women did both domestic and wage work.[23]

Regardless of their rate of participation in food preparation, the fact remains that "husband and child typically supplement, but do not replace the wife's efforts."[24] Or, as a Flin Flon woman remarked:

> My family help out with getting the meals. But only if they're here. And chances are they aren't around when the work has to be done. For them getting meals is something they do to help me out sometimes. For me it's something I got to do. If I'm not here to do it, it don't get done.
>
> (Generation II, b. 1935)

Despite changes in the work, food preparation still consumed a great deal of time. Most households ate three meals each day in addition to several snacks. Many women (eighty-three percent) had to pack a lunch box for their husbands as well.

> The thing about food and meals, about cooking you know, is that it is endless. Just as you get one meal done with, it's time to start the next. And you work for a couple of hours to make a meal, specially a nice one and it's gone in no time, just like you never did all that work.
>
> (Generation II, b. 1939)

While the amount of time required for meal preparation varied somewhat with the number of household members and the food preferences of the household, there was significant consistency in the amount of time women reported they spent on food preparation. However, this reported time allocation did not correspond very well to the amount of time actually spent on each of the tasks in twenty of the households in which I was able to observe the housewife at work. In one case, the woman said that she did not prepare breakfast. Shortly afterward, her preschooler woke up and she got him cereal with milk and sugar, toast and peanut butter and a glass of milk. It took her fifteen minutes to get it all organized and on the table. Later it took ten minutes to clean up after he had eaten. Table 5:3 compares the amount of time actually spent on each task with women's perceptions of the amount of time required.

Table 5:3

Average Amount of Time Spent on Food Preparation per Day

Task	Average estimated time n=88 active households	Average actual time n=20	Difference
Breakfast	15 min.	35 min.	20 min.
Lunch	20 min.	40 min.	20 min.
Supper	90 min.	135 min.	45 min.
Total	125 min.	210 min.	85 min.
Lunch box (n=73)	20 min.	30 min.	10 min.

The women underestimated by almost an hour and a half, the amount of time they spent preparing food each day. These averages did not include special food preparation, such as baking and preserving, which is done at regular intervals. Of the eighty-eight active housewives interviewed, only eleven women said that they never did any baking or preserving. All of the rest did some baking on an average of twice a week and fifty-two house-wives did preserving at least once a year:

> It's three meals a day and then some, every day and all day, seven days a week. And that doesn't include baking, preserving or canning which get fitted in in the spare time you can squeeze out of the week.
>
> (Generation III, b. 1945)

Food preparation consistently consumed the most time and energy of all housework tasks. One of the most central aspects of housework, it is a key ingredient in social relations, which means that it is surrounded by emotional and ideological notions.

The whole genre of cookbook literature is devoted to just this point. One cookbook published in Canada in 1901 argued that good cooking was especially important for the working class as their labour depends upon their health.

> ... To cook well is immensely more important to the middle class
> and working classes than to the rich, for they who live by 'the
> sweat of their brow' whether mentally or physically must have
> the requisite strength to support their labour. Even to the poor,
> whose very lives depend upon the produce of the hard-earned
> dollar, cookery is of the greatest importance. Every wife, mother
> or sister should be a good plain cook.[25]

Other cookbooks claim that good cooking is essential not only
for health but also for the survival of the family, the political and
social stability of the nation, and even the existence of "civilization."[26] One says, "The table is the centre of the family, the
centre of civilization."[27]

In general, cookbook ideology seems to be expressed in
practice. In one single-wage household the husband was on
bonus, which meant his pay depended on how hard he worked
(literally, he was the breadwinner). His wife commented:

> If he doesn't eat good, then he can't work hard and if he doesn't
> work hard, his pay is dropped so I figure that I got to cook good
> meals for him so we can all live off his wages.
>
> (Generation III, b. 1946)

Another woman said she considered good meals essential because:

> When we don't eat so good, everyone gets bitchy. I think my cook-
> ing keeps this family together.
>
> (Generation II, b. 1926)

All the women said they considered cooking to be one of the
most important parts of their housework, to a large extent
because they recognized the significance of food for both the
survival of the family and the reproduction of labour power. One
woman described the importance of food as she packed her
husband's lunch box:

> I always pack him a real good lunch with lots in it, even the day
> before pay day, so he can get through the day. If he don't have a
> good big lunch he just can't work.
>
> (Generation II, b. 1927)

Radio, TV and magazines also stress the importance of cooking
by devoting a great deal of time to it. Their concern, however, is
rarely to teach women how to prepare nutritious, inexpensive
meals in a short time with a minimum of work. Rather, they tend

to stress the creative aspects of cooking, urging women to elaborate their "culinary techniques." In this way they contribute to the prevalent notion that what women do at home is not work. Oakley notes that their aim is not "simple efficiency":

> Instead it is an elaboration of the task, designed to subtract it from the category of "work" and add it to the creative pleasure dimension. This treatment of cooking ... is a particularly clear demonstration of how the social denial of housework as work operates.[28]

When women get caught between the reality of their work situation and the ideology presented by the media, the results can be tragic. Some women responded with anger, recognizing the ideology for the fraud it is:

> Look at that shit they blast at us every day on TV about how lovely cooking is and how we should all spend our time cooking "creatively". Creative my foot!! Stupid shows like "The Galloping Gourmet" and all those ads. They are obviously made by people with oodles of money, no family and all the time in the world. It's so unreal it makes me angry.
>
> (Generation III, b. 1942)

Others internalized the contradictions and felt themselves to be incompetent:

> I watch all those TV shows and commercials and I read all the cooking articles in *Chatelaine* and it makes me realize how I don't cook good at all. I try to do what they suggest sometimes but it never works out right. I can't seem to organize myself to do it right. I wish I could make food like that on TV but I can't.
>
> (Generation III, b. 1947)

Cleaning

Just as cooking is "forever" work, cleaning involves many ongoing, repetitive tasks. The impact of technology on cleaning has eliminated much of this labour while retaining the structure of the job. Two technical developments have altered the way cleaning is done: the standardization of materials, and the development of specific cleaning appliances. But dirt cannot be centralized, so the worker has to move around the house to where the dirt is.

Under heavy cleaning, most housewives include such jobs as scrubbing floors, washing ceilings and walls, cleaning the stove, especially the oven — primarily jobs that are labour-intensive, dirty and time-consuming. Light cleaning includes such tasks as washing dishes, wiping kitchen counters, vacuuming or sweeping floors, cleaning the toilet and bathtub, and dusting. General tidying includes activities such as picking up toys and newspapers, emptying ashtrays, opening and closing the curtains at the appropriate times and putting things away in their assigned places.

Early house construction in Flin Flon made cleaning very difficult. Wood stoves and oil lamps gave off greasy smoke which adhered to walls and ceiling. Chamber pots retained the smell of urine which permeated bedroom furnishings and was hard to eliminate. Transporting fuel and water from a storage place to the stove or sink created dirt and puddles. However, as household construction was standardized, heating and lighting changed, and running water and sewers were introduced, cleaning became easier.

Household utensils and fabrics were similarly standardized. Until the turn of the century kitchen utensils were made from a wide variety of materials, such as tin, iron, copper, brass, silver, wood, zinc, agate and granite.[29] This range of materials created a great deal of work in the kitchen because each required a different chemical and procedure for cleaning. One housekeeping guide of the period listed ten "essential" cleaners.[30] Like kitchen utensils, each fabric used in the home required special chemicals and processes for cleaning. Fabrics included a variety of natural materials, mostly composed of cotton, linen and wool. One guide listed twelve common natural fibre fabrics.[31] A Flin Flon housewife recalled cleaning in the 1930s:

> I had a whole cupboard full of powders and liquids and every time I wanted to clean something I had to mix up a batch of the right stuff. There was a real knack to it — knowing which cleaners worked on what.
>
> (Generation I, b. 1897)

The introduction of new materials, such as stainless steel and plastics, eliminated the need for mixing and applying different chemicals and cleaning processes and allowed for the development of standardized, ready mixed cleaners. These new materials affected housework in several ways. The various chemicals and powders no longer had to be purchased, stored or mixed. Most utensils or fabrics could be washed together at the same time, eliminating the need for extensive sorting of items into different categories before cleaning. As the work processes became more uniform, they no longer required as much skill or knowledge.

The second major technological change in cleaning was the development of the vacuum cleaner and to a lesser extent the dishwasher. As Sigfried Giedion argues in *Mechanization Takes Command*, the mechanization of cleaning began as early as 1858 with the development of the carpet sweeper, the aim of which was to "dispense with back-bending and with the to and fro motion of the broom wielding hand."[32] Nevertheless, most women continued to clean their floors by hand, with a broom or a duster, until 1910 when electrically powered vacuum cleaners became available. By 1932 Christine Fredericks, an exponent of time and motion studies for the home, could argue that the vacuum cleaner was one of the most essential appliances in the home. "How many times in 365 days will she use the midget vacuum?" she asked. "Roughly at least 300 times a year."[33] She went on to say, "The power vacuum cleaner is so well known and accepted.... Next to the electric iron it is the power appliance most universally operated in the household."[34]

Flin Flon housewives agreed. Women who worked as housewives in the 1930s noted that vacuum cleaners were relatively inexpensive and extremely "useful," that is, labour saving and effective. Every household interviewed had a vacuum cleaner and housewives vacuumed an average of two or three times a week. Compared to a broom or carpet sweeper, vacuums are more efficient in picking up dust and dirt, require fewer motions to operate and do the job in less time.

Dishwashers, readily available by the 1960s, are not so obviously advantageous. Not only do they cost a lot and take up a significant amount of room, but the labour involved in preparing and loading them is almost as much as required for hand washing. Many housewives say that they are not worth either the expense or the labour involved. In Flin Flon only four women had one; they argued that it got the dishes very clean and that dishes could be stored in it. One woman with a household of nine people assured me that the number of dishes she washed each day warranted a dishwasher. Another woman suggested that husbands bought dishwashers for their wives because the men could get out of washing up that way:

> I used to tell him he should help with dishes, it was only fair; so one Christmas he bought me a dishwasher and now when I ask for help he says he bought me a dishwasher so I wouldn't have to do dishes so why am I complaining? (Generation III, b. 1955)

It is interesting that all four dishwashers were purchased by the men without their wives' knowledge.

Cleaning technology has its greatest impact on the work of heavy cleaning. In the tool-based household there was a yearly cycle to housework, the highlight of which was spring cleaning. An analysis of the diaries of two Flin Flon housewives for the year 1929 indicated that housework had a seasonal imperative to it. March and April were devoted to intensive spring cleaning, everything in the house was cleaned, aired, sorted and put away. In October the same women did a lesser fall cleaning during which they packed away summer clothes, unpacked winter wear and made the house ready for winter. These periods of heavy cleaning corresponded to seasonal changes, not only because the Canadian climate requires two completely different sets of clothing, but also because their houses got very dirty and stuffy and a full-scale cleaning was the only way to eliminate the accumulated grease and grime.

Because the modern house does not have the same kinds of dirt and modern cleaning techniques cut down on the amount that does accumulate, spring cleaning has ceased to be a particularly significant or disruptive event. The women I interviewed were vague about how often they did heavy cleaning. Some said they washed walls and ceilings of each room every couple of years; most washed windows twice a year when changing storm windows. Only cleaning the oven remained a regular task of heavy cleaning, and women said they cleaned their ovens about once every two months. As one young housewife noted:

> I know I don't have to work so hard as my mum to keep this house clean. It's real modern and I've got all the stuff I need to make cleaning easy. I don't have nearly the dirt to get rid of that she did.
>
> (Generation III, b. 1957)

Women did frequent light cleaning, however, which included vacuuming, sweeping, dusting, making beds, tidying up or straightening.

Women said that they vacuumed their living rooms and halls on average three times each week for about twenty minutes. They swept or vacuumed the kitchen daily for about ten minutes. Dusting was done an average of twice each week and took fifteen minutes. Making beds was done daily and took twenty minutes to half an hour. Tidying up or straightening was described as occurring "continuously," and women were reluctant or unable to estimate how much time it took. Table 5:4 compares the amount of time actually spent on each task with the amount of time housewives estimated they spent doing each job. Once again women underestimated; the amount of actual time their housework required each week was three hours more than their estimated time.

In *Purity and Danger* Mary Douglas argues that "uncleanliness is matter out of place" or that "dirt is essentially disorder." She goes on to suggest that a housewife conducts "busy scrubbings and cleanings" and organizes the storage of cleaning materials, not to eliminate potential health hazards or to rationalize her work, but rather as an attempt at symbolic presentation.[35] Such an analysis runs roughshod over the facts and insults the work that housewives do. While dirt is in part disorder, dirt is also dirt and disorder impedes daily life.

Housewives have two explicit goals when they do cleaning. The first is to ensure order, not for symbolic reasons but so that

TABLE 5:4

Average Amount Of Time Spent On Cleaning Per Week

Task	Average estimated time n=88 active households	Average actual time n=20	Difference
Vacuuming	60 min.	80 min.	20 min.
Sweeping	70 min.	105 min.	35 min.
Dusting	30 min.	55 min.	25 min.
Making beds	175 min.	280 min.	105 min.
Total	335 min.	520 min.	185 min.

household members can find things when they need them, so that things do not get broken, soiled or torn from misuse and so that the workplace is efficient. The second goal is to eliminate the dirt that attracts insects, mice and other vermin. Or as one woman put it:

> If I don't clean up after the children every day, I'd find rotting food in the furniture, flies swarming around the place, grit in the bed that scratches when you sleep and the house would be an uncomfortable place to be.
>
> (Generation III, b. 1947)

The cleaning process, however has a certain ambiguity: how clean is clean? Theoretically, one could clean endlessly and still never achieve total cleanliness. Standards of cleanliness are personal, and many housewives evaluate themselves by the cleanliness of their homes. Media presentations of housewives in their homes show shiny new floors and appliances, encouraging the image of the always tidy house. For some women the "impossible dream" becomes a personal goal and they feel endlessly frustrated when it cannot be reached. In this limited sense Douglas's analysis has validity. The level of cleanliness becomes symbolic of the efficiency, skill and hard work of a woman as housewife. But cleaning is also a frustrating process because as soon as it is done the house gets dirty again:

> The worst thing about cleaning this house is that it's endless. I scrub and dust and tidy and then I turn around and it's a mess again.
>
> (Generation II, b. 1926)

In this respect housework is like an assembly line. In industry such work would be defined as boring, frustrating and likely to lead to unrest among the workers. In the home, it becomes a frequent source of tension between the housewife and other household members:

> Nothing is so frustrating than to spend a whole day cleaning and then have someone mess it all up with dirty shoes or by throwing their stuff all around.
>
> (Generation II, b. 1923)

151

Laundry

For centuries the techniques by which North American house-wives did their laundry remained static. It was an arduous, physically demanding task which required the greater part of a whole day and had to be done on a regular basis, usually once a week and normally on Monday. Since the early nineteenth century domestic scientists and home economists were concerned with analysing and simplifying "blue Monday." The various descriptions ranging over more than one hundred years show a marked similarity that corresponds closely to the following description from Flin Fon in the 1930s.

Imagine, if you can, one of those blistery hot summer days, the kind when all you want to do is go sit in the lake. But it's Monday; so I can't. For Monday is washday. So I get up at 4:30 A.M. to start the fire in the stove — a fire and when it's already hot enough to fry eggs on the rocks! When the fire's going I fill the copper boiler with water and carry it from the tank to the stove and then lift it onto the stove — heavy work that and already the sweat is pouring down my back. It makes me hot just to think of it. Then I go get the washing. Baskets of dirty things — clothes, bed sheets, towels and his dirty work clothes and I carry them into the kitchen and sort them into piles and then by 6:30 I'm ready to start scrubbing. Each thing to wash you wet in the warm water and then throw it in the boiler to boil awhile. The steam rises everywhere till the whole house is like one of them Finnish saunas. Then you take a wooden spoon and start fishin'. One at a time you pull the steamy things out of the boiler and you hold them there heavy and steaming that they are — my, them wet things get heavy till your arm aches. Then when they cool enough to touch you start scrubbing, rubbing the thing against the scrub board and rubbing with soap and a scrub brush. Oh and I forgot the soap, which you couldn't forget because you had to get it ready the day before by taking a bar of soap and grating it into flakes so it would dissolve easier. So then you scrub each thing and there were hundreds and the steam is boiling and the clothes are hot and heavy and when you've scrubbed it you throws it into a pail of warm water for rinsing then you squeeze it out, and you have to squeeze so hard and your arms already tired and it so hot. Then you rinse again and wring and then pile all the stuff into the basket and carry it outside and one by one hang each piece on the line to dry and you have to hang them just right or you'll never iron the wrinkles out and that takes till 6:30 or 7:00 of an evening when he wants his supper and you go to sleep like the dead, hot and weary and worn to the bone. That were some hard work let me tell you and we never had no help from no one and that's what it used to be like to do my washing. Oh, but I forgot. All the while you had to keep stoking up the stove to keep it hot enough to keep the water boiling so's it got as I hated it, it was so hot and all the water splashed on the floor so when I finished I had to scrub the kitchen floor too. And we didn't have no plastic clothes line, only linen so it had to be strung up before clothes could be hung. And of course you were forever slipping in the water and losing your balance and hitting that fiery stove and of course the kids wanted looking after all day at the same time. Well that was Blue Monday all right.

(Generation I, b. 1896)

Throughout the various steps of the washing process the housewife usually worked alone, although occasionally with the help of children or friends or even a hired laundress. The woman stood for most of the day in a hot room working unprotected with fires, boiling water and wet clothes. She had to lift and carry heavy hot wet clothes, hang them on the line, and clean up the kitchen. After the clothes were dry, they were taken off the line, folded to prevent creasing, ironed, folded again and put away. While ironing and putting away was often left until the next day, these too were hot, wearisome tasks.

Irons had to be heated every five minutes on the stove, which of course meant that the stove had to be on all the time, even in summer. The textiles available required hand pressure. Like washing, ironing required the woman to stand while working.

A Flin Flon woman's diary entry for August 1930 describes her attitude toward laundry:

It was a hot hot day — too hot to move really but it was washday so I stoked up the stove this morning and I scrubbed all day. The sweat was just pouring off me in puddles. My back aches and my arms are tired and I'm bone weary tonight. The clothes are clean — folded waiting to be ironed tomorrow but it's terrible work. Just as fast as I wash they get dirty again. Laundry is the worst work a woman's got.

Her sentiment that laundry "is the worst work a woman's got" was echoed by housewives everywhere and was an important motivation for women to accept the major changes that occurred in the organization of the laundry processes.

Throughout the nineteenth century there was a rash of inventions and improvements as people experimented with ways of easing the burden of laundry work. Then, in the early 1920s with the development of small electric motors, the mass-scale distribution of washing machines began. Electric washing machines varied widely in the way in which they performed certain operations, in the extent to which they were mechanized and automatic and in the amount of labour they actually took over. As the manufacture of washing machines increased through the 1930s and 1940s, various improvements were incorporated. By the 1950s most washing machines on the market were fully automatic. By the early 1960s dryers were readily available as well, and a few manufacturers combined in the same machine all washing and drying procedures.

The mechanization and electrification of ironing was much simpler and proceeded more quickly. The traditional flatiron was successful as far as actual ironing went, but it required reheating every five minutes, and the fabric had to be sprinkled with water regularly. In 1906 the electric iron was first marketed. It was mobile, lightweight and had temperature control. Most significantly, the internal heat source eliminated the need to use the stove. Later, the steam iron resolved the problem of having to sprinkle the fabric.

For women with automatic washers, dryers and irons, laundry is vastly different from the earlier manual process. The technical developments of the laundry process eliminated significant amounts of labour. Electricity replaced human labour as the motive power in washing and removing water. The new processes eased the labour involved in carrying laundry and in ironing. In addition, the work involved in maintaining the wood stove, carrying water, preparing soap, starch and blueings and reheating flatirons was completely eliminated. These technical developments also eliminated many of the risks and much of the unpleasantness. Women were quick to obtain the new machinery as soon as it became available, and new housewives claim that a washer and dryer are among the first items they buy.

Flin Flon women, in fact, described purchasing washing machines before they had access to other facilities normally associated with washers. One woman described buying a gyrator washing machine in the early 1940s. She installed it in her kitchen despite the fact that she had no running water in her house. She considered it worth the initial expense and labour involved in carrying water to and from the machine. She observed that:

> ... sure I had to stand there all the time but I didn't have to scrub on a washboard. Hauling water and standing by was a picnic.
>
> (Generation II, b. 1907)

Another woman talked of her purchase of a wringer washer in the 1950s. This machine required her constant presence, but "it did all the hard work. I just stood there and fed things through!"

However, women perceived problems with some of the new developments related to laundry work. Modern textiles stain easily and are often harder to clean than cottons. Some fabrics melt easily when ironed. Recently, both research and women's experiences have suggested that modern textiles create certain health hazards.[36]

Flin Flon women also maintained, fairly consistently, that clothing dried on a line outdoors is cleaner, smells better and is generally nicer than machine-dried clothes. Many women hung their clothes out during the summer months using their dryers only on rainy days and in winter. Even on a sunny day in mid-winter some women hang out their "whites" because "the sun bleaches better than any bleach." An added advantage to using a clothes line is that it is cheaper. However, as line drying leaves cotton fabrics and towels stiff, some women perferred to machine dry them to eliminate ironing.

Of the women interviewed, all but ten had some type of electrically powered washing machine. All but fifteen had a dryer, and only eight had no iron. All of the women interviewed who had their own machines did at least two loads of wash each week. Women with babies had an additional load or two of baby clothes and frequently several loads of diapers each week, unless they spent money for disposable diapers. Of those ten women who did not have their own machines, only two sent clothes to the laundry. The rest washed some clothes at home by hand and took loads of washing to the laundromat. No one did her washing completely by hand.

It seems that changing fashion standards have had a major effect on the work of ironing. When asked what they ironed, women over forty unanimously responded by saying "everything." Subsequently, some of them qualified their assertion by "admitting" that they no longer iron certain items. Women under forty were much more likely to suggest that they only ironed a few "essentials," and fourteen women, eight of whom did not own irons, never iron anything. The younger women confirmed the impression that ironing has decreased in importance over the last fifty years. Most of them recalled their mothers ironing "everything." In many cases "everything" can be taken quite literally to include all those items washed. Women who ironed everything spent the best part of one day each week ironing. Women who did less, fitted ironing in with other tasks. A few women said they liked to do their ironing when they watch TV or have a friend in to chat.

Women's ability to estimate accurately the amount of time they spend on laundry each week contrasts with their underestimation in other household tasks. This is accounted for partially by the fact that automatic washers take a set length of time to complete their cycle. The aspects of work involved for women who have an automatic washing machine include collecting dirty clothes and sorting them according to colour, fabric and amount of dirt (average ten minutes). The dirty clothes are carried to the laundry area. The machine is loaded; laundry detergent and other cleansers, such as fabric softener and bleach, are added; finally the machine is turned on (average ten minutes). The machine proceeds to wash, rinse and spin dry the clothes without further intervention on the woman's part. When the washer is finished its cycle, the damp clothes have to be taken out and prepared for further drying (average five minutes). On an average, the washing cycle takes up twenty-five minutes of the housewives' time.

Using a dryer involves loading the dryer and turning it on for a total average of ten minutes. Using a clothes line requires much more time. The time involved depends on the things to hung up. A load of big sheets can take less than ten minutes to hang up, while a load of small baby clothes can take more than thirty minutes. Flin Flon women suggested that carrying the clothes outside and hanging them on the line usually took about twenty minutes, while taking them off the line took about fifteen minutes. Regardless of which drying method was used, clothes have to be folded and readied for ironing or put away (average twenty minutes). The total drying labour time using a dryer amounted to an average of thirty minutes. Using a clothes line averages sixty-five minutes. The total amount of actual labour time spent for each single load of laundry came to fifty-five minutes using a dryer or ninety minutes using a clothes line.

The number of loads of laundry a housewife does each week depends largely on the composition of her household. Every household interviewed did at least two loads each week of adult clothing and household items like sheets and towels. For every two schoolaged children women found they did another load of clothes. For every child in diapers women did an additional five loads each week. Thus, on an average, a woman with a husband and two schoolaged children did three loads of laundry each week. A woman with a husband, two schoolaged children and one preschooler in diapers did, on an average, eight loads of laundry each week. This means that, on an average, housewives spent somewhere between 110 minutes (1.83 hours) and 640 minutes (10.67 hours) each week doing laundry.

Although I do not have accurate records for the amount of time involved in manual washing processes, there are two sources of evidence which suggest that technology reduced the amount of time spent on laundry. The woman quoted at the beginning of this section began her washday at 4:30 A.M. and ended it at 6:30 or 7:00 P.M., a total of nine and one-half to ten hours. Two other diaries from the same period refer to washdays as lasting about eight hours and ten hours, respectively. If these figures are typical, they suggest that the amount of time spent on laundry has decreased with the invention of the washing machine and dryer. Only those women who have small children in diapers and who don't use a dryer are still putting in the same amount of time as women who washed by hand.

These figures seem to contradict Joann Vanek's findings, based on a series of time budget studies in the United States. She found that the amount of time spent in laundry has actually increased despite the technical changes. She also noted that no other task of housework has been so transformed and eased by technological developments as laundry, yet the amount of time spent on laundry has increased! Vanek suggests that this is because people have more clothes now and they wash them more often.[37]

There is some evidence from Flin Flon to support this explanation. Women of the first generation said that they washed sheets once a month; women of the third generation wash their sheets every week. One explanation of why Flin Flon women seem to do less laundry than their American counterparts may be that they have less clothing. On the other hand, the figures from Flin Flon suggest that laundry, like other components of housework, has become increasingly flexible. In other words, this evidence suggests that technological developments have a complex impact on housework. In this case, while the technology unquestionably eased the amount of labour and improved the working conditions, it also allowed for changing social standards of fashion and cleanliness to alter the amount of time expended.

CONCLUSIONS

There is a television advertisement for a particular brand of "instant dinner" which features a motherly looking woman who displays the product and asks, "Want to have more time to spend with your family and other important things?" One Flin Flon woman responded with fervour:

> Of course I do — dumb TV. My mother had no conveniences and she worked like a slave all day long. I want to keep my house nice — and I can because I have all these appliances to help — but I want to have time for my family, especially while the kids are young.

> (Generation III, b. 1947)

The explanation that women give for accepting new concepts, techniques and appliances is that it makes their work easier and more efficient by reducing the amount of their time and labour.

Housework has always been fragmented; there are no inherent work-related links connecting each of the processes. In the early period, they appeared to be more integrated because each task went on for a continuous period of time and one tended to follow the other. The introduction of machinery reduced the amount of labour time required at any one continuous stretch. As a result, the processes became increasingly discrete. Their only common link is that they are done in one location by the same worker for a common end.

Housework now involves generalized activity and supervision in four or five jobs. This means that, in the course of one day, the worker must move frequently from one job to another, rarely completing one task before having to start another. Such fragmentation results in doing multiple jobs at one time, which many women find tiring, and it means that housework is more flexible than it used to be. If the laundry is not done Monday morning, it can be thrown in the washer before bed Monday night and dried during breakfast Tuesday morning. Most modern housework tasks do not require intense concentration; they are repetitive and easily resumed if interrupted.

Housework provides the material basis for the rest of domestic work and for the social relations of the household members. As the focus of the work is the maintenance of the household and the people who live in it, it becomes a vehicle by which women express affection and do tension managing for their household members. Cooking a nice meal, providing clean sheets or eliminating dull, yellow floor wax become ways of expressing love. Technical changes and the resulting reorganization of labour have reduced housework time and have allowed the housewife to be more responsive to the social relations of the household. Thus, changes in housework have created a situation within which changes in the other components of domestic work could occur.

CHAPTER SIX

MAKING ENDS MEET

Consumptionism is the name given to the new doctrine; and it is admitted today to be the greatest idea that America has to give to the world; the idea that workmen and masses be looked upon not simply as workers and producers, but as consumers.... Pay them more, sell them more, prosper more is the equation.

Mrs. Christine Frederick,
Selling Mrs. Consumer (1929)

As the sphere of commodity production expanded and changed at the turn of the twentieth century, manufacturers needed to develop new markets. One area they focused on was the working-class household. As a consequence, the subsistence patterns of the household changed significantly, resulting in new work for domestic labour.

At the beginning of the twentieth century, modern advertising emerged as a whole new field devoted to encouraging people to buy. As part of its goal to urge people to consume, advertising became a powerful promoter of ideology and an instrument in the creation of new social needs. It had to "persuade people to buy, not to satisfy their own fundamental needs, but rather to satisfy the real historic needs of capitalist productive machinery."[1]

From the perspective of the working-class household, these changes had a profound effect on the structure of domestic labour. Because women were responsible for handling most of the household consumption, much of the advertising was directed at them. The advertising industry promoted a series of images about what constituted a "normal" household, a "successful" housewife and mother, a "happy, healthy" family.

More significantly, the creation of new social needs exploited and sharpened the general dissatisfaction many workers experienced. Advertising urged people to purchase goods and services by encouraging them to feel dissatisfied with what they currently had. An advertising executive from 1930 noted: "Satisfied customers are not as profitable as discontented ones."[2] As consumers, then, women confront a situation where, no matter what they do, they cannot fulfil the requirements of their work. It is their task to satisfy the needs of the members of the household. But those household members are daily inundated with forces aimed at creating new needs and keeping them in a state of permanent discontent. For working-class women this dilemma is compounded by the limitations imposed by the level of the wage.

In a small way this process was illustrated by what one Flin Flon woman called "the breakfast cereal swindle." Her two children, ages seven and nine, both refused to eat very much. She wanted them to eat more regularly, so she tried to buy foods they liked. When she asked what they would like to eat, they each named a different cereal they had seen advertised on TV and promised, if she bought it, to eat breakfast regularly. The woman bought two types of cereal and served the children their choice. But they refused to eat, requesting two other cereals that they had subsequently seen advertised. She bought those two cereals and again tried to get the children to eat. Again they would not eat, but suggested yet two more cereals. At this point the woman refused to purchase any more cereals. She complained about the role of advertising in encouraging her children to want endlessly different products instead of teaching them to eat well. She pointed out that it was impossible for her to satisfy her children as they kept wanting new products, "and I can't go on buying different cereals every day. I can't afford it."

Advertising plays on all the inherent ambiguities of domestic labour. It inundates women with information about new products, which will supposedly improve levels of household cleanliness, standards of nutrition, the quality of comfort of family members. Women want to improve the household standard of living so they have to pay attention to new information even when they know that advertisers are not concerned with the well-being of consumers and that the information may be misleading.

The creation of new needs based on dissatisfaction also means that the domestic worker can never be sure that household members will continue to like what they used to like. To carry out her work efficiently, she must be constantly attuned to the changing wants and needs of the people in her household. Given the limitations imposed by the wage level, the woman then has to rank those needs and wants to establish which ones can be met immediately, which must be postponed and which can never be gratified. It is at this point that her relationship to the household's wages becomes dominant.

WAGES AS THE INSTRUMENT OF CONSUMPTION

While the exchange of the wage for labour power seems to be simple, its structural relationship is complex. In fact, the wage is paid to ensure the maintenance and reproduction of labour power and, hence, pays for the subsistence needs of the worker and the worker's family. The discrepancy that exists between the surface appearance and underlying realities of the exchange of labour power for wages permeates women's domestic labour. In practice, wages are paid to wage earners and are theirs to dispose of at will. However, part of the sexual division of labour in the household means that the wages are distributed in such a way that they support the whole household.[3] The wife and husband have a common interest in the size of his paycheque (its real buying power) but they are, nevertheless, divided by the fact that he earns it for his work and she spends it in hers.

From the man's perspective, the wages are his. They are earned by his labour, by the "sweat of his brow," and they are paid to him whether or not he has a family. As the bread winner he recognizes that he is economically central to the household and he derives certain privileges from that position. The supreme importance of wages means that his needs, at least in his capacity as wage earner, have priority in the household. He has control and power over the distribution of the money that comes into the house in his wage packet.

From the woman's perspective, the wages may be her husand's but without them she cannot carry out her work. Her ability to do her domestic labour depends on his giving her a certain portion of them. Because the wages are paid to him, she is structurally dependent on his good will and generosity for both her own subsistence and the implementation of her work. This structural dependency is reinforced by all the other factors in their relationship that generate male dominance and female subservience.

The money form of wages has embedded in it a number of social relations. For the man it represents his labour. For both the husband and wife it represents their potential subsistence. For her it represents her powerlessness and dependency. As a result, women and men come together from different perspectives and understandings. The result is potentially explosive for both of them.

When tensions erupt over money they reflect all those feelings that smoulder beneath the surface. In an argument I witnessed a woman walked into her kitchen carrying several bags of groceries. Her husband got up from the livingroom and stood in the doorway watching her. She suggested that he help her. He responded:

> Help you! I help you when I give you my money that you use to buy that lot. Your job is spending it and just you see to it that you spend it carefully.

She blew up and yelled at him:

> Your money, your money. I work too. You think I like living on your money. I'd like to work, then I wouldn't have to spend your money, I could spend my own.

He laughed bitterly and sneered:

> I bet. You'd never work like I do. That's hard work, real work, that earns the money. And that money keeps you alive. Don't you forget it.

To which she responded in tears:

> I can't forget it. I wish to God I could forget it. Whatever I do, it's there. You earn the money and I spend it. Well do your own goddamn shopping from now on. You wouldn't be any good at it

anyway. If you did it, all your precious money would be gone in no time. So don't forget you need me too.

He turned and walked away as he muttered:

Women. You can't live with them and you can't really live without them.

(Generation III, woman b. 1940; man b. 1931)

FROM WAGES TO HOUSEKEEPING MONEY

The wages that the man receives must be transferred to the woman for housekeeping money. Because it is his money which he then gives to her, she has no automatic or direct means of getting access to it. The money transfer occurs in one of three ways:

1. The man voluntarily turns over all, or most, of his wages to the woman. She handles the money, pays the bills and gives him a personal allowance.

2. The man keeps all the money, pays the bills and gives the woman a certain amount for her housekeeping. When she needs money for personal expenses, she asks him for a specific amount.

3. The man puts the money in a mutually accessible place. Each pays the bills when they arrive. They discuss together how much money to spend on both housekeeping and personal expenses.

In households of the first generation sixteen (80 percent) followed the first pattern where the husband turns his wages over to his wife, and four (20 percent) followed the second pattern where the husband gives his wife a set amount.[4] In households of the second generation, sixteen (57 percent) followed the first pattern; five (18 percent) followed the second pattern; and seven (25 percent) followed the third pattern where they pool resources. In households of the third generation, seventeen (33 percent) followed the first pattern; twenty-three (44 percent) followed the second; and twelve (23 percent) pooled their resources. In other words, the prevalent pattern in Flin Flon was the first, in which the woman handles the money. It accounts for almost half (forty-nine) of the households interviewed.[5] The next most popular pattern was the second, in which the man controls the money completely and gives the woman a specific amount (thirty-two households). The third pattern occurred in only nineteen households.

There is an apparent democracy in the way the majority of households handled their finances. More than half of the women seemed to have ready access to money. But this is deceptive, for underlying even the most egalitarian sharing practices lurks the bread winner's power. In one household where the man cashed his paycheque and put the money in the kitchen drawer, the woman commented:

> He puts his paycheque in the drawer and I pay the bills and take what money I need. And I know I can spend it on what I want. But it's still his money and if I did anything he didn't agree with, like buy something I really want but he doesn't, then I know he'd get mad.
>
> (Generation III, b. 1961)

In another household where the man gave all his money to his wife and she paid for everything, the woman did not have any winter boots. She refused to buy any because:

> It's true I pay the bills and can decide what to spend our money on and he'd never complain if I bought something for the kids or for the house. But I don't like to spend money on me. It's his money that he makes for the family. I can get by okay with my running shoes; I don't really need boots. I'd hate to spend his money just on me.
>
> (Generation III, b. 1957)

In some cases, the man keeps tight control over the money. In the most extreme example I encountered, a husband of the third generation refused to give his wife any cash at all. She was forced to do her shopping by phone; then her husband picked up the order and paid for it himself. She had no money for her own use and had to ask him to purchase cigarettes, birth control pills and other personal items for her. He used his financial power to torment her, on occasion even withholding her birth control pills when he was angry with her. When she discovered that she was pregnant with her fifth child after one such dispute his response was "good, maybe another one will keep you in your place." While this situation was particularly vicious, it nevertheless illustrates the underlying power of the wage earner.

In those cases where the man gives the woman a housekeeping allowance, she is expected to pay for the items used in her work and for her personal expenses. In practice, allowances cover the expenses incurred for domestic labour but do not provide any money for a woman's personal expenses. While most Flin Flon women operating on an allowance managed to buy their cigarettes, contraceptives and the occasional cup of coffee in a restaurant, they had no money for other expenses, such as paying a babysitter, buying beer in a pub, paying for a movie. They were certainly unable to stretch their allowances to pay for clothing items or other personal effects. If they wanted money for entertainment, clothing or other incidentals, they had to ask for it.

Since they are not free to decide how to spend money, women usually cannot do anything without their husbands' prior knowledge. Economic power gives men tremendous social power and control over their wives:

> It's not that he minds giving me money when I ask. It's just that he always knows what I want to do with it and he always gets to voice his approval or disapproval. It feels like it used to be with my dad. It's his money so he gets to say what I do with it.
>
> (Generation III, b. 1948)

Because they have no assurance that their husbands will give them money when they request it, Flin Flon women resorted to all sorts of manipulations. In some instances, they used sexuality as a way of getting their husbands to give them money. In other instances, they cajoled, whined, begged and pleaded. One woman rather brutally described how she felt about getting money from her husband:

> Men are such sucks. They have this big fat ego and it needs feeding. When I need money I have to go through this whole song and dance about how wonderful he is and how big and strong and how I'd just be lost without him. And it works. He coughs up.
>
> (Generation II, b. 1928)

Even in households where resources were pooled, women still had to confront the fact of male power. When the household functioned smoothly and relations between the woman and man were amicable, male economic power was still latent, expressed in such observations as "he's real good that way:"

He brings home his paycheque and puts it in the kitchen drawer. Then I pay all the bills and take my housekeeping. The rest stays in the drawer and we help ourselves whenever either of us wants something. He's real good that way.

(Generation III, b. 1949)

He's real easy about money — lets me have whatever I want. But of course it's still his money and he *lets* me have it.

(Generation II, b. 1938)

When household relations break down, men's economic power becomes overt and potentially explosive. Women were aware of this potential explosiveness and dealt with it continually in their work. This was illustrated by the typical pattern of purchasing and consuming alcohol. While women frequently bought alcohol, they usually did so at their husbands' request. The alcohol was considered the husbands' property, and women often could not drink it unless their husbands agreed. One reason for this seemed to be that alcohol, even beer, was considered a luxury item. Because the husbands earned the money, they controlled the consumption of alcohol bought with it. A man described his understanding:

Way I see it, I earned that booze and no one but me is going to get it.

(Generation II, b. 1921)

A woman explained it more precisely:

I think that men feel like they make that money when they work, see. So it's theirs. Now they got to turn it over to their wives so's the woman can buy food. Otherwise they'd never eat. But booze now, that's different. So men don't want their wives drinking up their hard work and having a good time on it. See, most men think women got it easy — living off them. So they don't want to see us enjoying ourselves too much at their expense.

(Generation II, b. 1931)

CONSUMPTION MANAGEMENT

Once men have handed their wages, or a portion of them, over to their wives, the women confront the hardest and most pivotal aspect of their domestic labour. Because household survival depends on wages coming in regularly and on their being spent in a way that maximizes the level of subsistence, how women spend money has important consequences for their households.

Because as consumers women and men have no control over the prices charged for commodities, the money that the household must spend on subsistence items is determined by forces external to it. Similarly, household members have no control over the amount of money available to them. As workers, the men may be able to affect somewhat the level of wages. Wages are conditioned by the general standard of living, the types of commodities available, the items people want and think they need. Wages reflect the historical and social forces at work in any given period. In particular struggles, workers sometimes win wage increases for themselves. Their ability to struggle and win depends on the strength of the unions and on workers' willingness to fight collectively, but individual households have very little ability to influence these factors. The only flexibility and control available to the household members is in the sphere of consumption. This control is exercised in two ways. People can choose whether or not to buy a particular commodity. Once commodities have been purchased, the housewife can expand or contract her domestic labour, thereby altering their usefulness for her household. Usually these two possibilities overlap and merge into one process.

When the price of fresh milk increased by four cents a quart in 1976, three housewives decided that they were no longer prepared to spend that much money on milk. Instead, they bought powdered milk which was cheaper. The powdered milk however required much more planning and labour to ready it for household consumption. While fresh milk is immediately ready to drink, powdered milk has to be mixed in advance. One housewife estimated that the switch from fresh milk to powdered milk added at least ten minutes to her work time each day. She considered the increased time worth the money saved.

Control over consumption is not simply a matter of balancing wages with expenses. What particular commodities a household purchases is also determined by the preferences of individual members. In one of the households that switched from fresh to powdered milk, the children refused to drink powdered milk because they said it tasted "yucky." After several weeks of trying to convince them to drink the cheaper milk, the woman gave up and reverted to buying fresh milk. In this case, household tastes took precedence over economy.

The work of consumption management involves juggling the household income, commodity prices, household needs and the various preferences of household members. Like any juggling act, it requires a great deal of skill and sensitivity on the part of the domestic workers:

> Every payday I sit there holding the money and I think — this is it. I know what we need. I know what everyone likes. And I have to get what we need and as much as I can what they want and this [money] is all I got to do it with. I should be a magician.
>
> (Generation II, b. 1927)

The problems inherent in managing a household's consumption were highlighted by an incident between a woman and her husband when she served him meat loaf for supper. He commented that he did not like ground beef and asked why they could not have steak. She said they could not afford steak. He demanded to know why not, and they proceeded to fight over the cost of meat, the level of his wages, and their personal preferences for steak.

Underlying this fight were a set of defensive assumptions that each of them was making about their own work, each other's work and about their anticipated standard of living. The man was arguing for steak because he liked it and because it represented for him the best high-status meat available. She was arguing that they could not afford steak. He then felt attacked because this called into question his ability to earn good wages. He kept repeating that he earned good money. She felt there was an implicit criticism of her ability as a shopper, that somehow it was her carelessness or lack of skill that meant his wages could not be stretched to include steak. She defended herself by saying that he was out of touch with what things cost. His "stake in steak" was bound up with his image of himself as the bread winner. She felt that she was doing the best she could and that he was unfair in asking her to give his personal preference greater weight than the cost of living.

The housewife can manage consumption to make ends meet by intensifying her labour. A woman whose husband had a take home pay of $820 every two weeks had lived on those wages for two years. Unexpectedly his income dropped to $359 every two weeks for eight weeks due to an injury. Suddenly, she had to manage on $461 less. She described how she did it:

> I stopped buying good meat and got cuts that take a long time to cook. I didn't buy any ready-made foods like frozen vegetables or anything. Instead I bought turnips and carrots and potatoes. Jody [her son] needed new pants but instead of buying a new pair I made him some out of a worn-out pair of his father's. He needed new sneakers too so I put an ad on the radio asking about used sneakers and went to look at second-hand shoes.
>
> (Generation III, b. 1940)

She estimated that her changed cooking patterns increased her daily labour time by about half-an-hour. She spent five hours sewing the pants instead of half-an-hour buying them. Similarly, she spent about three afternoons going to look at used clothing rather than half-an-hour in the store buying shoes.

The work involved in this kind of management requires skill, but unfortunately consumption is not regularly recognized as work. Instead, it is usually associated with leisure and self-indulgence. Because men are only partially involved in shopping, and because it is their money which is spent, men regularly underestimate the work their wives do in consumption. They frequently accuse their wives of extravagance. The image of men as put-upon wage earners and women as mindless spenders is a dominant theme in North American folk culture. Women's work as consumers is mocked in comic strips in the Flin Flon daily and in other papers across the continent as Blondie forever wheedles money out of Dagwood to spend on what is portrayed as an endless orgy of whimsical, meaningless self-indulgence.

In her study of American housewives, Betty Friedan turned this folk image on its head and argued that housewives do not dupe their husbands into allowing them to indulge themselves. Instead, she argued, housewives are duped by the advertising industry into spending large amounts of money. This, according to Friedan, is a result of strategies developed by manufacturers and distributors to increase the domestic market for their products to ensure increased profits.[6]

However, as Ellen Willis pointed out, Friedan's argument is upside down as well. Women do not consume mindlessly in response to advertising. Nor do they consume in a futile attempt to ward off the malaise of the "problem that has no name."

Instead, they consume because that is part of their domestic work. Willis argued that psychic manipulation does not make people buy. Rather, "their buying habits are... a rational self-interested response" to the limited alternatives available to them. Further, spending money on consumer goods is not only part of a woman's work, it can also be "a healthy attempt to find outlets for her creative energies."[7]

In January 1976, The Bay in Flin Flon had a sale on bedding. Anticipating this sale, one housewife had saved some money out of her housekeeping allowance for the two preceding months. She bought $250 worth of linens. On the way home she congratulated herself on her foresight, on the fact that she had got such a good deal, ultimately saving several hundred dollars, and on the fact that she could now replace her worn out sheets and pillow cases. She was pleased and satisfied with her day's work. When her husband saw what she had bought and how much she had spent, he was furious and complained about how she was wasting money buying unnecessary items. She tried to explain to him:

> We need new sheets. The old ones are more than twenty years old and I've patched them and patched them so that now I'm patching patches. We really need them. And this was a really good sale. I saved lots of money. You should be pleased.
>
> (Generation II, b. 1922)

He was not pleased at all and tried to convince her to return them to the store. After he left she complained:

> I manage my house really carefully and I never spend more than we have and I only get what we need. I watch how I handle things really carefully. I wish he'd appreciate that.

Sometimes, no matter how skillful a woman is in handling money, there just is not enough to make ends meet. In that case, a woman may engage in activities which increase the amount of money available to the household. To do so she can take in work at home or get a job and by going out to work, become a wage worker herself.

TAKING IN WORK

There are a variety of ways for women to earn money by taking work into their homes. Usually this work is a logical extension of the domestic work they already do. It complements and intensifies their domestic labour without running into conflict with it.

Of the one hundred women interviewed, seventy-four had taken in work at some point in their lives. One of the most common tactics was to take in boarders. Sixty-nine of the one hundred had taken in boarders for at least one year to supplement household income. Because a certain percentage of the Flin Flon labour force is made up of single men, finding Company workers who want room and board is rarely difficult. This was a relatively easy way for women whose houses had an extra room to augment the household income. Having a boarder meant having an extra household member to cater to. It meant cooking bigger meals, packing an extra lunch box, doing more laundry, making another bed and caring for at least some of the needs of another adult. Nevertheless, most women said that having a boarder did not increase their domestic labour noticeably:

> It just means having an extra mouth to feed. I'd throw a few more dumplings in the pot, wash some extra clothes, make another bed. What's one more to care for when you're already doing the work?
> (Generation I, b. 1890)

Taking in boarders was often pleasant, especially if the boarder was compatible with other household members. Many women recalled their boarders with affection. Some had established fictive kin relationships with the young men and maintained personal ties with them long after the men had left their households:

> Having boarders was never a dull moment, all those young men. They meant extra work for the money but some of them was just like members of the family.
> (Generation I, b. 1889)

Another popular way of earning money inside the home was by providing child care for women who work for wages outside the home. Of the one hundred women interviewed, more than half (fifty-four) had taken care of other women's children as a way of earning money. Child care increases the load of domestic work, just as taking in boarders does, but without conflicting with it. Many women formed lasting family-like relationships with the children in their care. The guest of honour at a young man's wedding in 1976 was a woman who had cared for him from the time he was an infant until he was ten years old. He referred to her as "auntie" and in his speech he talked about his "two mothers."

Other kinds of work included taking in laundry, doing home baking, giving hair cuts and home perms, sewing, dressmaking or knitting, giving lessons in cultural or craft activities. Some forms of home-based money-making involved sales. Firms such as Avon and Tupperware do not retail through stores. Instead, salespeople, usually women, contract with the firm to distribute their products door to door. Tupperware salespeople organize parties to which a group of neighbourhood women are invited. The women have supper and visit and then the salesperson/hostess displays plastic kitchenware and takes orders from her guests.

The amount of money earned by these activities was usually low. However, for the women who do this kind of work the money served several functions. In some cases, it paid for particular expenses. A woman who took in boarders all through the 1930s estimated that the amount she got from her boarders paid for the doctors' bills and medical expenses of her chronically ill child. Another woman who did home child care during the 1940s used that money to pay for her household's food bills. In 1975, a young woman, whose husband was studying at a community college and whose income was quite low, gave hair cuts and home perms. The money she made enabled the couple to avoid going into debt for their regular living expenses.

While they found the money useful, not all women took on extra work simply to augment household incomes. Some women had lots of energy and delighted in pushing themselves. They thrived on the challenge of doing extra work. Others felt that by earning their own money they contributed in a significant way to the household income:

> I make some of the money we need. That way I feel like I really contribute to this house.
>
> (Generation III, b. 1957)

Other women recognized that by having some money of their own to control, they could counteract the powerlessness of being totally dependent on their husbands:

> Having my own money means I don't have to ask him every time I want something. It means I can buy him presents without him knowing about it beforehand.
>
> (Generation II, b. 1938)

Because taking in work requires that women stretch their domestic labour to include money-making activities, the amount of money that can be earned this way is limited. If women want to earn even more, they have to approach the problem from a different direction, that is, they have to contract their domestic labour to "free up" time to do wage work.

GOING OUT TO WORK

It's really a hard decision. We need the money and I wouldn't mind having a job just for interest sake. But can we afford it? What will happen to our family if I go out to work?

(Generation II, b. 1939)

Some women augment their household income by going outside the home to get jobs. Their ability to do so depends on both the availability of paid work for women and their ability to handle their outside jobs and their domestic labour responsibilities at the same time. Where taking in work complements women's domestic work, wage work contradicts it and the resulting pressures on women who do both jobs are heavy.

In advanced capitalist countries, women, as a category, act in some ways as a reserve army of labour with respect to the labour force.[8] From the perspective of the household, women move in and out of the labour force in response to pressures emanating from the world outside, although their ultimate ability to do so depends on the circumstances within the household.

Flin Flon, like other primary resource communities, has few jobs for women. While in recent years women have begun to make inroads into traditionally male spheres of work, such as logging and mining, frequently these jobs are restricted to single women.[9] Since 1973 the Company has hired a few women to work on the surface. They refuse to hire women underground, and they also generally refuse to hire married women with children. Since over half of the paid jobs in Flin Flon have always been with the Company, its discriminatory hiring policy has excluded married women from half the jobs in the community and from the best paying jobs as well. Those jobs available to women are in service, clerical or retail positions where the pay is traditionally poor. Consequently, there are not enough jobs for women who want them.

The owner of one of the first clothing stores in Flin Flon recalled what happened when he decided to hire a salesclerk in 1932:

I decided I could hire an assistant and I just casually mentioned it to one of my customers when she came in the store. By that

176

evening more than twenty women had been in to ask for the job.

(Generation I, b. 1907)

An older woman who had taken in boarders for many years commented that she would have preferred wage work but there was none available:

There just weren't jobs for women. This was a man's town. The only [wage] working women were the "ladies of the night." There was just no way for women to get work.

(Generation I, b. 1886)

It was only during the Second World War that the job situation improved somewhat for women when many of the men employed by the Company went overseas with the army. Women were paid good wages to replace the men:

In an effort to replace the dwindling labour supply, a total of 160 women are being employed on surface work.[10]

However, they were laid off as soon as the men returned:

I worked in the zinc plant during the war years. I really liked it. It wasn't good work but the money was good. But as soon as the war was over and there were men around, we got booted out. Then suddenly women weren't good enough workers anymore.

(Generation II, b. 1918)

As the town developed, proportionately more jobs for women became available. However, there are still more women who want jobs than there are positions open. When the city council advertised in 1976 for one experienced secretary, it received 124 applications from women in Flin Flon. In 1977 one of the retail stores advertised a position for an inexperienced check-out clerk. Forty-seven applications were received in the first two days.

The number of applicants for jobs is only a partial reflection of how many women would like paid work. Many women said they would like a job but as there were so few available, it wasn't worth their while to apply:

I'd like a job but I know I won't get one so I don't apply.

(Generation II, b. 1937)

Because there are so few jobs, many women do not even consider taking on paid employment. Despite the limited job market, however, over half (fifty-three) of the women interviewed had engaged in wage work at some time since they were married.

The pattern of wage work for women in Flin Flon is probably typical for many married women in urban centres in Canada. After leaving school they work for wages until their first child is born. Then they remain out of the labour force until the last child reaches high school or leaves home. At that point, they may enter the labour force again.

There has been a change in the pattern of employment for married women. While the percentage of the women interviewed who worked for wages before the birth of their first child was approximately the same, between 90 percent and 96 percent, for each generation, the percentage of women who worked for wages while they had at least one child under twelve increased in each generation (10 percent; 18 percent; 55 percent). While this increase may reflect features peculiar to Flin Flon's development, it also reflects a general trend in North America. Throughout the twentieth century the percentage of married women in the labour force has steadily increased. Since 1945 the percentage of those with dependent children has increased most significantly.[11] Although this pattern reflects the changing nature of the labour market and other forces external to the household, it also reflects certain features of the household.

THE DOUBLE DAY OF LABOUR

The working-class family household has rarely been able to subsist adequately on a single wage. Other household members, especially children and women, have supplemented the household cash income in a variety of ways. As industrial production and the state have taken over various aspects of domestic labour, women's labour has shifted from work done inside the home to wage work done outside the home.

It is quite possible that goods-producing activities and services will continue to be removed from the home. Such a tendency is not restricted by the nature of domestic labour. There are still large time-consuming tasks which could be extracted from domestic labour and taken over by paid labour. Tendencies in that direction, for example, are indicated by the recent growth of the fast food industry. To the extent that such a trend does continue, domestic labour will become ever more flexible.

Limiting such tendencies is the prospect that real wages in the current period will rise slowly if at all. One of the most important effects of the changes in domestic labour has been that women's labour time has been reduced to the extent that taking on wage work has become a real possibility and, simultaneously for many, a necessity. The amount of money coming into the household ultimately imposes certain absolute limits to the household's lifestyle beyond which the domestic labourer, no matter how skilled, cannot go. With the increase in consumer goods that have now become socially accepted necessities for the average household, a single wage is rarely sufficient to meet household needs. Thus, in the last thirty years more and more married women have been taking on wage work. As they do, they still retain responsibility for their domestic labour. Consequently, more and more women are now working a double day. As this trend continues it will magnify the contradictions experienced by women in both spheres of work. Going out to work both solves the problem of isolation and establishes the women as wage owners, thereby breaking down some of their economic dependency. It does not, however, get at the root of the burden of double day.

What are the implications for women who move into wage work? It is here that the oppressive nature of the sexual division of labour in capitalist society becomes most apparent. When married women move into wage work, they do not relinquish their domestic responsibilities. Instead, they must meet the requirements of two jobs: wage work and domestic work. These women continue to juggle the requirements of this double burden:

> Now that I'm working I never get a moment's peace. It's rush, rush, rush from when I get up till I go to bed. Before I got this job I used to think I never had time for myself. Now I have even less.
> (Generation II, b. 1927)

A number of studies have used time budget techniques to examine the nature of the sexual division of labour and its impact on women. By analysing the amounts of time spent by different categories of people in various activities they have come up with one measure of the implications of the sexual division of labour and of the double burden.

One of the most extensive of these studies was a cross-cultural investigation of the way time was spent in the everyday life of people in urban industrial centres in twelve countries, not including Canada.[12] As a basic category for comparison the study used employed men, employed women and full-time house-wives. It argued for a three-way division of human activities which differentiated physiological demands, work and leisure.

Comparing the categories of people, the researchers found that employed men spend more time per day in formal (paid) work situations than women do. This is partially due to the tendency for many women to work for wages part time. They also found that employed women spend about half as much time as housewives on domestic work. However, the double burden carried by employed married women meant that they actually worked more hours than either employed men or housewives. Of all the groups, they had the fewest hours to themselves. The full-time housewife, for example, rested on Sunday by decreasing her average daily labour time by half. The employed married woman on her days off wage work, doubled the amount of time spent on housework.

These general findings were corroborated by a Canadian study based on interviews with 340 couples in the Vancouver area.[13] The researchers found that men are only minimally involved in work around the house and that their involvement in domestic labour does not increase noticeably if their wives also take on wage work. Women, whether they do wage work or not, are primarily responsible for doing domestic labour. Married women who work for wages spend about twelve hours less per week doing domestic labour than full-time housewives. They also distribute their domestic time differently. [14] Wage working women in Vancouver, like those in the comparative study, spend more of their weekend time doing household work than do full-time domestic workers, and they meet these increased demands at the expense of their own leisure time. Based on their time budget analyses, these researchers recognize the central role women play by expending their labour time to meet the needs of

their household and the demands of the sphere of industrial production:

> When there are young children, and women contribute to an otherwise inadequate income, the greater requirements to which the household has to respond are being met almost entirely by women.[15]

What happens to domestic labour when the women doing it are also doing wage work? Meis and Scheu imply that domestic work is subject to Parkinsons Law, that is, that the amount of work to be done increases with the amount of time available in which to do it:

> Even though [wage] working women spend less time at it, there is some evidence to suggest that they also become more efficient.[16]

By implication they are suggesting that full-time domestic workers create unnecessary work for themselves. I think this assumption is incorrect. What happens, instead, is that when women take on wage work, the amount of money available to the household increases and hence they are able to buy more ready-made goods and services. They purchase convenience foods or eat out more often. They send their clothes to the laundry and hire babysitters. In other words, the necessary labour is transferred out of the household and done elsewhere, in factories or the service sector.

Women who take on wage work cannot, however, purchase all the goods and services of domestic labour. What happens is a process described by a Flin Flon woman who said: "I do less efficient work more efficiently." What she meant was that taking on wage work forced her to cut down on her domestic work. She became more efficient at doing her work, but at the same time she was forced to lower her standards of what was acceptable. This is a common pattern for women working a double day:

> I used to wash the kitchen floor every day. Now I only do it twice each week.
>
> (Generation III, b. 1945)

> Before I worked I cooked really good meals. I put a lot of effort and care into what I served my family. Now I cook really simple quick meals.
>
> (Generation II, b. 1919)

But doing this work less often is not a direct reflection of lowering standards. In the case of the woman who washed her kitchen floor less frequently, it is important to realize that her floor got less dirty when she went out to do wage work. When she was at home all day, she had a toddler with her and her schoolaged child came home at lunchtime and after school. Her kitchen was a centre of activity all day. Once she started working for wages her children were at a babysitter's all day and she was away from the house as well.

In some ways participation in wage work can force women to raise their domestic labour standards. A woman who had worked at home full time for twenty years got a job in an office where she had to wear "nice" clothes each day. She found that she had to wash her clothes more frequently, iron them more carefully and generally spend more time on the care of her clothing than she had previously:

> I used to work around the house in old slacks and I had to wash my clothes maybe once a week. Now I rinse out my nylons every night and I wash my blouses and underthings at least twice each week and sometimes more.
>
> (Generation II, b. 1929)

It is in this respect that the flexibility of domestic labour can trip women up. The standards for domestic work are not externally determined. Instead, they are set by the members of the household. Because there is no point at which it is possible to say that all domestic work is completed, women constantly feel pressured to do more. When their time is severely restricted by wage work obligations, they feel that they never get things done:

> I can never get on top of my housework. No matter how hard I work there is always a million things that I have to do right away. It makes me feel very rushed.
>
> (Generation II, b. 1934)

> Trying to keep up with things is dreadfully difficult. Just when I get one thing caught up, I realize there is something else that is crying out to be attended to.
>
> (Generation III, b. 1941)

Struggling to meet all the demands on their time, they have to make painful decisions about which areas to cut. Some women felt that they had to keep their house in good condition, and they chose to do so at the expense of time with their husbands and children:

> I like to keep the house nice. I just can't go to work if the place isn't nice. My husband complains. He says I should spend time with him and the baby and let the house go hang. But I'm just not made like that. I need a nice house.
>
> (Generation II, b. 1932)

Another woman whose children had all left home recalled making a similar choice:

> I worked when the children were young. At the time it seemed I had to but now looking back, I regret it. I don't know my children. We're not very close. And it's because when I worked, I had to take

care of my house too and I never had time for them. Now I wish I'd just forget about the house and spent time with them. Now I have plenty of time for my house and they've gone so I get no time with them.

(Generation II, b. 1926)

Other women chose to spend their time with their families and ignored the house:

I just figured my kids were more important than clean clothes and a tidy livingroom. So the house was always a pigsty.

(Generation II, b. 1927)

I knew I had to choose — a clean house or time with my kids. I chose the kids but I went slowly mad in that messy house.

(Generation III, b. 1946)

Flin Flon women unanimously supported the Vancouver study findings that women who hold two jobs do so at the expense of their own leisure time.

Table 6.1 compares the figures for twenty households in which the woman worked full time in the home, and the man

---

TABLE 6:1

Allocation of Time in Hours by Sex for Households with Full-Time Domestic Workers

n=20 couples

Wife   Husband

work day

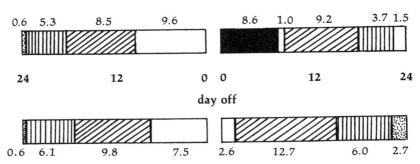

| 0.6 | 5.3 | 8.5 | 9.6 | | 8.6 | 1.0 | 9.2 | 3.7 1.5 |

| 24 | | 12 | | 0 0 | | 12 | | 24 |

day off

| 0.6 | 6.1 | 9.8 | 7.5 | 2.6 | 12.7 | 6.0 | 2.7 |

184

worked for the mining company. The allocation of time is divided into four major categories: wage work, domestic labour, personal care and leisure. Paid work includes not only the actual time spent at work but also the time spent getting to and from work. Domestic labour includes all the activities which have been discussed as housework and child care. It does not include the interpersonal and tension-managing aspects of domestic labour. Personal care includes sleep and hygiene, and leisure includes such activities as watching TV, visiting, reading and relaxing. This last category may be deceptive in that many women while they were relaxing or watching TV were also knitting or mending. These categories do not take into account the fact that at all times, even

TABLE 6:2

**Allocation of Time by Sex for Households
with Full-Time Wage Working Wives**

n=5 couples

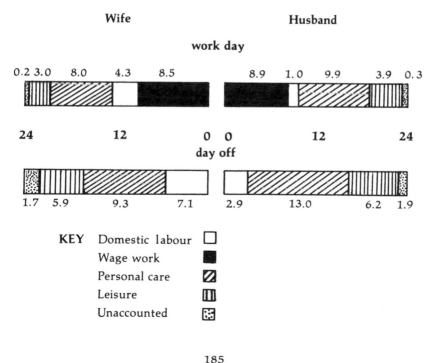

Wife				Husband			

work day

0.2 3.0   8.0   4.3   8.5   8.9   1.0   9.9   3.9   0.3

24   12   0 0   12   24

day off

1.7 5.9   9.3   7.1   2.9   13.0   6.2   1.9

KEY Domestic labour □
     Wage work ■
     Personal care ▨
     Leisure ▥
     Unaccounted ▧

185

while sleeping, women are responsible for the care of their young children and they must be ready to meet the needs of household members when they arise. A woman who gets up from her sleep to comfort a frightened child awakened by a nightmare will likely say that she slept through the night, denying that she spent half-an-hour tension managing. Table 6.2 uses the same categories to compare the time allocation in five households where the woman did the domestic labour and held a full-time, paying job as well.

The effects of wage work on women's time is more starkly revealed when women's time is divided into two categories: work time, which includes both categories of work, and personal time, which includes personal care and leisure. Table 6:3 shows the implications of the double burden on women's time. On a work day, an employed woman works 2.4 more hours than a full-time domestic worker. On her days off, the employed woman spends just about the same amount of time as the full-time domestic worker. As a result, employed women spend 2.8 hours less on personal activities. On their days off, they spend about the same amount of time.

The following account of a Flin Flon woman suggests how important those two hours are. This woman had three children at home, ages ten, thirteen and fifteen. She had been working as a clerk in a store full time for four years. Her husband worked steady days at the Company:

> My day starts about 6:30 when I get up and do a bit of housework — do a load of laundry or get supper started. I get the family up and make breakfast for everyone and lunch for the man and the two oldest. Then I leave for work. On my lunch hour I often come home to start supper — I just skip lunch on those days. After work, I have to get supper ready and then I clean up after — do the dishes, sweep the floor and then do the housework. I usually spend from seven to ten doing housework, then I relax till bedtime.
>
> (Generation III, b. 1933)

It means that for most of her waking day, even her lunch hour, she is working. The work is fragmented too. She has to switch from housework to wage work to cooking to wage work to housework. She can never follow one task through to its

TABLE 6:3

Allocation of Time for Full-Time Domestic
Workers Compared with Full-Time Wage Workers

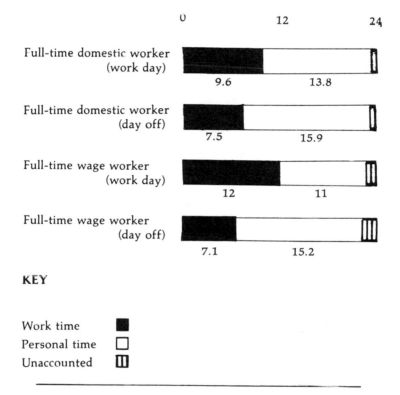

KEY

Work time ■
Personal time ☐
Unaccounted ▥

completion before she has to begin something else. She must constantly be aware of numerous activities and responsibilities. Another woman remarked:

I just always feel in a daze. Something is always nagging in the back of my head needing doing. I'm never on top of things. It makes me feel bad — harried and irritable.

(Generation II, b. 1941)

Within this range of conditions and effects, women make decisions about whether or not to do paid work. Like so many of the decisions which women must make about their domestic labour, this one cannot be made in a rational, objective way because the various implications cannot be known in advance:

> I want a job and we could really use the money I could earn. I just don't know what it will mean.
>
> (Generation III, b. 1955)

Often the results are not visible at the time; they only become apparent many years later. A woman who went out to work for wages in 1947 when her children were eight and ten developed ulcers and a heart condition twenty-five years later. Her doctor said that they were caused by stress, and she concluded that the stress came from holding two jobs:

> I wish I could have known at the time that it was too much. Now I am sick and crippled and I can't do anything about it. Working on top of a house and two kids was too much for me.
>
> (Generation II, b. 1917)

When a housewife takes on wage work herself, the impact of wage labour on domestic labour, however, is almost immediately visible. While her wages increase the total income of the household, her new job also increases household expenses. She may need more clothes for work. She may have to pay for child care and transportation. She has less time and energy available to exercise the "buffer" aspect of domestic labour and so will be forced to buy more prepared food and ready-made clothes. Housework has to be squeezed into the available non-wage work time. Added to the emotional drain inherent in domestic labour is the fact that she now acquires a new set of job-related tensions of her own.

Her domestic work now requires that she orchestrate three schedules, all of which may be "out of synch" with each other. The responsibilities of domestic labour impinge on her wage work rather than on her husband's, so that, for example, if the children are sick, she must take time off to care for them. The demands of her domestic work frequently prevent her from participating in work-related activities that occur after work hours. This is one reason why women find it difficult to become active in trade unions. Most significantly, she now experiences not only her oppression as a woman but also exploitation as a wage worker. The effects of wage labour on domestic labour vary with each of the specific components of the labour process. Each of the four aspects of domestic labour responds differently to the pressures of women's wage labour.

REPRODUCTION OF LABOUR POWER ON A DAILY BASIS

Once the wife starts to do wage work, she too becomes part of the household's production for exchange, and therefore the reproduction of her labour power increases in importance. However, a number of forces operate against her becoming as important as the man. The woman's labour power usually cannot be exchanged for as high a price as her husband's. As the exchange of his labour power brings more money into the household, his needs tend to remain predominant. While taking on wage work alters her position in the household, it does not lead to full equality between the woman and the man, nor does it eliminate the oppressive characteristics of her domestic labour.

A young woman, who had worked prior to the birth of her child, wanted to return to work when the child turned a year old. She and her husband had agreed that one of them should stay home to look after the child. He was willing to do so, but only if she could earn two-thirds of what he earned since they could not live on less. As he worked for the Company as a welder, there was no job in town that she could qualify for that would pay even half of his earnings. She felt trapped and furious.

> I have to get out of the house and get a job or I'll go crazy. He'd be better with the baby than me anyway. But there isn't any jobs I can get that pay good enough. So we're stuck with him working and me staying home.
>
> (Generation III, b. 1955)

Eventually they resolved their situation by moving to Calgary where she got a job as a line operator with the hydro company and he stayed at home with the baby.

Since the woman is responsible for the reproduction of labour power, she has to take care of her own needs. However, the tendency of the woman to deal with her own needs only after everyone else has been cared for continues when she takes on wage work. The whole thrust of domestic labour requires that she put the needs of others ahead of her own. The continued dominance of the male wage helps to perpetuate that tendency. As a result, even when women got paying jobs they recognized the greater significance of their husband's jobs:

His work is more important than mine because he makes more.
(Generation II, b. 1927)

He brings home more money, so we obviously need his work more. (Generation III, b. 1939)

Nevertheless, once the woman begins to bring home money, her position in the household shifts somewhat and her importance increases. Having her own money, which is paid to her and whose distribution she controls, modifies her dependency on her husband. She has a certain amount of money that she can spend as she chooses. Her money gives her a minimal independence:

The best part about working is having my own money. I don't have to ask for everything. I feel more like my own person.
(Generation II, b. 1925)

Having her own income also means that the woman can contribute to the subsistence income of the household. This gives her the strength to put forward more forcefully her wishes about how household income is spent:

Now that some of it is my money I don't mind arguing for what I want. He didn't want to buy a new car but I did and I was willing to pay for it myself so he didn't have a leg to stand on.
(Generation II, b. 1938)

Once she is doing wage work, a woman frequently begins to assert her needs simply out of necessity. The strains created by holding two jobs force some women to cut back on certain areas of domestic work. One of the first to be cut is that work which is least conscious and therefore most hidden. Tension managing and catering to the husband's needs is often drastically reduced.

This may occur because she is too tired. One husband commented that after his wife started wage work she no longer greeted him with a cup of tea and home baked "goodies":

> Used to be I'd get in from work and she'd be in the kitchen pouring tea and we'd sit together and have tea and goodies and chat about the day. Now she's tired when she gets in and she doesn't get in till after I do anyway. I really miss our teas.
>
> (Generation II, b. 1921)

Sometimes the strains make women conscious of the inequalities in the sexual divison of labour, and they refuse to cater to their husbands' needs as readily. A running tension in one household revolved around this issue. Both husband and wife returned from their jobs at the same time. The woman, however, went out of her way to pick up the children from the babysitter. When she arrived home tired and wanting a rest, he would demand his supper. Although she accepted that it was her responsibility to cook supper, she complained regularly at the injustice of the situation. From her perspective he got to relax while she picked up the children and then cared for them as well as getting supper. She argued that either he should help out by doing some of the work or they should take turns. He steadfastly refused. She commented bitterly:

> We both work and we both get home tired. He gets to lie around having beer and relaxing. I pick up the kids and then rush home and get supper and clean up and put the kids to bed and then he wants me to be all loving and happy and spend time with him.
>
> (Generation III, b. 1947)

Women reeling under the strain of their double work load cannot provide the same attention, sensitivity and concern for their husband's needs as full-time domestic workers can. Such husbands have to "fend for themselves" more often. Men lose some of their privileges and services when their wives go out to work for wages. Knowing this, some men oppose their wives doing so because they do not want to bear the cost. Others, while prepared for their wives to work for wages, fail to understand that the attention and tension managing are part of her domestic labour and feel that their personal relationship suffers because the women are working. The most sensative of husbands know why their wives have reduced the amount of time they will spend on their husbands. They accept it as an inevitable part of the job. However, none of the men seemed to realize that their wives wanted, or needed, more help than the men gave. The men unanimously appeared to consider the double burden to be part of being a woman:

It's true that she has to keep on managing the housekeeping while she's working. But that's women's work, isn't it?

(Generation III, b. 1946)

REPRODUCTION OF LABOUR POWER ON A GENERATIONAL BASIS

When childbearing was distributed throughout the greater part of women's fertile years, women tended to have several children at home for most of their working lives. They could only leave the house to do wage work if a substitute adult was available. Most working-class households could not afford to hire someone. They had to rely on such relatives as a grandmother, an unmarried aunt or an eldest daughter. In Flin Flon, especially in the first generation, such people rarely lived in the vicinity, and therefore that strategy was not readily available. The tendency was for women not to seek wage work but to stay at home with their children.

When the childbearing period was reduced, the pattern for most Flin Flon women included a period of six to ten years of intense child care while the children were young. After that, the woman was available to work for wages. As women tended to have fewer children, it became possible to pay a babysitter to look after one or two children in her own home.

The effect of the mother's employment on childrearing practices has been and still is the subject of an intense and heated debate among various "experts," such as psychologists, sociologists, doctors and educators.[17] The contradictory positions articulated in the debate by the "experts" permeates the attitudes and practices of the women actually in the situation. Objectively, employed women have less time available to spend with their children. One side of the argument maintains that this results in "maternal deprivation" and argues that children denied access to their mothers at all times will feel rejected, unloved and will turn to rebellious behaviour as a result. The other side argues that these children must assume greater responsibility for themselves and for other members of their household. This argument suggests that these children are more competent and independent.

Employed mothers, bombarded by these arguments, experience insecurity and profound guilt:

> Some people say a working [for wages] mother is good for a kid. Others say I'm depriving him. I don't know. How can I be sure? Maybe when he grows up I'll find it was bad for him. Then it will be too late. But he seems fine. But I'm never really sure.
>
> (Generation III, b. 1947)

> I like my job except I have to leave the kids with a sitter. She's terrific and really great with them but I never know if maybe I should stay at home with them. Am I doing the right thing by them?
>
> (Generation III, b. 1943)

When this confusion and guilt combines with the exhaustion some women regularly feel, the women are sometimes short-tempered and inclined to take those feelings of rage and frustration out on their children:

> Sometimes I get so mad at that kid, I just snap and lash out and hit him. I just can't take it. I feel bad. I think it happens when I'm tired.
>
> (Generation II, b. 1934)

Other women try to compensate by spending intense, one-to-one time periods with their children in the evening after work. Others talk about how much they enjoy being with their children after not seeing them during the day:

> I love the evenings. I'm so pleased to see the children and I plan to spend time with them each night and it's my favourite time of day. I love it. If I was home with them all day, I couldn't do it. I'd be too worn out.
>
> (Generation III, b. 1942)

Child care is the one component of domestic labour which often intrudes on wage work. If children are ill or hurt and require a parent's care, it is the mother, not the father, who must take time off wage work:

> Whenever one of the kids gets sick, the school always calls me at work. They never call his dad.
>
> (Generation II, b. 1930)

This is a double-edged dilemma. The assumption that women are responsible for child care means that they may lose money if they have to take time off work. If the required period of time is more than a few days, they may lose their jobs. Employers often use this situation as an excuse not to hire women, so some women are refused employment because they might have to lose time from work for child care:

> I worked as a secretary for an insurance company but when Johnny got measles I missed two weeks off work so the boss told me not to come back again. Later when I applied for a job with [a doctor's office] I was told I was too risky as I might have to take time off for my kids.
>
> (Generation II, b. 1938)

HOUSEWORK

Like child care, housework in the early period was so demanding that women could only go to work for wages if an alternate worker could be found. With the changes that have resulted from new processes and household technology, housework labour time has been reduced. In many cases, production time has also been reduced. The work has become more flexible and can more readily be fitted in around non-wage work time:

> I do a load of laundry every night. I throw a load in before I go to bed and then I put it in the dryer when I get up in the morning and it's ready to be put away when I get home from work.
>
> (Generation II, b. 1919)

As standards of housework are relatively flexible as well, women can cut back on certain aspects of housework by letting things slide for a while. Other household members can some-

times be drawn in to help out with various aspects of housework. However, as Meissner's time budget studies show men
do not increase their contribution to housework very much
when women take on wage work.[18] For example, a Flin Flon
woman who worked as a secretary had to stay at the office until
5:30 P.M. She regularly gave up her lunch hour to come home and
prepare supper. Her husband came in at 4:30 P.M. and, following
her instructions, put pots on the stove or turned the oven on at
certain times. This involved no more than five or ten minutes of
his time, but it meant that supper was cooked by the time she
returned. All she had to do was serve it:

> I really appreciate him doing that. If he didn't we wouldn't eat till
> nearly 7 P.M. and that's too late for the kids and I'd be starving
> too. He's been a real help that way since I started working.
> (Generation III, b. 1943)

Although they were both working outside the home, preparing
the meals, planning when different items should go on the stove
and at what heat, was still totally her responsibility. And no
matter how much women try to cut back, some degree of housework always remains.

THE WORKING CONDITIONS
OF DOMESTIC LABOUR

What does not disappear and what cannot be contracted is
general management, the overall, co-ordinating aspects of
domestic labour. Regardless of whether or not she works for
wages, how a housewife handles the money that comes into her
household determines how she can structure the other
components of her work. This is the ultimate expression of
household management, the process which integrates all the
components of domestic labour into one whole, continuous
work process. This general management is the total juggling act
and wage work adds yet another pin to be juggled. The success of
the juggler depends on her ability to be always in control, to
know which pins can fly free and which she must catch. If she
loses control, the pins start falling.

These fundamental characteristics of domestic labour generate occupational health and safety hazards. Because their work is fragmented and scattered, housewives must always be doing several things at once and can rarely complete one task before beginning several more. Women talked about how frustrating they found it, never being able to really finish anything. The endless, repetitive character of domestic labour was fatiguing and stressful. In other work situations such conditions would be a cause for concern about the workers' health and safety. Hidden in the household behind the myth that what women do is not work, these dangers create additional stress and pose serious physical hazards.

One Flin Flon housewife was holding her screaming baby while she stirred food cooking on the stove. Four schoolaged children burst in the front door, yelling for her attention. As the phone rang, a pot boiled over and her husband called from the bedroom asking her to keep the children quiet. She observed:

> The worst thing about this job is the working conditions. I always feel fractured because I always have to do several things at once. I feel so frazzled.
>
> (Generation III, b. 1947)

Few other jobs require workers to care for young children while simultaneously using sharp knives, handling boiling liquids or poisonous chemicals, or, in fact, concentrating on something else altogether. Households are notoriously unsafe and the housewife is vulnerable to all sorts of accidents and injuries. Flin Flon women recounted endless stories of these hazards:

> Last year it seemed we were having a rash of accidents so I kept track and sure enough, do you know, we had to go to the hospital once each week for three months in a row. Usually it was just little things — I burned my hand on the oven once and I fell downstairs carrying the laundry. The baby fell out of her highchair. My older boy poured hot coffee all over his front and my daughter got at the kitchen knife and sliced her hand open.
>
> (Generation III, b. 1945)

Other hazards are less obvious. The noise level produced by a screaming baby or by playing children can easily exceed levels considered safe in other jobs. When the baby is screaming at night, disrupting the woman's sleep, her fatigue and her concern about the child's welfare may turn into a lethal form of anxiety.

In other ways women's health suffers with their work. Often low incomes combined with the tendency to put family members' needs before their own result in the women eating poorly. Some eat very little and make up for it by drinking coffee and smoking cigarettes. Others overeat and gain a great deal of weight. Especially with small children at home, it is often difficult for women to get regular physical exercise and enough sleep.

Aspects of a woman's job require a high level of responsibility but give her very little recognition or reward. Often her legitimate concerns are dismissed by her husband, the family doctor and others as the musings of an "overprotective" mother or a neurotic wife. One mother felt that her six-month-old-baby was not developing as he should. She took him to the doctor who said he was fine and developing normally. She continued to express concern but everyone dismissed her worries. Finally, after several months, she insisted on taking the child to a specialist in Winnipeg who diagnosed the child as critically ill and requiring immediate treatment for a rare genetic disorder. The child died just before his first birthday and the Winnipeg specialist berated the mother for her "neglect" in not bringing him to the hospital sooner. In describing the events several years later, she observed:

> It was a no win situation. The doctor here blamed me for being overprotective. The doctor there blamed me for neglect. I knew the baby was sick and needed care but no one trusted my judgement.
>
> (Generation III, b. 1950)

The high level of responsibility, the isolation, the economic dependency and the endless tension managing all combine to make domestic labour a high stress job. Some women suffer from what doctors call "housewives' fatigue" — a chronic lethargy. To get temporary relief from this, many women turn to cigarettes, marijuana, alcohol or such prescription drugs as Valium:

> I smoke alot, and sometimes when things get really rough, I toke up [smoke marijuana]. Last year I was really despressed so my doctor gave me Valium and I've been taking it ever since. A lot of

the time I just feel spaced out so stuff doesn't bother me.
(Generation III, b. 1951)

Sometimes things get too difficult and it is not possible to escape through drugs. For some women depression and periodic nervous breakdowns become a chronic response to the irresolvable contradictions of their lives:

> My sister has been in and out of a mental hospital for the last five years. I think she is just so unhappy — she has five kids at home and no help and they are really poor. Sometimes she just can't cope anymore and she gives up.
>
> (Generation II, b. 1931)

Other women recognize some of the sources of their tension and try to reorganize their work to make life easier:

> It took me awhile to figure out what was going on. I was always tired, dragged out and run down. I was on Valium for awhile but I got fed up with it and one day I threw the pills away. Then I started examining my life and tried to change some things to make it better. I talked to other women and slowly began to get more control over my life. Things still get to me but now I think I understand why and I feel better.
>
> (Generation III, b. 1956)

The very structure of domestic labour imposes on women an endless barrage of pressure. Each facet of their work requires different skills. Managing each of the component work processes, trying to hold them together, and coping with their changing demands, creates an ongoing set of tensions. An older woman looking back over thirty years of domestic labour commented:

> I moved here just after the war and at that time I had four small children. I remember I used to think that things would be less chaotic when the children were grown up, or when I was more experienced, or when we had more money, or something. But instead, it's still chaotic — always has been and probably always will be. Just when you get one thing under control or fix things so your work should be easier, then something else comes along to mess life up again. I think that's just the nature of women's lives — chaotic.
>
> (Generation II, b. 1921)

Another woman elaborated on the same point:

> There's always a million things to do — dozens of different pressures. When I look back over my life that's the one thing that is constant. Just about everything has changed but there have always been those pressures and that unchanging tension.
>
> (Generation II, b. 1923)

All housewives say that pressure and tension are constants in their lives. What is striking about these tensions is the subtle way they have changed over the generations and the way that women have responded to them, by acquiescing, resisting and fighting back.

CHAPTER SEVEN

BREAD AND ROSES

The predicament of working class women is the most potentially subversive to capitalism.

Sheila Rowbotham

WHEN we step back from the daily experiences of individual women, the overall pattern of domestic labour becomes visible. It becomes possible to understand its totality — what domestic labour includes, how it fits with the other labour processes of industrial capitalism, and how it has changed. The main argument of this book is that the working-class household is sustained by two distinct but connected labour processes: wage labour and domestic labour. As the interior process, domestic labour has a two-fold characteristic. It is the production of family subsistence and, at the same time, the production of labour power.

The history of domestic labour through the twentieth century shows that the household changes in response to unplanned external forces. The family household is a vulnerable unit, subject to the pressures of, and limited by, the forces of industrial production and the state. Nevertheless, women and their families participate in these changes, trying always to maintain or to improve the quality of their lives. As a result, domestic labour is a residual labour; that is, those labours necessary for human subsistence that are not taken over by industrial production or the state are left to domestic labour. So, for example, food production was socialized in food processing plants across North America but food serving was not. Consequently, domestic labour took on the tasks of purchasing processed foods, making final preparations and serving the food to household members.

As residual labour, domestic labour is also the means by which new needs are introduced into the working-class household. For example, during the 1920s and 1930s changing concepts of early childhood development created a new need for intensified early child care practices. This resulted not in an expansion of day care services with professional child care workers but in a reorganization and intensification of the way women related to their children.

The new needs that are introduced into the household and met through the efforts of domestic labour are often introduced initially because of children. Children are vitally important in most families and parents often reallocate their time and material resources to meet the demands their children impose:

> I really want the best for my children. I keep my house really nice for them, so they will have good memories about the home they grew up in and if I think they need something, I'll get it for them, no matter what.
>
> (Generation III, b. 1945)

Many Flin Flon women explained that they were immediately receptive to new technical developments that would ease their housework because they hoped that these would give them more time to be with their children. Children themselves often introduce new needs into the household. They learn about new products and frequently pester their parents to make the purchase. Parents tend to want the best for their children and so are willing to adopt new procedures and products:

> My kids really wanted to take up hockey so we bought them skates and all that equipment. It really set us back, but for your kids, what can you do?
>
> (Generation III, b. 1941)

> When the babies were small we lived in a little house uptown. As they grew, we felt that they deserved a better house — one with more space, so they could have their own rooms and a playroom. So we sold the old house and bought this one. We'll be in debt for the rest of our lives, but I think it was worth it for them.
>
> (Generation II, b. 1932)

The straightforward way available to all women for changing their work involves easing the expenditure of their labour. All housewives constantly try to ease the amount of physical work

— to shift time away from laundry and dirty dishes — to make their time available for people — for their children, husbands, friends, their community, and even for themselves. Thus there is a constant impetus from the housewife to incorporate new household technology and techniques, to alter the interior dynamics of domestic labour.

These shifts and reallocations of women's labour time have not necessarily occurred smoothly or easily. Some Flin Flon women felt that the technical changes had diminished the satisfaction they got from housework:

> For all it was so difficult, there was something about housework in the old days that was very satisfying. I used to enjoy seeing my laundry hanging on the line or seeing a stack of wood I'd chopped myself. It's harder to see housework these days.
>
> (Generation II, b. 1930)

Women spend increasing amounts of time and energy caring for their children and socializing with their husbands. Tension managing of this sort can be emotionally exhausting for women and to be constantly sensitive to other people's needs seriously impinges on the ability of women to care for their personal needs and development. However, this "human" side of domestic labour is also the most rewarding and satisfying part, which gives meaning and worth to the rest of her work.

This aspect of domestic labour is most clearly embedded in the interpersonal relations of the family. Consequently, it is the most difficult to recognize as work despite its demanding and arduous character. This work can never be taken over entirely by either industry or the state for it is this part of domestic labour that is the central labour — the production of human beings, of life itself.

What is significant about the changes that have occurred in domestic labour, however, is that while these changes have reorganized the internal dynamics of domestic labour and profoundly altered the work for the women doing it, they have not substantially reorganized the situation of the worker herself nor the premises of the work itself.[1] The essential labour situation has remained unchanged.

Domestic labour is a continuous, ongoing process. Ultimately, its production time can never be eliminated as long as the production of human beings is based on subsistence obtained through privately owned wages. As long as the working class obtains its subsistence by means of the privately owned wage, then it must always have a private place wherein this process of sustaining life and reproducing labour power can occur. Therefore the core of domestic labour cannot be removed from the household. In this sense, despite all the changes that have occurred (and that will occur) in domestic labour, its fundamental organization has not changed. It remains private, isolated and the essential responsibility of women. As long as domestic labour is not socialized, it retains most of the residual work involved in the reproduction of human beings and their capacity to labour. Consequently, women's work is never done:

> It's endless, what we do. It's endless in the daily coming and going around the house. It's endless 'cause you do it till you die. It's endless, 'cause women always do it.
>
> (Generation II, b. 1937)

FACING THE PROBLEM

If women want to change the basic character of domestic labour, they are forced out of the realm of their own family household and into the terrain of politics. The very first step requires that women cut through the massive layers of mystification that hide the reality of domestic labour by becoming aware, or conscious, of what their real working conditions are.

Because housewives work in isolation in their own private homes, they often find it difficult to see beyond their own personal situation, to recognize that their domestic labour is more than a labour of love and to acknowledge the oppressive qualities of their work. When women do not understand the forces underlying their lives, they tend to blame themselves for the confusion they feel. Where their husbands can blame the Company for the alienation and frustration of wage work, women tend to experience a sense of frustration and guilt when they feel the same way about their work.

I interviewed a woman who, only three years before at age ninety, had retired after seventy-one years as a domestic labourer. She told me how for all those years she had always insisted that woman's place was in the home. She was convinced that her work was "just ideal for a woman. It was all any woman could want." But after she had retired, she had time to reflect on her long working career and she decided that she felt cheated:

> I think I made a mistake. If I had it to do over agin, I'd do it different. I think this woman's liberation is a good idea. I worked like a slave all my life. I did what people expected me to do and I never said no.... I used to think I was just so. If anybody had told me I didn't have it so good, I'd have laughed at them. But now I'm old and I can look back. It wasn't such a great life.
>
> (Generation I, b. 1883)

As she spoke I recognized an echo in myself. I understood how painful and humiliating it is for women to admit that they are oppressed.[2] Even worse, it is frightening. If women admit they are oppressed, they undermine their sense of self-worth, their pride and dignity. They undermine what sense of security they have in the world as it now is. And even more challenging, once women acknowledge their oppression, they confront the problem of figuring out what to do about it.

It takes courage to confront the problems and to begin fighting back. Whenever women resist their subordinate position, they face great upheavals in their lives. They often meet anger and resentment, not only from the world at large but, more painfully, from their dearest family and friends. One woman who had tried all her life to say no to the traditional subordinate position of women, described what happened to her:

> I always did things women weren't supposed to do. I didn't get married til I was real old. I went prospecting alone in the bush for years. I worked when my kids were small and I always spoke up for women's rights. Wasn't easy. My parents kicked me out of my home and wouldn't see me for forty years. People jibed me, saying reason I wasn't married were because no man would have such a battleaxe. There have been times when even my husband said I went too far, and he got real mad at me. Wasn't easy, but it were right. Women just have to take a stand.
>
> (Generation II, b. 1923)

Many women are so caught up in the relentless business of daily life that they end up avoiding the problem and not taking a stand. This leaves them vulnerable to all the contradictory pressures of life under capitalism. But many others are defiant and some are able to transform their defiance into active resistance and finally into political action to change the very structure of their work and hence the pattern of their lives.

FIGHTING BACK

Just as women's work in the home is hidden and yet central to the economy of industrial capitalism, so women's struggles with their work are often unseen. Yet they are important political struggles. The politics of domestic labour revolve around the central contradictions of the work. When women struggle to improve their working conditions, they both improve the quality of family life and, at the same time, resist and challenge the intrusion of capitalist relations into their daily lives.

Women's resistance is multileveled and complex. It begins in the home and radiates out into the community. Periodically it stretches even further into the very workings of the state or industrial production. It is uneven and erratic. But it is always there, lurking just beneath the surface.[3]

For wage workers, trade union and prolabour political parties provide organizational forms within which workers can develop their political consciousness and organize collective forms of struggle. For women doing domestic labour there have never been such organizations that could bring women together to discuss their situation, decide what can be done to improve it, and mobilize women into action. However, taking a stand alone is very hard, and individual action often remains at the personal level. To take the fight into social and political arenas, women need to get together with other women.

THE WOMEN'S LIBERATION MOVEMENT

One of the older women I interviewed had been active in the fight for women's suffrage at the turn of the century. She talked about the women's rights movement and the relationship between women and politics:

> Women's politics are like an iceberg. Only the tip shows and it never looks like much. But underneath is a vast mass of women, always moving — usually very slowly.... When I was young, women didn't even have the right to vote. Well, we thought about that and it didn't seem right so finally lots of women got together and worked for it and now we got the vote. Most people assume women will put up with things the way they are. But that isn't so. When women see a thing needs changing, things change.
>
> (Generation I, b. 1891)

In the late 1960s, in kitchens, offices and classrooms across North America, women began to think consciously about what it means to be a woman in male-dominated capitalist society. They met together and talked and discovered that the pain, fear, inadequacy and anger, which each had felt were her problems alone, were shared by many women. The effect was dynamic and the women's liberation movement was reactivated.[4]

Some Flin Flon women talked about the relief they felt when the women's liberation movement began public discussions and took direct action to challenge women's oppression:

> I cried the first time I saw some women on TV talking about things that I'd felt. Before that I always thought it was just me but when I realized other women felt the same, I felt so good.... I started reading everything I could get my hands on and talking to everyone.
>
> (Generation III, b. 1947)

While many Flin Flon women were untouched by the women's liberation movement, some felt their lives had been profoundly changed by it:

> I'm a different person now. I can't put my finger on what it is, exactly, but I know that women need to look out for themselves and look after each other as well.
>
> (Generation III, b. 1947)

One evening five women gathered together in one woman's house. They all brought their children, put them to sleep in another room and settled down with a pot of tea to watch a television special on the history of the women's movement. After the program, they spent several hours talking about it. During the discussion, three points came up that were particularly signficant. They all agreed, first of all, that they were amazed to learn that women have been involved in struggles for equal rights for hundreds of years. They were angry that they were unfamiliar with that history and excited to realize that their concerns were not new but had been shared by many women:

> I always thought this women's movement stuff was new. But those women in the show were saying the same stuff more than two hundred years ago! How come I never knew that?
>
> (Generation III, b. 1951)

> When I took history in school we learned about Nellie McClung and votes for women, but it was always a bit of a joke. Nobody took it very seriously. But that's the pits. If we don't take them seriously, no one will take us seriously and we'll just go on endlessly never changing anything. It makes me feel real good that lots of other women long ago did things that made it better for me. Maybe we can do things to make it better for our kids.
>
> (Generation III, b. 1948)

They were also impressed by the kinds of issues women have organized around in the past. A song called "Bread and Roses" had been played on the program, and the commentator had noted that the title reflects the two types of demands women have raised.[5] On the one hand, women fight for the material conditions that will make life easier — for bread. But as the song says, "hearts starve as well as bodies. Give us bread, but give us roses!" So women also fight for a better life.

> I really like that song. And that's exactly what we want — bread and roses — enough to eat and beautiful things to enjoy.
>
> (Generation III, b. 1950)

> I like the song too. It makes me think of all the things we should be asking for when we negotiate the contract with the Company. Not just for more money, but for more holidays and earlier

retirement and better health and safety regulations, so the men can live longer so our families have better times together.

(Generation III, b. 1948)

Finally, they began to clarify for themselves what the women's movement meant to them:

> You know, I used to think the women's movement was a bunch of "women's libber" kooks out there somewhere. But the more I think about it, and tonight's show made me think I'm right, the more I think the women's movement is something else. Maybe feminists are like trade unionists. You know, there are some trade union people who are always in the paper, who are the leaders of the big official organizations like the Manitoba Federation of Labour or whatever. Then there's just hundreds and thousands of ordinary workers all over the place. They go to work every day and they support their union and they don't think much about it most of the time. But when the crunch comes, they're on the right side. Maybe the women's movement is like that.

(Generation III, b. 1950)

Her friend elaborated:

> You mean, there's some women who get on TV and go on demonstrations and stuff but they're just the most visible. Then there's all those other women, like us maybe, who don't say very much but who do little things and if we all do little things, maybe it will add up.

(Generation III, b. 1948)

As these women were getting ready to go, carrying their sleeping children out to the cars, one of them stopped and said:

> I think the women's movement is any women who try to figure out what happens to women and then try to do something about it, to make it better.

(Generation III, b. 1951)

The women's movement is a network of individuals and different interest groups bound together by a loose feminist ideology and a commitment to struggle in various ways for equality for women. In a sense, the women's movement acts as a collective consciousness, which helps women develop an awareness of their situation and retain a memory of the different struggles women have engaged in.

As women become conscious of the conditions of their work, they begin to face the contradictions of their daily lives. Then they decide what their immediate needs are. Once they have determined those needs, they establish a series of demands based on where they decide they want to go. This means that the women's movement is constantly grappling with ideas about what kind of life women want to live. One of the most important lessons of the women's movement is that women need to talk to other women. By sharing their experiences they begin to recognize and understand the patterns that underlie their lives.

One night when all their husbands were on afternoon shift, four Flin Flon women decided to spend the evening together. They had originally planned the evening because none of them enjoyed being at home alone with the children. So they started by discussing how they felt about that. The next day, one of the women told me how excited she had been by what happened:

> We just talked all night. And I realized that they all felt just the same way I did. I thought it was just me that thought that way. I thought I was just being silly. But it wasn't just me — it was all of us…. So we started thinking about what we could do together that would make things better for us. And we're going to get together again, soon. It's just great!
>
> (Generation III, b. 1954)

By building such support networks with each other, women start to recognize the reality of their situations:

> For years I thought it was all my fault, that I was so unhappy and tense so much of the time. Finally when I understood it wasn't my fault, I felt so much better. I stopped guilt-tripping myself and began laying the blame where it belonged — on this society that puts women down all the time.
>
> (Generation III, b. 1951)

By beginning the painful process of separating their sense of identity from their work and of looking their situation squarely in the face, women begin to develop a genuine self-respect. Then they began to assert their needs, wants and autonomy. Once they generalize from their own personal situations to the larger question of the status of women in general, women start to change their lives.

OUT FROM THE KITCHEN

Probably the hardest step in the struggle for women's liberation occurs when women start to challenge the existing social relations in their own households. Many women start by insisting that what they do in the home is work and that it deserves respect. Others begin to challenge the sexual division of labour in the home. Domestic labour is necessary for survival; it is not innately "women's work." So some women begin by insisting that their husbands and children share in the work, so that women stop having to bear the brunt of it:

> Finally I just started to tell him, "Look it's your home too, so you have to do a share." At first he just started helping out. He'd do the dishes now and then, or mind the baby while I went out. But gradually he's started taking on more and more. I just push him a bit every so often.
>
> (Generation III, b. 1957)

Some men never give in and their resistance can be frightening. One woman described her husband's reaction when she asked if he would share the domestic labour with her:

> He hit the roof and yelled at me for weeks. Finally he issued me an ultimatum. If I ever made that kind of suggestion again, he would walk out of the door and I'd never see him again.
>
> (Generation III, b. 1953)

After much painful deliberation, this woman decided that she did not want to live under that kind of threat. Eventually she left him.

Other men are willing to try sharing domestic labour and a few have understood the importance of it. In one Flin Flon household, the couple developed what they considered to be an equitable divison of labour. He earned the wages by working for the Company. She worked at home doing all the laundry, house cleaning and all the child care while he was at work. They took turns doing the shopping, cooking and dishes, and they split the child care when he was not at work. She described her thoughts about this division:

I feel this way it's really fair. We both have our set work to do and then we split everything else down the middle. This way I feel like we live together in a partnership, not that I'm being supported by him or that I have to take care of him.

(Generation III, b. 1954)

He talked about what this meant for him:

It feels more co-operative this way. I feel like we both pull our weight. We both have about the same amount of work to do and we both get some time off. I really like feeling equally involved with the children. And because I do the work around the house, I know just how much she has to do, so I appreciate it. It feels better — sharing things.

(Generation III, b. 1949)

As men start to take on some of the responsibility for domestic labour, they develop an appreciation of how complex and demanding the work actually is. They begin to have a genuine respect for the work and for the women who do it. One husband had reluctantly started doing some of the domestic labour after his wife began a paid job. After about a month, he observed:

I never thought very much about what she did. I always thought it was pretty easy, being at home. Since I've started doing it, I realized how wrong I was. It's hard work, and there is so much of it. She's really something — doing all that stuff for so many years. And doing it really well too.

(Generation III, b. 1951)

As women negotiate with other household members for a more equitable division of labour, they can also enlist the help of the rest of their household in a larger struggle to change the external forces that limit domestic labour. This involves a two-pronged campaign, taking women into the community and into the wage workplace.

INTO THE COMMUNITY

Housewives have always been active in their communities, demanding a whole range of things that make life easier and better — schools, hospitals, paved roads and street lighting, parks and recreation centres. Periodically they organize around issues that are of specific interest to women. As they organize around various demands, housewives often link up with other individuals or groups so that they become part of community action and social protest movements. Sometimes these activities bring them into confrontation with government or other official agencies. Always such actions affect the women involved, giving them greater self-respect and pride and changing their relations to their work and their families.

In Flin Flon in the mid 1970s, the local hospital was planning a building campaign to add a new pharmacy. At that time, a number of women in the town wanted access to "bandaid" sterilizations. The hospital administration said it could not provide such operations because the hospital lacked the necessary equipment. The women then began to ask questions about who controlled hospital financing. They wondered why money was available to build a new drug dispensary but not to purchase particular surgical equipment.

Several women went to a hospital board meeting to ask these questions. They hoped to challenge the hospital administrators, to force a reconsideration of the allocation of funds. They met with some of the directors who listened to them politely and then sent them home, without even answering any of their questions. One of the women summed up their experience this way:

> We failed completely. But we learned something important. Those men wouldn't listen to five housewives. But they would listen if there had been more of us. We should have organized a public campaign so we could have gone representing hundreds of people, not just us.

(Generation III, b. 1948)

A few months later these women learned that the union was disturbed about the quality of health care provided to workers by the Company doctor. A few members of the union were talking about the possibility of using union funds to hire a doctor who would be independent of Company management. The women approached these men to suggest that perhaps the union's interests and the women's concern could be met if they worked together. One of the women commented:

213

I don't know if it will go anywhere but just meeting together is a good thing. With a larger group of concerned people, especially with the strength of the union behind us, we actually have a realistic chance of really doing something about medical care in this town. And talking together really helps. I never knew about the problems the men have at work before and I'm sure they never before really gave a care about us.

(Generation III, b. 1949)

In a mining community north of Flin Flon, a number of women were assaulted and raped over the course of several months.[6] The police assured the women that they were doing all they could to prevent further attacks, but the women were unconvinced and frightened. Both the police and town officials publicly urged women to stay at home until the attacks ceased. Several women, angered at this official response, decided to take matters into their own hands:

Telling us to stay home because it isn't safe is like saying it's our fault we get raped. I don't think the police really care about making it safe for women. They just want to avoid trouble so they want us neatly tucked away at home. Well, if they won't help us, we will do it ourselves.

The women organized several meetings and eventually set up a rape crisis centre. The centre provided emotional and legal support for rape victims and also operated an educational campaign to inform the police, city officials and others in authority of the importance of ending violence against women. The centre also organized what they called a "buddy system." If a women had to go somewhere alone at night, she could phone the centre and two other women would go with her to provide protection. One of the women involved in this centre talked about why it was so important:

Not only are we making the community a safer place for women — and heaven knows how important that is, but we are also teaching other people about what it's like to be a woman and in a small way we are changing that too. And for those of us involved in the centre, now we know that we can do something to make things better for us.

As women in different communities all across the country talk to each other about their needs, they begin to push for better services. They demand, and begin to build, a variety of women's centres where women can meet each other and get certain types of necessary services. In different cities groups of women have established rape crisis centres, hostels for battered wives, birth control, venereal disease and abortion referral centres, quality child care centres and special interest centres for immigrant, black and native women.

The more women get involved in these kinds of activities the more they learn that other women feel the same way they do. As they learn the skills necessary to organize in the community, they stop feeling impotent and begin to recognize their own strength and power. A woman from another northern community in Manitoba told me how she felt after being involved in the local women's centre:

> I felt so great! I used to go to the centre and just stand there amazed and think — Oh wow! We did this. We did it ourselves — just a group of women.... We thought it would be neat to have a place where women could go to meet other women, to drop in for a cup of coffee and let their kids play in the playroom, to get information that women need. And three years later our idea was reality. And now that we have the centre, women all over town keep asking how we ever managed without it. What I learned from this is that if women get together and want something badly enough, they can make it happen. We did it!

LINKS WITH THE UNIONS

As women grapple with the various ways available to improve their working conditions and their lives, they eventually have to deal with the nature of their husbands' wage work. Because domestic labour is predicated on wage labour, women have a vested interest in their husbands' struggles in the wage workplace. However, because there is such a separation between the home and the wage workplace, it is often difficult for women to act on their own interests. Even when they do, they often have to overcome the resistance not only of their husbands but of the union leadership as well. Periodically they also have to deal with management attempts to manipulate them into anti-union positions.

From the earliest days of union organizing in Canada and the United States, women have been actively involved in building and supporting the labour movement. Like so much of women's history and working-class history, this activity is not well known! In the last few years, feminist researchers have begun to uncover the history of women's involvement as wage workers themselves and as daughters, wives and mothers of union men. A series of films such as *Salt of the Earth, Harlan County, With Babies and Banners* and *The Wives' Tale — l'Histoire des Femmes* have demonstrated the subtle and complex relationship between union politics and family politics.[7]

Flin Flon women of all generations were ambivalent about their relationship with the union and the politics of their husbands' workplace. Some women felt that the separation between men's work and women's work was so great that they wanted nothing to do with what happened to their husbands at work. As one women expressed it:

> I do my work at home and as long as he brings home his pay steady, I don't want to know what happens to him at work and I don't care about the union.
>
> (Generation II, b. 1934)

Other women resented the time and energy that union politics demanded. They felt excluded:

> He's always off at the Labour Temple [the union hall], every free minute he gets. I wish he'd stay home more. I don't know what he does down there.
>
> (Generation III, b. 1950)

Those who understood how much their lives were affected by their husbands' wage work often wanted to get involved but were not sure how to go about it:

> I feel so strongly about that. I wish I could get involved somehow. I'd like to go to union meetings and tell them what I think. But they'd never let me in.
>
> (Generation III, b. 1953)

In their day-to-day workings, unions rarely give any thought to the families of their members. At Christmastime, they often throw a party for the children and occasionally hold fundraising parties during the year. Only during times of real crisis do the unions attempt to reach beyond their membership for support.

In Flin Flon this reaching out for support has occurred during strikes.

During the early 1930s, workers at the Company tried to form a union to protect their interests. Many of the women in the community supported these efforts and when the workers finally went on strike in June 1934 the women formed a strike support committee which played a central role throughout the month-long strike:

> Well, it were our men working there. The hours were long, the work was dangerous, and the pay — you couldn't support a family on the pay! So it was our strike too. So we went down there and did everything that needed doing.
>
> (Generation I, b. 1912)

The women walked the picket lines, prevented strike breakers and scabs from crossing the lines and fought with the RCMP to defend the union:

> It was a Saturday, I think, when there was going to be a vote against the union. We went down to the community hall and all us women went up on the steps and blocked the doorway. I had two eggs in my pocket and I waited til a bunch of strike breakers was trying to get through and I threw my eggs — they made a lovely mess. Well, we were strong that day and all their police with their guns and all those bullies — we stood firm.
>
> (Generation I, b. 1911)

The Flin Flon Strike, 1934

Although this strike ended essentially in a defeat for the workers, the experience had a lasting effect on many of the women involved. For some, it was their first experience working collectively with other women. It broke down many of the barriers that had previously isolated women in their homes and it gave them a stronger sense of belonging to a larger community, of having responsibilities beyond their families:

> Before the strike, I stayed at home with my family. I didn't know many people and I wasn't interested in the union. But during the strike I got to know a lot of other women and afterwards I felt more part of the town.
>
> (Generation I, b. 1904)

> Standing on those steps, arm in arm with those other women, I realized something. I used to think they were real different from me — one was Ukrainian and one was a Pole. They talked different and kept to themselves. But during the strike, they stuck up with me and they became my friends.
>
> (Generation I, b. 1911)

For some women, participating in the strike helped them change their relationship with their husbands. One woman told me how when she was a child her mother used to tell her, with great delight, about the way the strike changed her marriage:

> She used to say that before the strike my father never paid her much heed. He always told her not to bother with "men's work." But after he saw her on the picket line yelling at the police, he always used to ask her opinion. And he used to say "My wife is smart and tough."
>
> (Generation II, b. 1937)

Similar patterns emerged during the 1971 strike. One woman described her feelings just before the strike vote was taken:

> I didn't know where I stood. I really didn't want a strike. I knew we couldn't manage on strike pay. But I knew we needed more money, so I was sort of for the strike. I felt really mixed up and afraid.
>
> (Generation III, b. 1951)

Once the strike was actually on, she overcame her ambivalence and threw herself into the activities:

> Once we were on strike I knew I had to support it, so I did.

The strike situation clarified the class differences that existed in Flin Flon. Management sometimes tried to manipulate the women, playing on their ambivalent feelings or on their loyalty to the town:

> I had been really active in the town. After the strike had been on for awhile, [a Company manager] met me on the street and asked me to have a coffee with him. He told me how the strike was hurting the town and said that the Company was thinking of pulling out altogether as the operation wasn't profitable. He asked me to use my influence to get the men to settle so as to save the town.
>
> (Generation II, b. 1918)

One woman described an incident where personal friendship and class differences came into conflict. Before the strike, she and the other woman had been good friends. After the strike there was no basis for friendship anymore:

> Our husbands were on strike, so a bunch of us housewives went walking the picket line. Then this woman I know come out of the managers' housing where she lives and walked over to me. "Susie," she said. "I come out when I saw you here. We're friends, Susie," she says. "I want to talk to you." Then she told me how we women were all the same and how we should all get together to end the strike. "You're a housewife, the same as me," she says. Well, I thought about it afterwards. Her husband is a boss. He's on salary and I bet he earns three times what my husband does. My husband's just a mucker and his wages are low. I don't think her and me are the same. It's true we're all housewives, but there's a difference.
>
> (Generation III, b. 1949)

Another woman talked about the importance of women organizing themselves:

> I went up to the Labour Temple to help out. One of the men there said sure they wanted women's help so I should go help serve coffee to the picketers. That didn't seem like much help, so I went home and called some of my friends. We got together and organized a woman's picket.
>
> (Generation II, b. 1937)

Such experiences are really important in bringing women out of their homes and into the political arena. They break down the women's individual isolation and start to cut across the profound divisions that fragment the working class. However, most union leaderships have failed to recognize this and have down played the importance of family and community support. A Flin Flon woman described what happened to the wives' support committee after the strike:

> Before the strike the union didn't have any interest in us. But then during the strike they needed all the help and support they could get, so they was real glad we were there. But after the strike was over, they weren't interested in us any more.
>
> (Generation II, b. 1934)

This has been a typical pattern of trade union politics. Time after time women act behind the scenes and in the streets in support of the union. When the union clearly needs support it appreciates the women, but when the immediate crisis is over, it sends the women home. In the film about the role of American women in the Flint (Michigan) General Motor's strike of 1937, one of the women summed up what happened to the Women's Emergency Brigade after the strike:

> Following the strike, the Emergency Brigades were effectively dispersed; there was none of the usual thing of financing, or encouraging on the part of the men. What happened in effect, if you can imagine this, from the International on down, everybody in it said, "Thank you, Ladies. You have done a wonderful job, we appreciate it very much; but now the laundry is piled up, the dishes are piled up, and the kids need attention."[8]

In Flin Flon during the 1976 contract negotiations between the Company and the union, the women's lack of power became apparent. Whatever the outcome of the negotiations, women's lives and their working conditions would be deeply affected. But the women had no formal way of participating in the debates of the union membership nor any say in the negotiating itself. One woman commented:

> What they decide affects us all in this town, the whole town. If they settle for a bad contract, we [women] will have to make do on less. If they strike, we will have to make do on nothing. Wives should have some say in the contract.
>
> (Generation II, b. 1926)

Another woman observed:

> That's my life they're voting on. I should get a chance to vote too.
>
> (Generation III, b. 1950)

Some of the women went to the union leadership and proposed that women should be allowed to participate in the decision making. The leadership ignored their request and the women were left annoyed and frustrated.

> How I run my household is all up in the air while those men fight about their contract. Women should have a say.
>
> (Generation II, b. 1934)

As these negotiations continued and it seemed that another strike might occur, women in Flin Flon became even more concerned about their inability to influence the situation.

The federal government had imposed wage and price controls, and everyone in town knew that the workers would probably take a cut in real wages. One afternoon four women were discussing the situation over coffee in the cafeteria of one of the department stores. All of them were housewives; one of them worked parttime in the store as a waitress. Their discussion indicated how well they understood the situation and showed their despair at not knowing how to act and what to do. The waitress commented:

> The union may strike over this contract but with this wage controls they won't get anywhere. The first thing we have to do is get rid of wage controls, and the only way that will happen is if every worker in this country walked off the job and refused to go back to work until the controls are lifted.... If I thought half the people in this store would come with me, I'd go out now
>
> (Generation II, b. 1926)

Her friend continued:

> You have to get the brass of the MFL [Manitoba Federation of Labour] or the CLC [Canadian Labour Congress] to organize something like that. And they don't want to do it. That's what we need all right. And not just union people either, but everyone.
>
> (Generation II, b. 1929)

The third woman nodded and observed:

> This strike that's maybe coming up here — it will affect the whole town. If the union goes out, there'll be no pay. Families won't have any money. The stores won't sell anything. But what can we do about it, except sit back and wait to see what happens.
>
> (Generation II, b. 1923)

The conversation ended as the fourth woman concluded:

> Knowing what to do isn't all that hard. It's knowing how to do it that's the problem.
>
> (Generation II, b. 1933)

This conversation demonstrates that the women have a sophisticated appreciation not only of their own personal situation but of the conditions facing the working class of Canada as a whole. Their awareness, and the consciousness of many of the women I met in Flin Flon, calls into question the traditional assessment that housewives are either politically conservative or politically unconscious. It does, however, raise some absolutely crucial issues: How can women win their needs? How can women organize? Who are their allies?

THE RISING OF THE WOMEN

There are no simple answers to these questions. Challenging the way domestic labour is organized means challenging the most basic structures of male-dominated industrial capitalist society. This takes women out of their households and into two arenas: the first, sexual politics and the women's liberation movement; the second, class politics and the workers' movement.

The specific strategies and tactics that working-class women develop emerge directly from their experiences in day-to-day struggles in the home, in the community and in the paid workplace. Their struggles challenge the sexual division of labour which so profoundly divides the working class. Their struggles also help to unite all oppressed and exploited people in their fight to build a world free from oppression and exploitation. As the final verse of "Bread and Roses" envisions:

> The rising of the women
> Means the rising of the Race.
> No more the drudge and idler —
> Ten that toil where one reposes,
> But a sharing of life's glories:
> Bread and Roses! Bread and Roses!

Some feminists have argued that the one issue women could organize around is the demand for wages for the work they do in the home. These advocates of wages for housework argue that if women organize around a wage demand, they will expose and clarify the hidden relationship between housewives and capital.[9] They also maintain that women's wagelessness is the root of their powerlessness and that demanding a wage is a way both of insisting on material recognition of domestic labour as work and of attaining the financial means to independence for women. The wages-for-housework advocates argue that if housewives organize around the demand for wages, their struggles will move from the isolated, private and personal realm of the family into a social struggle that will link them with other working-class political struggles.

I asked Flin Flon women what they thought of the wages-for-housework demand. While they were unanimous in agreeing that they would like an income of their own, they were quick to raise a number of criticisms. They were cynical about who would actually pay for the wage:

> Well, I'd like to get my own wage — be nice to have the money. And it would make what I do seem more like real work. But they wouldn't just give us money. We'd pay for it ourselves in the long run through our taxes.
>
> (Generation II, b. 1934)

Some suggested that if the state paid wages, it would start to supervise and investigate the women receiving wages. Isolated in their own homes, these women would have difficulty resisting such intrusions:

> It would be just like being on welfare or mother's allowance. They'd say — you get money from us so we have the right to inspect you. Then if they didn't like how you spent their money or ran your home — they'd take the money away, or fine you or put you in jail for misuse of funds....
>
> (Generation III, b. 1949)

Others pointed out that in different ways, the state has periodically paid women for aspects of domestic labour. They suggested that a wage payment could easily be abused and used to oppress women even more:

Well, whenever they want us to make more babies, they increase the baby bonus or change the family tax laws. So the government could decide to pay women according to how good a wife and mother they are. Then we'd all have to have dozens of kids and keep spotless houses and do home baking and never complain.
(Generation III, b. 1951)

The most important criticism of the payment of wages-for-housework is that it does not in any way attempt to break down the sexual division of labour:

It just kind of assumes that women always have to do housework. But we want men and kids doing it too. If we got paid to do it, no man would ever help us. Instead they'd say, "It's your job. You get paid for it — you do it." My husband says that to me already. If I really got paid, he'd be ten times worse.
(Generation III, b. 1948)

Nor does the demand attempt to break down the isolation and privacy of the working-class household. Instead, if women were paid wages for housework, the isolation of individual women working privately for their own families would be reinforced:

I think getting paid to stay home would be worse. It would be impossible to ever get out of the house then.
(Generation II, b. 1939)

Very few groups have actually campaigned specifically for housewives, and therefore the women involved in the wages-for-housework campaign deserve credit. However, their campaign is essentially a dead-end one, which will not eliminate the contradictions of domestic labour and which may well divert women's energies away from more useful struggles.

Women need instead to engage in struggles which will break down their isolation and atomization, overcome the contradictions of domestic labour and begin to heal the rifts between women and men. They need to transform the way their lives are currently organized to create a situation where people can make real choices about how they want to live their lives — choices based on real, viable alternatives. Women need to develop organizational forms to help them fight. This means building the autonomous women's liberation movement to help women get together to formulate demands, to develop tactics and strategies and to assert themselves in carrying them out. It also means building links between the women's liberation movement and other groups, particularly the workers' movement.

There have been times when working-class women, and especially housewives, have not been of central concern to either the women's liberation movement or the workers' movement. But as Rowbotham argues, "the movement of working-class women is ... essential" and is "the most potentially subversive to capitalism" because women are located both in the home doing domestic labour and in the paid labour force as wage workers. They bear the brunt of both class exploitation and sex oppression. She goes on to argue that working-class women "... need each other, they need the support of male workers, and their fight at work connects immediately to their situation at home. Their organization and militancy is vital not only for women's liberation but for the whole socialist and working class movement."[10]

The militancy of working-class women proceeds on three fronts. The first is the paid labour force, where the overall demand is for the abolition of the sex-segregated labour force and ultimately for the creation of a division of labour where people work to satisfy their own needs rather than to make profit for other people. More women than ever before are doing paid work. Since 1931 the percentage of married women in the paid labour force has increased from 10 percent to almost 60 percent. But women still earn very little. On the average women earn 56 percent of what men earn.[11] And the material conditions of their work immediately generate a series of issues which are political. Women need the right to equal jobs and equal pay. They also need the education and training that will prepare them for these jobs.

Women's groups across the country have begun organizing around these issues. Equal pay coalitions have been formed to monitor pay discrimination and to fight for equal pay. In some cities groups of women have formed women-into-industry campaigns. Supported by local unions, these groups have filed formal charges of discrimination against certain major companies, and their victories have resulted in a few women being hired in what previously were exclusively male jobs.[12] In Flin

Flon in the mid 1970s, the Company hired women to work in the plant for the first time since the Second World War. While the Company steadfastly refused to hire women for underground work which included the highest paid jobs, other companies across the country have slowly begun to hire women in heavy industry and mining.[13]

In those paid occupations that have traditionally hired mostly women, the majority of workers are unorganized and underpaid. Campaigns to unionize these women workers and to increase their pay rates, have begun in certain occupations, with the bank tellers, for example.[14] Within the labour movement as a whole, women's caucuses have been formed to force the trade unions to take up women's issues, such as sexual harassment on the job, paid maternity (and paternity) leaves and nurseries in the workplace. Women are also working with men to improve working conditions generally by struggling for such things as health and safety regulations, a shorter work week with no loss of pay ("thirty for forty") and guaranteed jobs for all.

Because unions are crucial not only to defend workers' rights on the job but also to act as the focal point of many united actions, the unions need to become more attuned to women's needs. If, for example, unions provided child care at meetings, their female members would be able to participate more regularly. If the unions then encouraged their male members to use the child care provided, they would be helping to break down the sexual division of labour in the home and would win more support from their members' wives. Based on a recognition of the crucial relationship between wage and domestic labour, unions need to establish an ongoing union role for the families of their members. It is particularly important, especially in places like Flin Flon where there is one major employer, for housewives to have a real voice and an ongoing role in the union.

As women begin to win rights in the paid labour force, the economic necessity for women to marry will disappear, and women will be in a better position to choose their own lifestyles and personal relationships. However, while engaging in paid work breaks down women's isolation and gives women a certain amount of economic independence, it does not get at the root of the problem of women's work in the home. Nor does it diminish the tensions women experience from their double day of labour.

The struggle on the second front therefore is in the household where women strive to get all members to share equally the work of domestic labour. At the same time, some people have tried to break down the isolation of the family household by creating community co-operatives, which help eliminate private domestic labour. Such organizations as credit unions, food, housing and child care co-operatives provide households with much-needed services while giving their members experiences that help them formulate ideas about other lifestyles.

The struggle to socialize as much domestic labour as possible leads to the third front, to the struggles for a redistribution of the social surplus away from private profit to meet the needs of the majority of people. This means demanding a change in social policy, and it brings women into direct confrontation with the state. Essentially, women need a government that is sympathetic to women's needs so that women and their families, and not big business, are the top priority in government planning. This means that women and their allies need to fight for social ser-vices that will relieve the pressures of domestic labour and reduce its isolation in a humane way. So far struggles for these social services have been the least successful, and success on this front will require innovative thinking.

In many ways, these struggles arouse the greatest fear in people. There is a great deal of talk about how socializing domestic labour destroys the family. However, it is the contra-dictions inherent in domestic labour and in the sexual division of labour in the family that put so much destructive pressure on family members. Once women are no longer prisoners of domestic labour, they are free to develop themselves and are able to enter into relationships as loving human beings rather than out of economic necessity. Therefore it is profoundly in women's interests to fight for a range of services that will ease the burden of domestic labour while allowing for individual preferences and choice.

There have been some imaginative attempts in this direction. As consumers, some housewives have extended their normal practice of comparison shopping by forming price watch committees. Groups of women check out prices and insist that store managers not raise their prices above what the women decide is fair. Day care action groups have demanded free, quality child care on a twenty-four-hour daily basis, so that it is available whenever parents need it.

Other community groups have demanded quality subsidized housing so that families can live more comfortably and adequate health care facilities so that women no longer have to nurse their families alone. Some have called for inexpensive restaurants serving healthy food so that women do not need to cook so often. As an alternative, there could be "collective kitchens" where people from a neighbourhood cook for the whole group and then either eat together or take the precooked food home. Similarly, people could drop their laundry off at cheap neighbourhood cleaners and pick it up later. This would ease the laundry burden for individual women and would eliminate the need for so many privately owned washers and dryers. One Flin Flon women described her vision this way:

> What I'd really like to do is to change pretty well everything about the way people get fed, clothed, and live. It takes lots of time, lots of work, and not just one person to make such big changes. It seems if you don't do something, no one will, but if one person starts and keeps things going, others will.
>
> You can't just talk about it; you have to do it. For instance, we need good day care — like *real* good day care — and cheap restaurants which serve healthy food, not crap and sugar. You need lots of women and men working together.[15]

While struggling for each of these issues is important, the most effective struggles are those which link up with others to form a united effort to fight on many fronts at once:

> A bunch of us women decided we needed a day care centre to look after our kids. We got a little group together and we did all the things we had to do. We filled out forms and wrote letters to the premier and met all the rules and regulations, but finally we figured we weren't going to get anywhere. The government said we could open a day care but it wouldn't give us any money! ... Then we found out other people were mad because the government wouldn't pave the highway near them and others wanted better health care service in the North.... And then when

all of us got together, and it was an election year too, we started a
"better services in the North" committee. Eventually we got most
of what we wanted.

(Generation II, b. 1929)

One of the most impressive examples of a united front, where
people fought on all three fronts for a number of interlocking
issues, occurred in Sudbury, a mining city in northern Ontario.
During the winter of 1978-79, the Sudbury Steelworkers Union
Local 6500 went on strike against Inco. The wives of the male
workers decided to organize a women's support group, called
Wives Supporting the Strike.[16] Unlike many of the husbands at
the beginning of the strike, this group understood that the strike
concerned not just the union and its members but also the
families of the strikers and other members of the Sudbury community:

When the men go on strike, the women are on strike too. And our
workload doesn't ease at all, and there's less money around....[17]

Throughout the nearly nine months of the strike, this women's
group carried on a series of activities designed to ease the
pressure on strikers' wives and families. They organized baby-
sitting co-operatives, car pools, potluck suppers, neighbourhood
entertainment and group suppers:

Nobody had any money, see, and some women were really scared.
So we took care of each other. For instance, once we organized a
huge bean supper and fed hundreds of people supper. We learned
we could cope.[18]

By providing moral and material support they helped each other
survive the terrible strain that families endure during a strike.
Indirectly, they were also developing ways of collectivizing
domestic labour.

The Wives Supporting the Strike group also attempted to
educate the strikers' wives about the union and about the strike.
Many women did not have access to information about important issues such as how strike pay levels are determined, why the
strike was important, and how they could support the strike:

Some women just didn't know anything, so they were scared.
They wanted to see the strike end, so they weren't supporting
their husbands at all. One man who had started by supporting the
strike started to back off when he got so much flak from his wife.

But when we explained everything to her and answered all her questions, then she felt good about it and understood, and now she feels okay and is supporting the union and he feels much stronger too.[19]

Members of this committee also joined the picket line, raised money for the strike and travelled around the country informing people in other centres about the strike to build support wherever possible.

In March 1979 a group of women representing Wives Supporting the Strike drove to Toronto to participate in a rally and demonstration that had been organized to celebrate International Women's Day.[20] The organizers had four main slogans: "Jobs! Full Social Services! Control of Our Bodies! Lesbian Rights!"[21] The Sudbury women joined in the demonstration. After the march was over, one of the women said:

I agreed to come because we want to win our strike, and we can only do that if we have support from people all over Canada. So we came to tell you about us.... And I couldn't come unless my

Sudbury wives supporting the strike march in International Women's Day demonstration, Toronto, 1979

husband looked after the kids, so he's at home doing what used to be my work, while I'm here supporting his.... And we just marched, not just for our union, but for day care and equal pay and even abortion and rights for lesbians. So here I am, a house-wife from Sudbury, on a women's liberation march because — because winning our strike is all tied up with those other things.[22]

One of the main reasons why the Sudbury strikers were able to hold out so long and finally win the battle was because of the support of these women. In organizing their support, the women themselves profoundly changed their views of their own lives:

I'll never be quite the same again. Now I have a vision of another way. I guess I learned that ordinary women like me can fight a big multinational company like Inco, and win — can challenge the government.... I learned that there are other ways of organizing our daily lives, ways of living as a community together, ways of being husbands and wives that I never imagined before.... Maybe all together, we could make a better world.[23]

Working-class women are starting to realize that the present form of the family holds them back. They are beginning to understand that the way work is divided between the sexes in-juries both women and men. The demands that these women are making to improve their daily lives require fundamental changes in the way society is organized.

The way forward will not be easy It will demand all the imag-ination, courage and determination that women can muster. But together we are strong and we will win "bread and roses" for ourselves and for each other.

POSTSCRIPT

In 1981 I returned to Flin Flon to see the changes that had taken place in the five years since I had done the original study. In this follow-up study, I sought out only women of the third generation and was able to locate forty-nine of the original fifty-two.

Things had indeed changed. I found that the majority of the women, all of whom had children under twelve, were working outside the home for pay. Given the new demands of their paid employment, they were forced to reorganize their domestic labour in various ways. Some women insisted that their paid work must never interfere with their ability to run their households. They maintained high standards and did all their domestic labour themselves. As a result, they were constantly overworked and stressed. Some of the other women also believed that employed women should continue to be responsible for domestic labour. However, they acknowledged the stress involved in juggling two jobs and coped by lowering their standards and by asking their husbands to "help out" more often. Despite such help, they still bore the major responsibility for organizing and doing domestic labour. Just over half of the women argued that because they were employed, their husbands should share the domestic labour. These women were actively engaged in struggling with their husbands for a more equitable redistribution of the workload.

This study indicated that the changing pattern of women's paid employment is creating a crisis in the way labour is distributed and accomplished in the family household. In the labour force, women attempting to change sexual divisions have the support of the women's liberation movement, the trade union movement and sometimes the law and other institutions such as human rights commissions. In contrast, women in the home are on their own. There are no organizations that provide a social context within which they can evaluate their experiences. As a result, the women I interviewed all felt isolated. They perceived the changes that were affecting them not as part of a large-scale transformation in the patterns of work and family life, but as personal problems unique to their own marriages. (For a more detailed report of this study, see my article, "Two Hands for the Clock: Changing Patterns in the Gendered Division of Labour,"*Studies in Political Economy* 12 (Fall 1983), pp. 27-44.)

CHAPTER 1, pp. 11-21.

1 Monique Proulx, *Five Million Women: A Study of the Canadian Housewife* (Ottawa: Advisory Council on the Status of Women, 1978). For a discussion of the increased participation of married women in the paid labour force see Patricia Connelly, *Last Hired, First Fired* (Toronto: The Women's Press, 1978). For a discussion of the numbers of women who are full-time housewives and what happens when they take on paid work as well, see *The Report of the Royal Commission on the Status of Women in Canada* (Ottawa: Information Canada, 1970), p. 33; or Pat Armstrong and Hugh Armstrong, *The Double Ghetto* (Toronto: McClelland and Stewart, 1978).

2 For a discussion of the historical development of these two spheres see Eli Zaretsky, "Capitalism, the Family and Personal Life," *Socialist Revolution* 13 and 14 (January-April 1973); and 15 (May-June 1973).

3 Quotations such as this one are drawn from my interviews with Flin Flon housewives, which were conducted specifically for this study. To identify the speaker, I have indicated in which of three generations she set up her household in Flin Flon and the date of her birth. For a fuller explanation, see pages 38-41.

4 Frederick Engels, *The Origin of the Family, Private Property and the State* (New York: New World Paperbacks, 1972), pp. 71-72.

5 For three examples see Harry Braverman, *Labor and Monopoly Capital: The Degradation of Work in the Twentieth Century* (New York: Monthly Review Press, 1974); Michael Burawoy, *Manufacturing Consent: Changes in the Labour Process under Monopoly Capitalism* (Chicago: University of Chicago Press, 1979); Andrew Friedman, *Industry and Labour: Class Struggle at Work and Monopoly Capitalism* (London: Macmillan, 1978).

6 As far as I can determine, the term "domestic labour" was first applied to women's work in the home in an article by Wally Seccombe, "The Housewife and Her Labour under Capitalism," *New Left Review* 83 (January-February 1974). Subsequently, the term was taken up by numerous authors in what became known as "the domestic labour

debate." The most recent publication on this topic is a collection of essays, which includes an extensive annotated bibliography, edited by Bonnie Fox, *Hidden in the Household: Women's Domestic Labour Under Capitalism* (Toronto: The Women's Press, 1980). For a more detailed theoretical argument about the importance of a twenty-four-hour perspective, see Margaret Luxton and Wally Seccombe, "The Making of the Working Class: Two Labours, Not One" (paper presented at the annual meeting of the Canadian Sociology and Anthropology Association, June 1980, Montreal, Quebec).

7 Once in the employ of capital, the worker's labour power actually becomes a part of capital — the elastic or variable part. Karl Marx, *Capital, Vol. 1: A Critique of Political Economy* (London: Penguin Books, 1976).

8 For a full elaboration of the Marxist theory of the proletarian condition and the necessity of a private household sphere, see Wally Seccombe, "Domestic Labour and the Working-Class Household"; and "The Expanded Reproduction Cycle of Labour Power in Twentieth-Century Capitalism," in Fox, *Hidden in the Household,* pp. 25-99; pp. 219-268.

9 A household may refer to any number of possibilities ranging from that of one person living alone in a rented room to that of several adults and children living together in a privately owned house. In fact, people live in many different types of households. The capitalist mode of production allows for such a variety in household living arrangements, but the nuclear family form remains typical. It is the particular form that is reinforced by the state and ideologically encouraged in a thousand ways. It is possible to live as a proletarian outside of nuclear family households, but it is not easy. In one way or another, those who make a habit of rejecting nuclear family living arrangements are considered abnormal.

10 Domestic labour is women's work par excellence. However, this does not mean that only women do domestic labour. All men help out occasionally and some men do their own domestic labour regularly. In some households, domestic labour is organized collectively so that all the members of the household divide the work equally. See Margaret Luxton, "Urban Communes and Co-ops in Toronto" (M. Phil. dissertation, University of Toronto, 1973). Those people who can afford to can either pay others (cleaning ladies, nannies) to do their domestic labour for them in their homes or purchase these services elsewhere (restaurants, cleaners, hotels, prostitutes). Despite these alternatives, domestic labour is still primarily women's work. See Ann Oakley, *Women's Work: The Housewife Past and Present* (New York: Vintage Books, 1976).

11 While it has its roots in pre-existing household and family forms, the working-class household, as a part of working-class social relations, emerged as a new social form with the rise of capitalism. Too often investigators assume that the household is determined by capital, forgetting that it is formed and shaped by class struggle. For a discussion of the historical development of the working-class household, see E.P. Thompson, *The Making of the English Working Class* (Harmondsworth, England: Pelican Books, 1968); Eli Zaretsky, "Capitalism, the Family and Personal Life"; Peter Sterns, *Lives of Labour: Work in a Maturing Industrial Society* (London: Croom Helm Publishing, 1975); Jane Humphries, "The Working Class Family, Women's Liberation and Class Struggle: The Case of Nineteenth Century British History," *The Review of Radical Political Economics: Women, Class and the Family* 9, no. 3 (fall 1977).

12 John Littlejohn, *Westrigg: The Sociology of a Cheviot Parish* (London: Routledge and Kegan Paul, 1963), pp. 122-123.

13 Schwartz Cowan has noted, "The industrialization of the home was a process very different from the industrialization of other means of production, and the impact of that process was neither what we have been led to believe it was nor what students of the industrial revolution would have been led to predict." Ruth Schwartz Cowan, "The 'Industrial Revolution' in the Home: Household Technology and Social Change in the Twentieth Century," *Technology and Culture* 17, no. 1 (January 1976), p. 1.

14 Joann Vanek, "Keeping Busy: Time Spent in Housework, United States, 1920-1970" (Ph.D. dissertation, University of Michigan, 1974).

15 Karl Marx, *Capital, Vol. 2* (London: Progress Books, 1969), p. 127.

CHAPTER 2, pp. 23-41.

1 This chapter was coauthored with Paul Campbell, who also conducted much of the research on which it is based.

   Readers may be interested in how Flin Flon got its name. During the early 1900s, a team of gold prospectors exploring the northern Manitoba bush near Churchill River found a book by the side of the portage. *The Sunless City*, by J.E. Muddock, published in England in 1905, tells the tale of a shopkeeper and amateur scientist, Josiah Flintabbaty Flonatin, who when his business goes bankrupt takes the small submarine he has built and sets off to explore a bottomless lake. He finds a hidden city where gold is so plentiful that it lies untouched in heaps by the roadsides. Even more startling are the inhabitants of this land of Esnesnon (nonsense). Not quite human, their skins are blue, they have tails, and most shocking for Flin, the women rule the land!

In a dry style that seems to attack the English women's struggle for equal rights, the author shows Flin so horrified by this reversal of female/male relationships that he helps the men instigate a revolution, aided by a princess who has betrayed the women because she has fallen in love with Flin! Thus ends the story. When the prospectors came upon a conical formation, a hole in the rock face of an unfamiliar lake, they decided that it might be Flin's lake, and so they began to call it Flin Flon.

2 For a discussion of the characteristic features of Canadian single industry, primary resource communities, see Rolf Knight, *Work Camps and Single Enterprise Communities in Canada and the United States: A Working Bibliography* (Toronto: Scarborough College, University of Toronto, 1972); Rex A. Lucas, *Minetown, Milltown, Railtown: Life in Canadian Communities of Single Industry* (Toronto: University of Toronto Press, 1971); Ira Robinson, *New Industrial Towns on the Canadian Resource Frontier* (Chicago: University of Chicago Press, 1962).

3 Lucas, *Minetown, Milltown, Railtown*, p. 52; Ronald Frankenberg, "In the Production of their Lives, Men (?) ... Sex and Gender in British Community Studies," in *Sexual Divisions and Society* (London: Tavistock Publications, 1976).

4 The argument I am making here is that shared class experiences override other differences, such as ethnicity. While ethnic differences continue to be important, they are not the determining factor. Hence, all women have about the same amount of money to spend on food. What they spend it on reflects personal and cultural choices but these differences are virtually insignificant to the organization of domestic labour.

5 For references on mining in the Americas around the turn of the century, see T.A. Rickard, *A History of American Mining* (New York: American Institute of Mining Engineers, 1932); C.C. Spence, *Mining Engineers and the American West: The Lace Boot Brigade* (New Haven: Yale University Press, 1970); R.E. Lingenfelter, *The Hardrock Miners: The History of the Mining Labour Movement in the American West, 1863-1893* (Los Angeles: University of California Press, 1974). For information on the impact of these experiences on Canadian mining, see any issue of *The Canadian Mining Journal* or Charles Mitke, "Relations of Standardization to Mine Management," *The Canadian Mining Journal*, 10 December 1920, pp. 1019-1022; E.S. Moore, *American Influence in Canadian Mining* (Toronto: University of Toronto Press, 1941); D.M. Le

Bourdais, *Metals and Men: The Story of Canadian Mining* (Toronto: McClelland and Stewart, 1957); Paul MacEwan, *Miners and Steelworkers: Labour in Cape Breton* (Toronto: Samuel Stevens Hakkert, 1976).

⁶ The original inhabitants and users of the region were Indians, mainly Cree speakers. For a variety of reasons, most of them racist, Company managers did not employ local people. Thus, although the man who actually found the original site was David Collins, an Indian trapper, neither he nor any of the other Indian people of the area received compensation for their land or recognition of their services.

⁷ Quoted in Valerie Hedman, Loretta Yauck and Joyce Henderson, *Flin Flon* (Flin Flon, Manitoba: Flin Flon Historical Society, 1974), p. 19.

⁸ Harry Braverman, *Labor and Monopoly Capital: The Degradation of Work in the Twentieth Century* (New York: Monthly Review Press, 1974).

⁹ For a discussion of the uneven development of household technology, especially for working-class households, see Susan Kleinberg, "Technology's Stepdaughters: The Impact of Industrialization upon Working Class Women" (Ph.D. dissertation, University of Pittsburgh, 1973).

¹⁰ George Waring, *How to Drain a House: Practical Information for Householders* (New York: D. Van Nostrand, 1895).

¹¹ This research method is known as participant observation.

¹² The interview schedules were derived from: Elizabeth Bott, *Family and Social Network* (London: Tavistock Publications, 1971); William Firth, Jane Hubert, and Anthony Forge, *Families and Their Relatives: Kinship in a Middle-Class Sector of London* (London: Routledge and Kegan Paul, 1969); Ann Oakley, *The Sociology of Housework* (Bath: Martin Robertson, 1974); Richard A. Berk, Sarah F. Berk, and Catherine W. Berheide, "Household Work in the Suburbs: The Job and Its Participants" (unpublished paper, Northwestern University, 1976); and "The Non-division of Labor" (unpublished paper, Northwestern University, 1976); Helena Lopata, *Occupation: Housewife* (Toronto: Oxford University Press, 1971).

¹³ I am grateful to Maureen FitzGerald, who suggested researching family albums as a way of reconstructing social networks through time.

CHAPTER 3, pp. 43-79.

¹ The most important lack of alternatives is the fact that heterosexual monogamous marriage is generally considered to be the only normal life choice for everyone. People who choose to be single, to have children alone, to have no children, to live with several people, lesbians, homosexuals and bisexuals, even couples who live together

without marrying — all are subjected to some degree of social sanction and disapproval. As long as this is so people cannot "choose" freely to marry.

2 The situation of women wage earners with respect to the sex-segregated job market and the unequal pay differentials between women and men was well-documented in 1970 by the *Report of the Royal Commission on the Status of Women in Canada* (Ottawa: Information Canada, 1970). More up-to-date figures from the Department of Labour, Women's Bureau, are summarized by Pat Armstrong and Hugh Armstrong, *The Double Ghetto* (Toronto: McClelland and Stewart, 1978). These more recent figures confirm that the pay differential between women and men is, if anything, increasing.

3 L.D. Easton and K.H. Guddat, ed. and trans., *Writings of the Young Marx on Philosophy and Society* (New York: Doubleday, 1967), p. 292.

4 Ibid.

5 For a study of the impact of shift work on the social relations of the family, see P.E. Mott, *Shift Work: The Social, Psychological and Physical Consequences* (Ann Arbor, Michigan: University of Michigan Press, 1965), p. 18.

6 Winnipeg Women's Liberation, *Newsletter*, February 1978.

7 This is a typical pattern for working-class families. Denis et al. cite the example of the man who threw his supper into the fire even though he admitted that it was particularly good food. His wife had gone out and arranged for another woman to prepare his meals for him. They quoted him when he explained that he threw out the dinner because it was his wife's job to prepare his meal and she could not allocate her work to someone else. N. Denis, F. Henriques, and C. Slaughter, *Coal is Our Life: An Analysis of a Yorkshire Mining Community* (London: Tavistock Publications, 1969), p. 182.

8 Michael Young and Peter Willmott in *The Symmetrical Family: A Study of Work and Leisure in the London Region* (London: Routledge and Kegan Paul, 1973) suggest that the shorter week for wage workers and the improved situation for domestic workers created by household technology have resulted in a new type of family relations where the sexual division of labour is breaking down. They note that men have begun to spend a bit more time around the house helping out with domestic work and that women are increasingly taking on wage work. They hypothesize from these observations that a basic equality is evolving within the family. They are able to make such a statement only because they have never stopped to investigate what actually does constitute domestic labour. While it is true that men are helping out more around the house, they are still "helping out." The

internal household labour is still the primary responsibility of women.

9 While marriage laws vary, one universal feature is the recognition
that legal marriage must be "consummated"; that is, sexual inter-
course must take place. If it does not, the marriage may be annulled,
which essentially means that the marriage never occurred.

10 Lillian Rubin, "The Marriage Bed," *Psychology Today,* August 1976,
p. 44.

11 Michael Schneider, *Neurosis and Civilization* (New York: The Seabury Press, 1975).

12 For a summary of the major studies on North American sexuality
since Kinsey see Ruth Brecker and E. Brecker, *An Analysis of Human
Sexual Response* (New York: Signet, 1966); M. Hunt, *Sexual Behavior in
the 1970s* (Chicago: Playboy Press, 1974); Shere Hite, *The Hite Report*
(New York, Dell Books, 1976).

13 Rubin, "The Marriage Bed," p. 92.

14 Ibid., p. 47.

15 Charnie Guettel, *Marxism and Feminism* (Toronto: The Women's Press,
1974), p. 14.

16 M. Borland, ed., *Violence in the Family* (Manchester: Manchester University Press, 1976); V. D'Oyley, ed., *Domestic Violence* (Toronto: Ontario Institute for Studies in Education, 1978); J.M. Eekelaar, and S.N.
Katz, *Family Violence* (Toronto: Butterworth, 1975); Linda MacLeod,
Wife Battering in Canada: The Vicious Circle (Ottawa: Canadian Advisory
Council on the Status of Women, 1980); J.P. Martin, ed., *Violence and
the Family* (New York: John Wiley, 1978); J. Renvoize, ed., *Wed of Violence* (London: Routledge and Kegan Paul, 1978).

17 For a good discussion on how and why women subordinate their
needs to those of their husbands, see Laura Oren, "The Welfare of
Women in Labouring Families: England 1860-1950," in M. Hartman
and L.W. Banner, eds., *Clio's Consciousness Raised: New Perspectives on the
History of Women* (New York: Harper and Row, 1974); M.L. McDougall, "Working Class Women During the Industrial Revolution, 1780-
ton Mifflin, 1977); Jane Humphries, "The Working Class Family,
Women's Liberation, and Class Struggle: The Case of Nineteenth
Century British History," *The Review of Radical Political Economics: Women, Class and the Family* 9, no. 3 (fall 1977).

18 In Lewis Carroll's *Through the Looking Glass* (London: Penguin Books,
1971), Alice meets the Red Queen and they begin to run just as fast as
they can because they want to stay in the same place. Alice suggests
that this is unusual but the Queen assures her: "Now here you see, it

takes all the running you can do to keep in the same place. If you want to get somewhere else, you must run at least twice as fast as that." A number of women who had read this story saw a similar pattern in their own lives.

19 For information on the role of women in miners' strikes in North America, see M.E. Parton, ed., *The Autobiography of Mother Jones* (Chicago: Charles H. Kerr, 1974); and Kathy Kahn, *Hillbilly Women* (New York: Avon Books, 1973). The important part that women play in primary resource strike situations was graphically portrayed by Barbara Kopple in her film *Harlan County, USA* (1975). For a sketchy outline of the role of women in the Flin Flon strikes, see Valerie Hedman, Loretta Yauck and Joyce Henderson, *Flin Flon* (Flin Flon, Manitoba: Flin Flon Historical Society, 1974). *The Wives Tale/ L'histoire des femmes*, is a film about the 1978 strike against Inco in Sudbury, Ontario.

CHAPTER 4, pp. 81-114.

1 Sally MacIntyre, "'Who Wants Babies?' The Social Construction of 'Instincts'," in *Sexual Divisions and Society: Process and Change* (London: Tavistock Publications, 1976).

2 Juliet Mitchell, *Women's Estate* (London: Penguin Books, 1971), p. 119.

3 Ibid., pp. 117-118.

4 Margaret Mead, Introduction to *Introduction to Socialization* (St. Louis: C.V. Mosby, 1972), p.ix.

5 Ann Oakley, *The Sociology of Housework* (Bath: Martin Robinson, 1974), p.102.

6 Simone de Beauvoir, *The Second Sex* (New York, Bantam Books, 1970), p.49.

7 Helena Lopata, *Occupation: Housewife* (Toronto: Oxford University Press, 1971, p.190.

8 For an analysis of the connections between the medical profession, the processed foods industries and women's attitudes and habits regarding breast feeding, see War on Want, *The Baby Killer* (War on Want Publications, 1977); J. Cottingham, "Bottle Babies," *Isis*, December 1976.

9 Hannah Gavron, *The Captive Wife: Conflicts of Housebound Mothers* (London: Routledge and Kegan Paul, 1966).

10 Pauline Bart, "Depression in Middle-Aged Women," in *Women in Sexist Society* (New York: Basic Books, 1971).

CHAPTER 5, pp. 117-159.

[1] Leonore Davidoff, "The Rationalization of Housework," in *Dependence and Exploitation in Work and Marriage* (London: Longmans, 1976).

[2] For a discussion on the history of housework, see Siegfried Giedion, *Mechanization Takes Command: A Contribution to Anonymous History* (New York: W.W. Norton, 1969); Heidi Hartmann, "Capitalism and Women's Work in the Home 1900-1930" (Ph.D. dissertation, Yale University, 1974); Susan Kleinberg, "Technology's Stepdaughters: The Impact of Industrialization upon Working Class Women" (Ph.D. dissertation, University of Pittsburgh, 1973).

[3] Christine Fredericks, *The Ignoramus Book of Housekeeping* (New York: Sears Publishing, 1932), p.83.

[4] For a graphic description of this dependency on household production for the period immediately preceding the establishment of Flin Flon, see E. Rowles, "Bannock, Beans and Bacon," in *The Workingman in the Nineteenth Century* (Toronto: Oxford University Press, 1974), pp.156-164.

[5] Ellen Richards, *The Cost of Food: A Study in Dietaries* (New York: John Wiley, 1910); and *The Cost of Shelter* (New York: John Wiley, 1911); Christine Fredericks, *The Ignoramous Book of Housekeeping.*

[6] In 1977 a group of people in Flin Flon set up a health food co-op. They purchased supplies in bulk from a wholesaler in Edmonton. When the order arrived they took turns packaging and distributing the food. Subsequently, other entrepeneurs opened a health food store.

[7] Helena Lopata, *Occupation: Housewife* (Toronto: Oxford University Press, 1971), p.165.

[8] Ann Oakley, *The Sociology of Housework* (Bath: Martin Robinson, 1974), p.5.

[9] Lopata, *Occupation: Housewife*, p.115.

[10] Sarah Berk, Richard Berk, and Catherine Berheide, "The Non-division of Household Labour" (paper presented to the American Anthropological Association, February 1976), p.31.

[11] After the event, a number of households equipped their houses with wood-burning stoves, so that they would have a source of heat that they could control.

[12] Catherine Beecher and Harriet Stowe, *The American Woman's Home or Domestic Science* (New York: J.B. Ford, 1869).

[13] Giedion, *Mechanization Takes Command*, p.518.

[14] Oscar Anderson, *Refrigeration in America: A History of a New Technology and Its Impact* (Princeton, N.J.: Princeton University Press, 1953).

15 G. Peltz, *The Housewife's Library* (Guelph, Ont.: World Publishing, 1883).

16 M. Parloa, *Miss Parloa's New Cook Book* (Boston: Estes and Lauriat, 1881); Eliza Parker, *Economical Housekeeping* (Toronto: J.S. Robertson, 1886); Grace Denison, *The New Cook Book* (Toronto: Rose Publications, 1906).

17 Berk, Berk and Berheide, "The Non-division of Household Labour."

18 Oakley, *Sociology of Housework*, p.59.

19 Ibid., p.119.

20 Ibid., p.59.

21 Ibid., p.100.

22 Berk, Berk and Berheide, "The Non-division of Household Labour," p.9. Their figures show women doing 88 percent of tasks, while husbands contributed to 16 percent and children to 12 percent.

23 Martin Meissner, E. Humphries, S. Meis, and J. Scheu, "No Exit for Wives: Sexual Division of Labour and the Cumulation of Household Demands" (unpublished paper, University of British Columbia, 1975), p.7. The authors report that 93 percent of the housewives interviewed spent time cooking during the week as compared to 27 percent of their husbands (n=340 couples).

24 Berk, Berk and Berheide, "The Non-division of Household Labour," p.24.

25 *Ye Old Miller's Household Book* (Toronto: Campbell Flour Mills, 1901), p.7.

26 Annie Gregory, *Canada's Favourite Cook Book* (Brantford, Ont.: Bradley-Garretson Co., 1902); H. Wiley and M. Maddocks, *The Eaton Pure Food Cook Book* (Toronto: The T. Eaton Co., 1931).

27 L'école normale de St.-Pascal, *Manuel de Cuisine Raisonnée* (Quebec City: L'action sociale, 1919), p.62.

28 Oakley, *Sociology of Housework*, p.58.

29 Peltz, *The Housewife's Library*; B. Jeffries, and J.C. Nichols, *Household Guide or Domestic Cyclopedia* (Toronto: J.L. Nichols, 1897).

30 Charles Tuttle, *The Dominion Encyclopedia of Universal History and Useful Knowledge* (Montreal: Bigney, 1877).

31 *Smiley's Cook Book and Universal Household Guide* (Chicago: Smiley Publishing, 1901).

32 Giedion, *Mechanization Takes Command*, p.548.

33 Fredericks, *Ignoramous Book of Housekeeping*, p.50.

34 Ibid., p.57.

35 Mary Douglas, *Purity and Danger* (London: Routledge and Kegan Paul, 1966), pp.40; 2; 68. Lenore Davidoff has written a very interesting article in which she applies Douglas's concepts of ritual pollution and

symbolic behaviour to housework. She argues that housework is an attempt "to impose cultural patterns on the natural world." The main thrust of her article, however, suggests that such an analysis is appropriate for upper-class and middle-class housewives. It is not appropriate for working-class housewives. An analysis that compared housework in working-class homes with that done in middle-class and upper-class homes would shed some important light on this question of the symbolic and ritual aspects of housework (Leonore Davidoff, "The Rationalization of Housework," p.125).

36 The best example is that of nylon underwear which tends to promote vaginal infections, unlike cotton fabrics which absorb vaginal discharges and minimize infections. Some children's pyjamas are made of flammable material, and there are some people who maintain that natural fibres are generally healthier.

37 Joann Vanek, "Keeping Busy: Time Spent in Housework, United States, 1920-1970" (Ph.D. dissertation, University of Michigan, 1974), p.119.

CHAPTER 6 pp. 161-199.

1 Stuart Ewen, *Captains of Consciousness: Advertising and the Social Roots of the Consumer Culture* (Toronto: McGraw-Hill Ryerson, 1976), p. 35.

2 Ibid., p.39.

3 For a discussion of the history and political implications of the family wage, see Michelle Barrett and Mary McIntosh, "The 'Family Wage': Some Problems for Socialists and Feminists" (paper presented at the Conference of Socialist Economists, Leeds, England, July 1979).

4 Studies of British working-class households indicate that the normal practice is for a husband to hand over part of his wages to his wife. These women rarely know how much their husbands earn. See Michael Young and Peter Willmott, *Family and Kinship in East London* (London: Penguin Books, 1957); N. Dennis, F. Henriques, and C. Slaughter, *Coal is Our Life: An Analysis of a Yorkshire Mining Community* (London: Tavistock Publications, 1969)....

5 It may be that money transfer patterns have been affected by changes in the way men are paid. The Company employees are currently paid by cheque and in most households women and men share a joint chequing account. As a result, Flin Flon women know the amount of each pay cheque and have access to any money desposited in the account.

6 Betty Friedan, *The Feminine Mystique* (New York: Dell Books, 1963).

7 E. Willis, "Consumerism and Women," *Women in Sexist Society* (New York: Basic Books, 1971), pp. 658, 663.

8 The issues in this debate are best summarized in Harriet Holter, *Sex Roles and Social Structure* (Oslo: Universitets Forlaget, 1972); Ann-Marie Henshel, *Sex Structure* (Toronto: Longmans, 1973); Pat Armstrong and Hugh Armstrong, *The Double Ghetto* (Toronto: McClelland and Stewart, 1978); Patricia Connelly, *Last Hired, First Fired* (Toronto: The Women's Press, 1978).

9 For a discussion and analysis of women as wage earners in primary resource industries, see B.C. Employers' Council, *Female Employment in Non-traditional Areas: Some Attitudes of Managers and Working Women* (Vancouver, B.C. Employers' Council, 1975); *Newfoundland Signal 1*, no. 10, 13 February 1975; Judylaine Fine, "Go North, Young Woman," *Chatelaine*, April 1976; B.C. Ministry of Economic Development, *Report of the B.C. Manpower Sub-committee on North East Coal Development*, Vancouver: B.C. Ministry of Economic Development, 1976.

10 *Engineering and Mining Journal* 144 (1943), p. 117.

11 Patricia Connelly, *Last Hired, First Fired*.

12 John Robinson, Phillip Converse and Alexander Szalai, "Everyday Life in Twelve Countries," in *The Use of Time* (The Hague: Mouton, 1972).

13 S. Meis and J. Scheu, "All in a Day's Work" (paper presented to the Canadian Anthropology and Sociology Association, May 1973); Martin Meissner, E. Humphries, S. Meis, and J. Scheu, "No Exit for Wives: Sexual Division of Labour and the Cumulation of Household Demands" (unpublished paper, University of British Columbia, 1975); Martin Meissner, "Sexual Division of Labour: Labour and Leisure," in *Women in Canada* (Toronto: New Press, 1973).

14 Meis and Scheu, "All in a Day's Work," p. 9.

15 Meissner, "Sexual Division of Labour," p. 9.

16 Meis and Scheu, "All in a Day's Work," p. 9.

17 This debate had concentrated on the issue of whether or not women should do wage work while they have dependent children. Some have argued that employed mothers are better with their children because they are less smothering than nonemployed mothers (Alice Rossi, "A Good Woman Is Hard To Fine," *Transaction* 2 [1964], pp. 20-23); or they are less likely to live vicariously through their children (Betty Friedan, *The Feminine Mystique*). Others have argued that children of employed mothers suffer from "maternal deprivation" because they are neglected (Benjamin Spock, *Baby and Child Care* [Markham, Ont.: Simon and Schuster, 1968]; F.I. Nye and L.W. Hoffman, *The Employed Mother in America* [Chicago: Rand McNally, 1963]). For a good summary of these issues that starts from the premise that many mothers are employed and investigates the results, see Judith

Brown, "The Subsistence Activities of Women and the Socialization of Children") paper presented to the American Anthropological Association, 1972, Toronto, Ontario).

[18] Meissner, *Sexual Division of Labour*, p. 16.

CHAPTER 7, pp. 201-231.

[1] Allison Ravetz, "Modern Technology and an Ancient Occupation: Housework in Present-Day Society," *Technology and Culture* 7, no. 2 (spring 1965).

[2] After much deliberation, I have chosen to use "they" rather than "we" in the rest of this chapter. However, I include myself in everything that follows.

[3] For a history of women's resistance, see Sheila Rowbotham, *Women, Resistance and Revolution* (London: Penguin Books, 1972).

[4] For a discussion of the second wave of the women's liberation movement, see Juliet Mitchell, *Women's Estate* (London: Penguin Books, 1971); Sheila Rowbotham, *Woman's Consciousness, Man's World* (London: Penguin Books, 1973); and Robin Morgan, *Going Too Far* (New York: Random House, 1979).

[5] In 1912, twenty thousand workers in Lawrence, Massachusetts, went on strike. Inspired by their banners, James Oppenheimer wrote the lyrics, which Caroline Kohlsaat set to music. The song is reprinted in Edith Fowke and Joe Glazer's *Songs of Work and Protest* (New York: Dover Publications, 1973).

[6] The following information about other northern Manitoba towns, and the interview material, was gathered during my trip to three communities from 6 December to 11 December 1977.

[7] See also Milton Cantor and Bruce Laurie, *Sex, Class and the Woman Worker* (London: Greenwood Press, 1977).

[8] Susan Reverby, "With Babies and Banners: Story of the Women's Emergency Brigade — a review," *Radical America* 13, no. 5 September-October 1979).

[9] Nicole Cox and Sylvia Federici, *Counterplanning from the Kitchen, Wages for Housework: A Perspective on Capital and the Left* (New York: Falling Wall Press and New York Wages for Housework Collective, 1975).

[10] Sheila Rowbotham, *Woman's Consciousness, Man's World*, p. 124.

[11] Pat Armstrong and Hugh Armstrong, *The Double Ghetto* (Toronto: McClelland and Stewart, 1978).

[12] "First Four Women Start Jobs at Stelco," *Globe and Mail*, 27 March 1980; and personal communications with Debbie Field, a member of the committee.

13 From personal communication with two researchers: Kate Braid of Simon Fraser University, Burnaby, British Columbia; and Leslie Martin, University of Toronto, Toronto, Ontario.

14 For a discussion of one such campaign, see The Bank Book Collective, *An Account to Settle: The Story of the United Bank Workers (SORWUC)* (Vancouver: Press Gang Publishers, 1979).

15 This is from an interview with a Flin Flon housewife, which appears in The Everyday Collective's *Everywoman's Almanac 1980* (Toronto: The Women's Press, 1980).

16 The information in the following discussion of Sudbury is derived from newspaper articles written at the time, public rallies and forums, and personal communication with a few of the women involved.

17 "Workers' Wives Organize Support During Inco Strike," *Globe and Mail*, 10 October 1978.

18 Personal communication, 16 December 1978.

19 Personal communication, 21 January 1979.

20 International Women's Day (March 8) has been celebrated since the late nineteenth century; it is a day when women demonstrate their solidarity and demand their rights as women.

21 International Women's Day Committee leaflet, distributed at the demonstration held in Toronto, 10 March 1979.

22 Personal communication, 10 March 1979.

23 Personal communication, 10 March 1979.

BIBLIOGRAPHY

Anderson, Oscar. *Refrigeration in America: A History of a New Technology and Its Impact.* Princeton, N.J.: Princeton University Press, 1953.

Aries, Philippe. *Centuries of Childhood: A Social History of Family Life.* New York: Vintage Books, 1962.

Armstrong, Pat and Armstrong, Hugh. *The Double Ghetto: Canadian Women and their Segregated Work.* Toronto: McClelland and Stewart, 1978.

Bacon, Elizabeth. "The Growth of Household Conveniences in the U.S., 1865-1900." Ph.D. dissertation, Radcliffe College, 1942.

Bank Book Collective. *An Account to Settle: The Story of the United Bank Workers (SORWUC).* Vancouver: Press Gang Publishers, 1979.

Bart, Pauline. "Depression in Middle-Aged Woman." In *Women in Sexist Society,* edited by Vivian Gornick and Barbara K. Moran. New York: Basic Books, 1971.

Baxandall, Rosalyn; Ewen, Elizabeth; and Gordon, Linda. "The Working Class Has Two Sexes." *Monthly Review* 28, no. 3 (1976), pp. 1-10.

B.C. Employers' Council. *Female Employment in Non Traditional Areas: Some Attitudes of Managers and Working Women.* Vancouver: B.C. Employers' Council, 1975.

B.C. Ministry of Economic Development. *Report of the B.C. Manpower Sub-Committee on the North East Coal Development.* Vancouver: B.C. Ministry of Economic Development, 1976.

Becker, Gary S. "A Theory of the Allocation of Time." *Economic Journal* 75 (September 1965), pp. 493-517.

Beecher, Catherine, and Stowe, Harriet B. *The American Woman's Home or Domestic Science.* New York: J.B. Ford, 1869.

Benston, Margaret. "The Political Economy of Women's Liberation." *Monthly Review* 21, no. 4 (1969), pp. 13-27.

Berheide, Catherine W.; Berk, Sarah E.; and Berk, Richard A. "Household Work in the Suburbs: The Job and Its Participants." Unpublished paper. Northwestern University, 1976.

Berk, Richard A.; Berk, Sarah F.; and Berheide, Catherine W. "The Non-Division of Household Labour: A Preliminary Analysis." Paper presented to American Anthropological Association, February 1976.

Berk, Sarah F., ed. *Women and Household Labour*. London: Sage Publications, 1980.

Berkner, Lutz. "Recent Research on the History of the Family in Western Europe." *Journal of Marriage and the Family* 35 (August 1973), pp. 395-405.

Blood, Robert O. and Wolfe, D.M. *Husbands and Wives: The Dynamics of Married Living*. Glencoe, Ill.: The Free Press, 1960.

Bloom, Lynn. "'It's All for Your Own Good': Parent-Child Relationships in Popular American Child Rearing Literature, 1820-1970." *Journal of Popular Culture* 10 (1976).

Blumenfeld, Emily. "Child Rearing Literature as an Object of Content Analysis." *The Journal of Applied Communications Research*, November 1976.

Bond, Kathleen Gale. "Wife's Eye View." *North* 8, no. 2 (1961), pp. 22-25.

Borland, M., ed. *Violence in the Family*. Manchester: Manchester University Press, 1976.

Bott, Elizabeth. *Family and Social Network*. 2nd ed. London: Tavistock Publications, 1971.

Braverman, Harry. *Labor and Monopoly Capitalism: The Degradation of Work in the Twentieth Century*. New York: Monthly Review Press, 1974.

Brecher, Ruth, and Brecher, E. *An Analysis of Human Sexual Response*. New York: Signet, New American Library, 1966.

Bridenthal, R., and Koonz, C., eds. *Becoming Visible: Women in European History*. Boston: Houghton Mifflin, 1977.

Brown, Judith K. "The Subsistence Activities of Women and the Socialization of Children." Paper presented to the American Anthropological Associates, 1972, Toronto, Ontario.

"Bucans, Company Town." *Winnipeg Women's Liberation Newsletter*, February 1976, p. 14.

Burawoy, Michael. *Manufacturing Consent: Changes in the Labor Process under Monopoly Capitalism*. Chicago: University of Chicago Press, 1979.

Campbell, Paul; Luxton, Margaret; and Petersen, Kathryn. "Labour, Science and Technology, and Ideology: A Study of Prescriptive Literature on Women's Domestic Work, 1830-1930." Unpublished paper. University of Toronto, 1974.

Cantor, Milton, and Laurie, Bruce, eds. *Sex, Class and the Women Worker.* London: Greenwood Press, 1977.

Caulfield, Mina. "Imperialism, the Family and Cultures of Resistance." *Socialist Revolution* 4, no. 20. (October 1974).

Carroll, Lewis. *Through the Looking Glass.* Reprint. London: Penguin Books, 1971.

Connelly, Patricia. *Last Hired, First Fired: Women and the Canadian Work Force.* Toronto: The Women's Press, 1978.

Cottingham, J. "Bottle Babies." *ISIS*, December 1976.

Coulson, Margaret; Magas, Branca; and Wainwright, Hilary. "The Housewife and Her Labour under Capitalism — A Critique." *New Left Review* 89 (January-February 1975), pp. 59-71.

Cowan, Ruth Schwartz. "A Case Study of Technology and Social Change: The Washing Machine and the Working Wife." In *Clio's Consciousness Raised,* edited by M. Hartman and L.W. Banner. New York: Harper and Row, 1974.

———. "The 'Industrial Revolution' in the Home: Household Technology and Social Change in the Twentieth Century." *Technology and Culture* 17, no. 1 (1976).

Cox, Nicole, and Federici, Sylvia. *Counterplanning from the Kitchen, Wages for Housework: A Perspective on Capital and the Left.* New York: Falling Wall Press and the New York Wages for Housework Collective, 1975.

Danziger, Kurt. *Socialization.* London: Penguin Books, 1970.

Davidoff, Lenore. "The Rationalization of Housework." In *Dependence and Exploitation in Work and Marriage,* edited by Diana Barker and Sheila Allen. London: Longmans, 1976.

de Beauvoir, Simone. *Old Age.* London: Weidenfeld and Nicolson, 1972.

———. *The Second Sex.* New York: Bantam Books, 1972.

Denison, Grace E. *The New Cook Book: A Volume of Tried and Tested and Proven Recipes of the Ladies of Toronto and other Cities and Towns.* Toronto: Rose Publications, 1906.

Dennis, N.; Henriques, F.; and Slaughter, C. *Coal Is Our Life: An Analysis of a Yorkshire Mining Community.* London: Tavistock Publications, 1969.

Dixon, Marlene. "The Centrality of Women in Proletarian Revolution." *Synthesis* 1, no. 4 (spring 1977).

Douglas, Mary. *Purity and Danger.* London: Routledge and Kegan Paul, 1966.

D'Oyley, V., ed. *Domestic Violence: Issues and Dynamics.* Toronto: Ontario Institute for Studies in Education, 1978.

L'école normale de St.-Pascal. *Manuel de Cuisine Raisonnée.* Quebec City: L'action sociale, 1919.

Eekelaar, J.M., and Katz, S.N. *Family Violence: An International and Interdisciplinary Study.* Toronto: Butterworth, 1975.

Ehrenreich, Barbara, and English, Deirdre. "The Manufacture of Housework." *Socialist Revolution,* October-December 1975, pp. 5-41.

Eichler, Margrit. "Sociological Research on Women in Canada." *The Canadian Review of Sociology and Anthropology* 12, no. 4 (November 1975) pp. 474-481.

Engels, Frederick. *The Origins of the Family, Private Property and the State.* 1884. Reprint. New York: New World Paperbacks, 1972.

Ettorre, E.M. *Lesbians, Women and Society.* London: Routledge and Kegan Paul, 1980.

Everyday Collective. *Everywoman's Almanac 1980.* Toronto: The Women's Press, 1979.

Ewen, Stuart. *Captains of Consciousness: Advertising and the Social Roots of the Consumer Culture.* Toronto: McGraw-Hill Ryerson, 1976.

Fee, Terry. "Domestic Labor: An Analysis of Housework and Its Relation to the Production Process." *The Review of Radical Political Economics* 8, no. 1 (1976), pp. 1-9.

Feinstein, Karen W. *Working Women and Families.* London: Sage Publications, 1979.

Fine, Judylaine. "Go North, Young Woman." *Chatelaine,* April 1976.

Firth, Raymond; Hubert, Jane; and Forge, Anthony. *Families and Their Relatives: Kinship in a Middle-Class Sector of London.* London: Routledge and Kegan Paul, 1969.

"Flin Flon Mine." *Canadian Mining and Metallurgical Bulletin.* July 1930.

"Four Women Start Jobs at Stelco." *Globe and Mail,* 27 March 1980.

Fowke, Edith, and Glazer, Joe. *Songs of Work and Protest.* New York: Dover Publications, 1973.

Fox, Bonnie, ed. *Hidden in the Household: Women and Their Domestic Labour Under Capitalism.* Toronto: The Women's Press, 1980.

Frankenburg, Ronald. "In the Production of their Lives, Men (?) ... Sex and Gender in British Community Studies." In *Sexual Divisions and Society: Process and Change,* edited by Diana Barker and Sheila Allen. London: Tavistock Publications, 1976.

Frankford, Evelyn, and Snitow, Anna. "The Trap of Domesticity: Notes on the Family." *Socialist Revolution*, July-August 1972.

Fredericks, Christine. *The Ignoramus Book of Housekeeping.* New York: Sears Publishing, 1932.

Freidan, Betty. *The Feminine Mystique.* New York: Dell Books, 1963.

Friedman, Andrew. *Industry and Labour: Class Struggle at Work and Monopoly Capitalism.* London: Macmillan, 1978.

Galbraith, John K. *Economics and the Public Purpose.* New York: Houghton Mifflin, 1974.

———. "The Economics of the American Housewife." *Atlantic Monthly,* August 1973.

———. "How the Economy Hangs on Her Apron Strings." *Ms.,* May 1974.

Gallagher Ross, Kathleen. *Good Day Care: Fighting for It, Getting It, Keeping It.* Toronto: The Women's Press, 1978.

Gardiner, Jean. "Political Economy of Domestic Labour." In *Dependence and Exploitation in Work and Marriage,* edited by Diana Barker and Sheila Allen. London: Longmans, 1976.

———. "Women's Domestic Labour." *New Left Review* 89 (January-February 1975).

Gauger, William. "Household Work: Can We Add It to the GNP?" *Journal of Home Economics* (October 1973), pp. 12-15.

Gavron, Hannah. *The Captive Wife: Conflicts of Household Mothers.* London: Routledge and Kegan Paul, 1966.

Gerstein, Ira. "Domestic Work and Capitalism." *Radical America* 7, no. 4 and 5 (1973), pp. 101-128.

Giedion, Siegfried. *Mechanization Takes Command: A Contribution to Anonymous History.* New York: W.W. Norton, 1969.

Girard, A. "Le budget-temps de la femme mariée dans les agglomérations urbaines." *Population,* no. 4 Paris: L'institut national d'études demographiques, 1958.

Gregory, Annie. *Canada's Favourite Cook Book.* Brantford, Ont.: Bradley-Garretson, 1902.

Gross, B., and Gross, R. *The Children's Rights Movement.* New York: Anchor Press, 1977.

Guettel, Charnie. *Marxism and Feminism.* Toronto: The Women's Press, 1974.

Harrison, John. "The Political Economy of Housework." *Bulletin of the Conference of Socialist Economists,* winter 1973, pp. 35-52.

Hartmann, Heidi Irmgard. "Capitalism and Women's Work in the Home, 1900-1930." Ph.D. dissertation, Yale University, 1974.

Hedman, Valerie; Yauck, Loretta; and Henderson, Joyce. *Flin Flon.* Flin Flon, Man.: Flin Flon Historical Society, 1974.

Heitlinger, Alena. *Women and State Socialism: Sex Inequality in the Soviet Union and Czechoslovakia.* Montreal: McGill-Queens University Press, 1979.

Henshel, Anne-Marie. *Sex Structure.* Toronto: Longmans Canada, 1973.

Herrick, C.T. *In City Tents: How to Find, Furnish and Keep a Small Home on Slender Means.* New York and London: G. P. Putnam and Sons, 1902.

Hite, Shere. *The Hite Report.* New York: Dell Books, 1976.

Hodgetts, J.E. *The Canadian Public Service: A Physiology of Government, 1867-1970.* Toronto: University of Toronto Press, 1973.

Holter, Harriet. *Sex Roles and Social Structure.* Oslo, Norway: Universitets Forlaget, 1972.

Howe, Louise Kapp. *Pink Collar Workers Inside the World of Women's Work.* New York: Avon Books, 1977.

Humphries, Jane. "Class Struggle and the Persistence of the Working Class Family." *Cambridge Journal of Economics* 1, no. 3 (September 1977).

———. "The Working Class Family, Women's Liberation, and Class Struggle: The Case of Nineteenth Century British History." *The Review of Radical Political Economics* 9, no. 3 (fall 1977), pp. 25-42.

Hunt, M. *Sexual Behavior in the 1970s.* Chicago: Playboy Press, 1974.

Jeffries, B., and Nichols, J.C. *Household Guide or Domestic Cyclopedia.* 23rd ed. Toronto: J.L. Nichols, 1897.

Kahn, Kathy. *Hillbilly Women.* New York: Avon Books, 1973.

Kendrick, John W. "Studies in the National Income Accounts." In *Contribution to Economic Knowledge through Research.* 47th Annual Report of the National Bureau of Economic Research. New York, 1967.

Kleinberg, Susan. "Technology's Stepdaughters: The Impact of Industrialization upon Working Class Women." Ph.D. dissertation, University of Pittsburgh, 1973.

———. "Technology and Women's Work: The Lives of Working Class Women in Pittsburgh, 1870-1900." *Labour History* 17, no. 1 (winter 1976), pp. 58-72.

Knight, Rolf. *A Very Ordinary Life.* Vancouver: New Star Books, 1974.

———. *Work Camps and Single-Enterprise Communities in Canada and the United States: A Working Bibliography.* Toronto: Scarborough College, University of Toronto, 1972.

Komarovsky, Mirra. *Blue-Collar Marriage.* New York: Vintage Books, 1962.

Kuhn, Annette, and Wolpe, Annmarie *Feminism and Materialism: Women and Modes of Production.* London: Routledge and Kegan Paul, 1978.

Lacasse, Francois D. *Women at Home: The Cost to the Canadian Economy of the Withdrawal from the Labour Force of a Major Proportion of the Female Population.* Studies of the Royal Commission on the Status of Women in Canada, no. 2. Ottawa: Information Canada, 1971.

Landes, Joan B. "Women, Labor and Family Life: A Theoretical Perspective." *Science and Society* 41, no. 4 (winter 1977-1978) pp. 386-409.

Le Bourdais, D.M. *Metals and Men: The Story of Canadian Mining.* Toronto: McClelland and Stewart, 1957.

Lingenfelter, R.E. *The Hardrock Miners: The History of the Mining Labor Movement in the American West, 1863-1893.* Los Angeles: University of California Press, 1974.

Littlejohn, John. *Westrigg: The Sociology of a Cheviot Parish.* London: Routledge and Kegan Paul, 1963.

Lopata, Helena *Occupation: Housewife.* Toronto: Oxford University Press, 1971.

Lower, A., and Innis, Harold. *Settlement on the Logging and Mining Frontier.* Toronto: Macmillan, 1936.

Lucas, Rex A. *Minetown, Milltown, Railtown: Life in Canadian Communities of Single Industry.* Toronto: University of Toronto Press, 1971.

Luxton, Margaret. "Urban Communes and Co-ops in Toronto." M. Phil. dissertation, University of Toronto, 1973.

Luxton, Margaret, and Seccombe, Wally. "The Making of a Working Class: Two Labours, Not One." Paper presented at the annual meeting of the Canadian Sociology and Anthropology Association, June 1980, Montreal, Quebec.

MacEwan, Paul. *Miners and Steelworkers: Labour in Cape Breton.* Toronto: Samuel Stevens Hakkert., 1976.

MacIntyre, Sally. "'Who Wants Babies?' The Social Construction of 'Instincts'." In *Sexual Divisions and Society: Progress and Change,* edited by Diana Barker and Sheila Allen. London: Tavistock Publications, 1976.

MacLeod, Linda. *Wife Battering in Canada: The Vicious Circle.* Ottawa: Canadian Advisory Council on the Status of Women, 1980.

Malos, Ellen. "Housework and the Politics of Women's Liberation." *Socialist Review* 8, no. 1 (January-February 1978), pp. 41-73.

Martin, J.P., ed. *Violence and the Family.* New York: John Wiley and Sons, 1978.

Marx, Karl. *Capital, Volume I: A Critique of Political Economy*. 1867. Reprint. London: Penguin Books, 1976.

———. *Capital, Volume 2*. 1893. Reprint. London: Progress Press, 1969.

———. *Writings of the Young Marx on Philosophy and Society*. Translated and edited by L.D. Easton and K.H. Guddat. New York: Doubleday, 1967.

McDougall, M.L. "Working Class Women During the Industrial Revolution, 1780-1914." *Becoming Visible: Women in European History*, edited by R. Bridenthal and C. Koonz. Boston: Houghton Mifflin, 1977.

Mead, Margaret. Introduction to *Socialization: Human Culture Transmitted*, by T.R. Williams. St. Louis: C.V. Mosby, 1972.

Meillassoux, Claude. *Femmes, Graniers et Capitaux*. Paris: Francois Maspero, 1975.

Meis, S., and Scheu, J. "All in a Day's Work." Paper presented to the Canadian Anthropology and Sociology Association, May 1973.

Meissner, Martin. "Sexual Division of Labour: Labour and Leisure." Unpublished paper. University of British Columbia, 1975.

Meissner, Martin; Humphreys, Elizabeth; Meis, Scott; and Scheu, William, "No Exit for Wives: Sexual Division of Labour and the Cumulation of Household Demands." Unpublished paper. University of British Columbia, 1975.

Mitchell, Juliet. *Women's Estate*. London: Penguin Books, 1971.

Mitke, Charles A. "Relations of Standardization to Mine Management." *The Canadian Mining Journal*, 10 December 1920, pp. 1019-1022.

Molyneux, Maxine. "Beyond the Domestic Labour Debate." *New Left Review*, July-August 1979, pp. 3-28.

Moore, E.S. *American Influence in Canadian Mining*. Toronto: University of Toronto Press, 1941.

Morgan, Robin. *Going Too Far: The Personal Chronicle of a Feminist*. New York: Random House, 1979.

Morton, Peggy. *A Woman's Work Is Never Done*. Toronto: Hogtown Press, 1970.

Newfoundland Signal 1, no. 10 (13 February 1975).

Nye, F.I., and Hoffman, L.W. *The Employed Mother in America*. Chicago: Rand McNally, 1963.

Oakley, Ann. *The Sociology of Housework*. Bath: Martin Robinson, 1974.

———. *Woman's Work: The Housewife Past and Present*. New York: Vintage Books, 1976.

Oren, Laura. "The Welfare of Women in Labouring Families: England 1860-1950." In *Clio's Consciousness Raised: New Perspectives on the History of Women,* edited by M. Hartman and L.W. Banner. New York: Harper and Row, 1974.

Parker, Eliza R. *Economical Housekeeping: A Complete System of Household Management.* Toronto: J.S. Robertson, 1886.

Parloa, M. *Miss Parloa's New Cook Book: A Guide to Marketing and Cooking.* Boston: Estes and Lauriat, 1881.

Parton, M.F., ed. *The Autobiography of Mother Jones.* Chicago: Charles H. Kerr, 1974.

Peltz, G. *The Housewife's Library.* Guelph, Ont.: World Publishing, 1883.

Proulx, Monique. *Five Million Women: A Study of the Canadian Housewife.* Ottawa Advisory Council on the Status of Women, 1978.

Rainwater, Lee; Coleman, R.P.; and Handel, G. *Workingman's Wife.* New York: McFadden-Bartell, 1959.

Rapp, Rayna. "Family and Class in Contemporary America: Notes Toward an Understanding of Ideology." *Science and Society* 42 (fall 1978), pp. 278-301.

Ravetz, Allison. "Modern Technology and an Ancient Occupation: Housework in Present-Day Society." *Technology and Culture* 7, no. 2 (spring 1965).

Reiter, Rayna. Introduction to *Toward an Anthropology of Women,* by R. Reiter. New York: Monthly Review Press, 1975.

Renvoize, J. *Web of Violence.* London: Routledge and Kegan Paul, 1978.

Report of the Royal Commission on the Status of Women in Canada. Ottawa: Information Canada, 1970.

"Report on Flin Flon." *The Canadian Mining Journal* 50 (September 1929) pp. 836-838.

Richards, Ellen. *The Cost of Food: A Study in Dietaries.* New York: John Wiley, 1910.

———. *The Cost of Shelter.* New York: John Wiley, 1911.

Rickard, T.A. *A History of American Mining.* New York: American Institute of Mining Engineers, 1932.

Reid, Margaret G. *Economics of Household Production.* New York: John Wiley, 1934.

Robinson, Ira. *New Industrial Towns on the Canadian Resource Frontier.* Chicago: University of Chicago Press, 1962.

Robinson, John; Converse, Philip; and Szalai, Alexander. "Everyday Life in Twelve Countries." In *The Use of Time*, edited by Alexander Szalai. The Hague: Mouton, 1972.

Rossi, Alice. "A Good Woman is Hard to Find." *Trans-action* 2 (1964), pp. 20-23.

Rowbotham, Sheila. *Women, Resistance and Revolution*. London: Penguin Books, 1972.

Rowles, E. "Bannock, Beans and Bacon." In *The Workingman in the Nineteenth Century*, edited by Michael Cross. Toronto: Oxford University Press, 1974.

Rubin, Lillian. "The Marriage Bed." *Psychology Today*, August 1976.

———. *Worlds of Pain: Life in the Working-Class Family*. New York: Basic Books, 1976.

Russell, Loris S. "The First Canadian Cooking Stove." *Canada* 3, no. 2 (December 1975), pp. 34-35.

Schneider, Michael. *Neurosis and Civilization: A Marxist/Freudian Synthesis*. New York: The Seabury Press, 1975.

Seccombe, Wally. "Domestic Labour and the Law of Value." Unpublished paper. Toronto: Ontario Institute for Studies in Education, 1978.

———. "Domestic Labour and the Working Class Household." In *Hidden in the Household*, edited by Bonnie Fox. Toronto: The Women's Press, 1980.

———. "Domestic Labour: Reply to Critics." *New Left Review* 94 (November-December 1975), pp. 85-96.

———. "The Expanded Reproduction Cycle of Labour Power in Twentieth-Century Capitalism." In *Hidden in the Household*, edited by Bonnie Fox. Toronto: The Women's Press, 1980.

———. "The Housewife and Her Labour under Capitalism." *New Left Review* 83 (January-February 1974), pp. 3-24.

Sidel, Ruth. *Urban Survival: The World of Working Class Women*. Boston: Beacon Press, 1978.

Smiley's Cook Book and Universal Household Guide. Chicago: Smiley Publishing, 1901.

Smith, Dorothy E. "Women, the Family and Corporate Capitalism." In *Women in Canada*, edited by Marylee Stephenson. Toronto: New Press, 1973.

Spence, C.C. *Mining Engineers and the American West: The Lace Boot Brigade*. New Haven, Conn.: Yale University Press, 1970.

Spock, Benjamin. *Baby and Child Care*. Reprint. Markham, Ont.: Simon and Schuster of Canada, 1968.

Sterns, Peter. *Lives of Labour: Work in a Maturing Industrial Society*. London: Croom Helm Publishing, 1975.

Szalai, Alexander, ed. *The Use of Time: Daily Activities of Urban and Suburban Populations in Twelve Countries*. The Hague: Mouton, 1972.

Thompson, E.P. *The Making of the English Working Class*. Harmondsworth, England: Pelican Books, 1968.

Tuttle, Charles. *The Dominion Encyclopedia of Universal History and Useful Knowledge*. Montreal: Bigney, 1877.

Vanek, Joann. "Keeping Busy: Time Spent in Housework, United States, 1920-1970." Ph.D. dissertation, University of Michigan.

Walker, Kathryn E. "Homemaking Still Takes Time." *Journal of Home Economics* 61 (1969), pp. 621-624.

———. "How Much Help for Working Mothers: The Children's Role." *Human Ecology Forum* 1-2.

———. "Time Spent in Household Work by Homemakers." *Family Economics Review*, September 1969.

———. "Time Used by Husbands for Household Work." *Family Economics Review*, June 1970.

War on Want. *The Baby Killer*. War on Want Publications, 1977.

Waring, George E. *How to Drain a House: Practical Information for Householders*. New York: D. Van Nostrand, 1895.

Weinbaum, Batya, and Bridges, Amy. "The Other Side of the Paycheck: Monopoly Capital and the Structure of Consumption." *Monthly Review* 28, no. 3 (July-August 1976), pp. 88-103.

Weiner, Lynn. "The Housewife's Hymnal: A Case Study of the *Ladies Home Journal*." Paper presented to Berkshire Conference on the History of Women, October 1974, Radcliffe College.

Welter, Barbara. "The Cult of True Womanhood, 1820-1860."*American Quarterly* 18 (1966), pp. 151-174.

Wiley, H., and Maddocks, M. *The Eaton Pure Food Cook Book*. Toronto: The T. Eaton Company, 1931.

Williams, Thomas R. *Introduction to Socialization: Human Culture Transmitted*. St. Louis: C.V. Mosby, 1972.

Willis, Ellen. "Consumerism and Women." In *Women in Sexist Society*, edited by Vivian Gornick and Barbara K. Moran. New York: Basic Books, 1971.

Willis, Paul. *Learning to Labour: How Working Class Kids Get Working Class Jobs.* Westmead, England: Saxon House, 1978.

Wilson, J.D.; Stamp, R.M.; and Audit, L.P. *Canadian Education: A History.* Toronto: Macmillan, 1970.

Wilson, Johanna Gudrun. *A History of Home Economics in Manitoba, 1826-1966.* Winnipeg: Economics Association Centennial Project, 1968.

Women's Bureau, Ontario Department of Labour. *Women in the Labour Force-Fact Sheet No. 2.* Toronto: Ontario Ministry of Labour, 1978.

Women's Work Study Group. "Loom, Broom and Womb: Producers, Maintainers and Reproducers." *Radical America* 10, no. 2 (March-April 1976) pp. 29-45.

"Workers' Wives Organize Support during Inco Strike." *Globe and Mail,* 10 October 1978.

Wright, Julia M. *The Complete Home: An Encyclopedia of Domestic Life and Affairs.* Brantford, Ont.: Bradley, Garretson, 1879.

―――. *Practical Life.* Brantford, Ont.: Bradley, Garretson, 1881.

Ye Old Miller's Household Book (formerly *The Dominion Cook Book*). Toronto: Campbell Flour Mills, 1901.

Young, Michael, and Willmott, Peter. *Family and Kinship in East London.* London: Penguin Books, 1957.

―――. *The Symmetrical Family: A Study of Work and Leisure in the London Region.* London: Routledge and Kegan Paul, 1973.

Zaretsky, Eli. "Capitalism, the Family and Personal Life." *Socialist Revolution* 13 and 14 (January-April 1973); and 15 (May-June 1973).

UPDATE

Barrett, Michèle. *Women's Oppression Today: Problems in Marxist Feminist Analysis.* London: Verso, 1980.

Barrett, Michèle and Mary McIntosh. *The Anti-Social Family.* London: Verso, 1982.

FitzGerald, Maureen, Connie Guberman and Margie Wolfe, eds. *Still Ain't Satisfied: Canadian Feminism Today.* Toronto: Women's Press, 1982.

Rosenberg, Harriet. "The Home is the Workplace: Stress, Hazards and Pollutants in the Household," in Wendy Chavkin, ed., *Double Exposure: Women's Health on the Job and at Home.* New York: Monthly Review Press, 1984.

―――. "The Political Economy of Pain: Motherwork Under Capitalism," in Meg Luxton and Heather Jon Maroney, eds., *Women in Canada: Political Economy and Political Struggles* (forthcoming).

Strasser, Susan. *Never Done: A History of American Housework.* New York: Pantheon, 1982.